Capitalist Agriculture and the Global Bee Crisis

Capitalist agriculture relies heavily on the pollination work of bees, but this system harms bees in innumerable ways. Indeed, human agriculture is one of the main culprits for the declining populations of wild bees and the declining health of honey bees. This book presents a political ecology of pollination that critically examines how managed honey bees and wild bees are harmed by capitalist agriculture.

The book focuses on the three most urgent problems: the standardization and simplification of landscapes through monocultures; the use of pesticides including neonicotinoids, other insecticides, herbicides, and fungicides; and the embeddedness of commercial, migratory beekeeping in the capitalist agriculture system which, among other things, has the potential to spread pests and pathogens across continents. At the heart of this crisis is the power and influence that a small group of agrochemical corporations have over national and international agricultural policy. The book argues for an interspecies alliance of small-scale farmers, bee advocates, beekeepers, environmentalists, and bees themselves, along with a vision for an agricultural system that nurtures multispecies flourishing.

This book will be of significant interest to readers of political ecology, animal geographies, environmental anthropology, food system studies, and critical animal studies.

Rebecca Ellis holds a PhD in Geography and Environment (2021) from Western University in London, ON, Canada. Her research project, "Pollinator people: An ethnography of bees, bee advocates and possibilities for multispecies commoning in Toronto and London, ON", examined the entangled and embodied relationship between people and urban bees. She received her BA (2008) and MA (2010) in Anthropology from Western University. Her MA research focused on the role of community gardens in a rapidly gentrifying neighbourhood in Toronto, Canada. Her research interests include animal geographies, political ecology, social reproduction theory, and sustainable food systems. Rebecca works as an adjunct professor at Western University and Algoma University. In addition to studying bees, agriculture, and sustainable food systems, she is a beekeeper, urban farmer, and long-time community activist.

Routledge Frontiers of Political Economy

Capitalist Agriculture and the Global Bee Crisis
Rebecca Ellis

China, Trust and Digital Supply Chains
Dynamics of a Zero Trust World
Warwick Powell

Macroeconomic Modelling, Economic Policy and Methodology
Economics at the Edge
Edited by Mikael Randrup Byrialsen, Hamid Raza and Finn Olesen

Economics, Anthropology and the Origin of Money as a Bargaining Counter
Patrick Spread

Bernard Schmitt's Quantum Macroeconomic Analysis
Alvaro Cencini

Blockchain and the Commons
Vangelis Papadimitropoulos

Globalization and the Decline of American Power
The Political Economy of the American Fall
Cyrus Bina

Marx and Le Capital
Evaluation, History, Reception
Edited by Marcello Musto

For more information about this series, please visit: www.routledge.com/Routledge-Frontiers-of-Political-Economy/book-series/SE0345

Capitalist Agriculture and the Global Bee Crisis

Rebecca Ellis

LONDON AND NEW YORK

First published 2023
by Routledge
4 Park Square, Milton Park, Abingdon, Oxon OX14 4RN

and by Routledge
605 Third Avenue, New York, NY 10158

Routledge is an imprint of the Taylor & Francis Group, an informa business

© 2023 Rebecca Ellis

The right of Rebecca Ellis to be identified as author of this work has been asserted in accordance with sections 77 and 78 of the Copyright, Designs and Patents Act 1988.

All rights reserved. No part of this book may be reprinted or reproduced or utilised in any form or by any electronic, mechanical, or other means, now known or hereafter invented, including photocopying and recording, or in any information storage or retrieval system, without permission in writing from the publishers.

Trademark notice: Product or corporate names may be trademarks or registered trademarks, and are used only for identification and explanation without intent to infringe.

British Library Cataloguing-in-Publication Data
A catalogue record for this book is available from the British Library

Library of Congress Cataloging-in-Publication Data
Names: Ellis, Rebecca, author.
Title: Capitalist agriculture and the global bee crisis / Rebecca Ellis.
Description: First edition. | New York, NY : Routledge, 2023. |
Includes bibliographical references and index.
Identifiers: LCCN 2022013369 (print) | LCCN 2022013370 (ebook) |
ISBN 9780367695613 (hardback) | ISBN 9780367695620 (paperback) |
ISBN 9781003142294 (ebook)
Subjects: LCSH: Bee culture. | Agriculture--Economic aspects. | Political ecology.
Classification: LCC SF523 .E53 2023 (print) | LCC SF523 (ebook) |
DDC 638/.1--dc23/eng/20220322
LC record available at https://lccn.loc.gov/2022013369
LC ebook record available at https://lccn.loc.gov/2022013370

ISBN: 978-0-367-69561-3 (hbk)
ISBN: 978-0-367-69562-0 (pbk)
ISBN: 978-1-003-14229-4 (ebk)

DOI: 10.4324/9781003142294

Typeset in Bembo
by Taylor & Francis Books

This book is dedicated to bees and the people who love them. Collectively, we are planting the seeds for other, better worlds for all living beings.

Contents

	Acknowledgments	viii
1	Introduction: The global pollinator crisis and human agriculture	1
2	Bees in the Capitalocene	19
3	The *Apis*-industrial complex: The commodification of the lives and work of honey bees	39
4	Toxic flowers and uncertain science: Pesticides and bees	64
5	Bee-washing: Agrochemical corporations and struggles over neonicotinoids	85
6	Which bees shall we save?: Debates over honey bee harm to native bees	107
7	Pollinator people: Hopeful possibilities for multispecies flourishing in cities	129
8	Building movements to confront capitalist agriculture	152
	Index	167

Acknowledgments

This book would not have been possible without the loving support of my partner, Sean Kaiser, who took on a disproportionate amount of laundry and parenting while I wrote. My friend and co-parent, Steve D'Arcy, was a big source of intellectual support especially during the times that writing a book felt overwhelming. My Ph.D. supervisor, Tony Weis, intellectually challenged me throughout my Ph.D. which has helped turn me into a better researcher and writer. Parts of this book are based on my Ph.D. research, during which I interviewed and spent time with beekeepers, gardeners, and urban farmers and I am endlessly appreciative of these insightful, generous, and thoughtful research participants. I am thankful to my mom, Sandra Ellis, and my in-laws, Susie and Peter Kaiser, who let me use their spaces for periodic writing retreats. I would not have finished the book without being able to spend time away from home. While away on those retreats my dogs, Georgia and Arthur, provided constant, loving companionship.

Lastly, I am deeply thankful to the beekeepers, gardeners, peasants, farm workers, and small-scale farmers who dream of a better world – and agricultural system - for all. The struggle continues and I believe we will win!

1 Introduction

The global pollinator crisis and human agriculture

Human lives, past and present, are entangled with bees of all species. Much of the food we depend on for our everyday sustenance – berries, fruit, nuts, seeds, and vegetables – requires the work of bees. Additionally, humans like many other species of animals have long enjoyed honey, the sweet and sticky food made in abundance by a variety of bee species. But the human and bee relationship is even more entangled than this: an estimated 80% of terrestrial plants from the largest trees to low-growing ground covers, rely on the pollination work of bees to reproduce (Packer 2011). While the lives of humans and bees are inextricably intertwined, something has disrupted the human and bee relationship. Wild bees are increasingly at risk of defaunation or extirpation due to the combined effects of climate change, pesticide use, and loss of habitat and forage (Siviter et al. 2021; Dance et al. 2017; Gill and Raine 2014; Goulson et al. 2015). Domesticated bees, most notably honey bees, face increasingly high mortality rates due to pests and pathogens, pesticides, and poor nutrition (Steinhauer et al. 2018; Tsvetkov et al. 2017; Woodcock et al. 2017; Smith et al. 2013). The long-standing human and bee relationship is at risk due to human activity. But not all human activity harms bees. Capitalist agriculture is the biggest risk to the health of bee of all species. This book will explore the ways in which bees of all species are negatively impacted by capitalist agriculture, particularly the way in which this form of agriculture standardizes and simplifies landscapes and commoditizes the work of bees.

Bees: a background

Although there are many kinds of animal pollinators including mammals such as nectar-eating bats and birds such as hummingbirds, insect pollinators are by far the most numerous and important pollinators of plants (FAO 2008). Many different groups of insects engage in pollination including beetles, flies, wasps, butterflies, and moths. However, bees are the group of insects that are the most efficient and effective pollinators in the world (FAO 2008). Worldwide, there are over 20,000 different species of bees living on every continent, except for Antarctica (FAO 2018). Taxonomically, bees are vegetarian digger wasps and, as such, share a common ancestor as well as many characteristics with wasps.

DOI: 10.4324/9781003142294-1

Bees' status as vegetarian in contrast to their omnivorous wasp cousins is why bees are such prolific pollinators. They rely on plant sources for both protein and carbohydrates; primarily getting these essential nutrients through pollen (protein, essential for the development of larvae) and nectar (carbohydrates, essential for adult bees). Pollen is fed to larvae and is an important part of the diet of mature bees. Bees, unlike many other 'accidental' pollinators, intentionally gather pollen and, by doing so, expertly pollinate flowering plants.

Due to their gregarious pollination, bees have been crucial to the human diet likely since the earliest evolution of our species. In many areas of the world, foraging human societies relied on berries, fruit, and nuts to provide essential nutrients and calories. These foods are largely derived from plants that need animal pollination to produce fruit and seeds. When humans began to intentionally cultivate plants, the pollination work of bees became even more crucial to the human diet. The 'free gift' of pollination (Ellis et al. 2020) provided by bees has enabled the flourishing of human agriculture throughout the world. For much of human agrarian history, abundant ecological lifeworlds provided bees with ample forage and habitat nurtured by diverse farming and gardening practices (Ellis et al. 2020). Until the 20th century, many farms around the world were polycultures in which a wide variety of crops were grown. The common practices of leaving pollinator flower patches, cultivating a variety of crops, leaving fallow land, and planting hedgerows along fields allowed for bee flourishing. To flourish is to grow in conditions in which needs are not only met, but exceeded, allowing individuals and species to thrive. To flourish requires ecological lifeworlds that are dynamic and abundant. Mutual flourishing within ecological lifeworlds and between species of animals (including humans) and plants, requires interspecies sharing and cooperation.

About 10,000 years ago honey bees were domesticated in what can be called hive beekeeping (in which they are kept in human-created hives) in the Fertile Crescent, although they should be understood to only be semi-domesticated animals largely due to their natural swarming behaviour (Seeley 2019). The species *Apis mellifera*, or the Western honey bee, is the world's most widely managed honey bee species, and the only one currently living in the United States and Canada. In the wild *Apis mellifera* typically makes their home in cavities such as the hollow sections of the trunks of large trees or crevices in rocks, and will expand their colony – and honey production – depending on the size of the cavity. Over time, people discovered that *Apis mellifera* is an adaptable species of bee that will also make their homes in human-created cavities. Although the exact process of the domestication of *Apis mellifera* is unknown, it likely began with humans providing cavities that mimicked their preferred home, with intentional beekeeping, or apiculture, beginning in Egypt and spreading to many parts of North Africa, the Middle East, and Europe (Crane 1999) where it was intertwined with agriculture for millennia.

The domestication of honey bees and the rise of agrarian societies

The relationship between human agriculture and bees is long and entangled. In most parts of the world, humans relied on the work of bees of all species to produce abundant sources of food, especially fruits, nuts, and some vegetables. Even before honey bees were domesticated by humans, the relationship of humans to bees through specific practices central to agrarian societies – the cultivation of certain crops and the saving of seeds was entangled in mutually beneficial ways. Although not present in the archaeological record, it is posited that the ancestors of modern humans engaged in honey hunting in regions in which honey-producing eusocial bees lived (Crane 1999).

Honey collection from non-domesticated bees

Honey, its production by honey bees, and the desire of humans to consume it, is an important part of the long, entangled relationship between bees and people. For most of this relationship, humans acquired honey by engaging in various honey collection practices including honey hunting and the tending of wild honey bee nests. Honey collection involves locating nests of honey-producing bees and removing some of the honey and wax in ways that leaves the colony intact and reduces stings to the honey hunter. In many places of the world in which people currently engage in honey collection from non-domesticated bees, the nests are considered to be owned by a family, kin-group, or entire community (Crane 1999). Honey collection and nest-tending practices include a variety of practices, knowledge, and tools that differ greatly based on the individual person, community practices, region, and species of bee. In some areas of the world, depending on which species of honey-producing bee was most prevalent, this was a dangerous and highly skilled practice as it involved climbing up cliffs or very high trees to take the honey from defensive and stinging bees (Crane 1999). Honey hunting practices did not only include the gathering of honey, but often also included the stewarding of the trees in which the bees chose to nest, protecting the trees for years, and passing down knowledge about honey hunting and honey tree stewardship to other members of a family or community. The practice of honey hunting was often part of a broader forest management strategy used for procuring honey, nuts, fruits, firewood, and other important resources (Tsing 2003).

The stewarding of food forests has a long history in many parts of world, but particularly in tropical regions, continuing to the present day in some parts of the world. Forest stewardships practices included the collection and planting of seeds and the ongoing maintenance of stands of nut, fruit, or 'honey' trees. Fruit trees, berry trees, and nut trees have been important in the diets of many groups of people throughout the world because of the availability of important nutrients, sugar and fat. Many foraging societies were seasonally nomadic, and there is evidence that stands of fruit and nut trees in some dense forests were nurtured by the same kin-group for decades, giving that kin-group customary rights to the fruit and nuts (Tsing 2003). Honey bee colonies are perennial and can live continuously for many years often in the same spot, so kin-groups among some people in the world also had customary rights to trees in which wild bee colonies lived (Tsing 2003).

Without bee pollination, most fruit and nut trees would not develop the nutrient-rich foods sought after by humans and many other animals. Honey hunting, and the accompanying stewarding of food forests, can be considered a mutually beneficial relationship between honey bees and people, albeit one in which the bees have not consented. The intentional planting and active nurturing of fruit and nut trees by people is beneficial for bees seeking out ample sources of both nectar and pollen. While many trees have good nectar flow when in bloom, they are perhaps more important as essential sources of pollen for bees (Hill and Webster 1995). Human-planted stands of fruit and nut producing trees are highly beneficial for many species of bees and represents one of the longest-standing mutually beneficial food-generating practices between bees and humans, likely existing thousands of years before the rise of grain-based agriculture, the emergence of stationary agrarian-based societies, and the domestication of honey bees.

Honey collecting and hunting practices are varied and diverse around the world, with much of the knowledge about specific practices and knowledge based on ethnographic research on communities in which these practices still exist. While over-generalizing these practices is not useful or accurate, there are a few important aspects of this relationship between people and honey-producing bees. One, this relationship has likely existed for thousands of years in regions of the world in which honey-producing eusocial bees live, although artifacts of it are unlikely to show up in the archaeological record. Two, this relationship was not simply about getting access to honey, but about stewarding trees in which bees nest, while getting access to a valuable whole food product and was tied to complicated community ownership rules. Three, honey collecting in many ways resembles beekeeping and so it complicates the timeline of and some conceptions about the domestication of honey bees.

Domestication of Apis mellifera *and the semi-domesticated nature of honey bees*

Societies in which humans engaged in diverse types of agriculture were numerous, and preceded the development of the grain-based, largely sedentary societies associated with a shift to agrarianism. It is important to note that horticultural practices overlapped with foraging societies in many parts of the world, the idea that human societies were bound and static based on their food-based means of production is not accurate. In fact, human societies that tended to flourish and persevere were the ones that had diverse forms of food-procurement including hunting, foraging wild food from plants, cultivating some plants, and nurturing stands of fruit and nut producing trees. With the rise of grain-based systems of agriculture in Southwest Asia, Northern Africa, and Southern Europe, came dramatic changes to the lives of people living in those regions as well as the lives of the animals in which those people were entangled. Grain-based systems of agriculture, settled along waterways, led to more sedentary and larger-scale agrarian societies (Scott 2017). While most grains are wind-pollinated and do not rely on the work of animal pollinators, the creation of large-scale permanent or semi-permanent human settlements based on the growing of grains meant that other forms of agriculture including the growing of food-producing plants that rely on animal pollination also became common and increased in scale. Occurring over many thousands of years, the development of these permanent, large-scale grain-based societies led to the domestication of some species of animals (Larson et al. 2014), including herding animals such as cows, goats, and sheep, as well as cats and honey bees. The domestication of these animals differed greatly based on species and geographical region but most experts believe the process was neither linear or simple and likely involved a variety of pathways as well as false starts, and interruptions (Larson et al. 2014). The domestication of herding animals, cats, and honey bees was a transformative and distinctive aspect of large-scale agrarian societies beginning in and around Northern and Eastern Africa, Asia, and, to a lesser extent, South America (Larson et al. 2014).

The exact ways in which honey bees were domesticated is, of course, unknown and like other forms of animal domestication probably happened in a variety of different ways depending on region and the subspecies of honey bee. The most probable reason honey bees were domesticated was so humans could have safe and regular access to honey and, to a lesser extent, wax. Instead of climbing a tree or scaling a cliffside, it would be much easier and safer to have a readily available source of honey close to human settlements. Honey bees were not initially domesticated or managed by humans for their pollination work because bees of all species, as well as other animal pollinators, would have lived in abundance in regions where forage and appropriate nesting materials and sites existed. There would have been no need for humans to actively move pollinating honey bees onto their spaces – only to create the conditions in which they could thrive. Although the pollination work of managed bees would have been beneficial in areas of largescale and settled agriculture, it would have been abundant without the need for human intervention. The pollination work of bees only becomes scarce, entailing moving honey bees onto agricultural landscapes relatively recently, when monocropping of pollinator-dependant crops became common and wild populations of pollinators become scarce (Ellis et al. 2020).

There are several species of honey-producing bees including honey bees in the *Apis* genus, and stingless bees in the *Melipona* genus,[1] that are managed by humans for honey and pollination, likely for thousands of years. However, one species has come to dominate the beekeeping industry – *Apis mellifera*. *Apis mellifera* was much easier to domesticate than other species of honey bees, due to their nesting and reproduction habits, and, as a result, this species of honey bee has become thoroughly embedded within capitalist agriculture throughout the world. *Apis mellifera* nests in cavities, often choosing hollowed-out trees or other enclosed and protected spaces such as cracks and crevices in cliffs and caves. There are numerous bees in their colonies and the colony expands to fit the space of their nest. When a colony of *Apis mellifera* finds a good spot to nest, close to ample sources of forage and protected from both wind and water, they will stay in that nesting site for many years, sending out swarms to find new nest sites when their numbers get too large for the space. Due to these characteristics if humans create an acceptable nesting site for a colony of this species of honey bee, it will stay in that site, producing honey and wax, for many years. *Apis mellifera* can survive in cooler climates, something not true for stingless bees who live extensively in tropical areas of the world, making them easy to move to cooler regions of the world as agrarian-based societies expanded.

The swarming behaviour of *Apis mellifera* likely made them easier to (semi) domesticate. Swarming is honey bee reproduction on the colony level in which half the colony and the old queen leave to find a new place to nest, while the remaining bees raise a new queen. Other species of *Apis*, most notably *Apis cerana*, or the Asian honey bee, swarm but they do so more frequently and often without warning, making it harder for beekeepers to keep a colony in a hive (Theisen-Jones and Bienefeld 2017). Beekeeping with *Apis cerana* requires beekeepers to consider themselves stewards more than keepers, as these bees have a high amount of autonomy from beekeepers. While swarming can be troublesome for beekeepers to manage, it is one of the ways that they have traditionally established new hives before there was a sub-industry devoted specifically to rearing queens. In fact, catching swarms and putting them into human-created nest sites such as straw skeps, tree hives, logs, crevices in rocks and stone walls is likely how honey bees were initially domesticated (Crane 1999).

Humans likely employed diverse strategies to influence where honey bees lived, to get easy access to honey and wax long before they were officially considered to be domesticated animals. When people located a honey bee nesting site, they would not only take honey but also maintain the ability of the colony to flourish in that spot through activities such as protecting the nesting site from predators and extreme weather. Before honey bees were domesticated, people probably engaged in colony splitting, mimicking the swarming behaviour of honey bees, setting the new colony in adequate, but not necessarily human-created, nesting sites. These types of practices would not show up in the archaeological record. The point at which honey bees are determined to have been domesticated is often thought to be when *human-created* hive bodies and beekeeping tools appear in the archaeological record.

There are debates among honey bee scientists and beekeepers about whether honey bees are actually domesticated, especially in comparison to other species of domesticated animals who are dependent on humans for survival and differ greatly from their wild counterparts. While different 'breeds,' sometimes called 'races' of *Apis mellifera* exist, so-called domesticated honey bees remain physiologically very close to their wild counterpart (Seeley 2019). They have a high degree of agency from beekeepers, especially through their swarming behaviour which can be impossible to control once a colony makes the decision to swarm (Seeley 2011). Honey bees go feral quickly, and often successfully, also largely due to their swarming behaviour. The success of feral honey bees has only been hampered recently with the rise of pests and pathogens, especially the parasitic varroa mite (Seeley 2019). Preeminent entomologist Thomas Seeley considers *Apis mellifera* honey bees to be semi-domesticated, managed but not fully domesticated by humans (Seeley 2019). He argues that, unlike domesticated animals, artificial selection of specific traits in honey bees has only been practiced for the past century and as a result there are no distinct breeds of honey bees in a genetic sense. The subspecies of *Apis mellifera* that exist are due to natural selection, not human breeding (Seeley 2019). They readily return to the wild, living without human intervention and, as Seeley illustrates, "these wild colonies show us that honey bees have not yielded their nature to us, for whenever they live on their own, they still follow a way of life set millions of years ago" (2019, p. 98).

However, honey bees cannot be considered wild animals because they are actively bred and intensively managed by humans for their role as honey producers and pollinators. They retain a high level of agency but beekeepers control many aspects of their lives, including finding ways to disrupt swarming, splitting colonies, raising queens, and artificially feeding them sugar syrup and pollen patties. Furthermore, the ways in which they have been moved across the world and integrated into systems of agriculture on every scale means that they, as a species, lack true autonomy. They have been moved across landscapes in ways that they never would have been able to without considerable human intervention including landscapes in which they are highly vulnerable, requiring more intervention from humans. For example, when honey bee colonies are moved to regions with a high amount of monoculture agriculture, their diets may need to be supplemented by humans in order for them to survive. Likewise, although honey bees have strategies to survive very cold winters, the colony mortality rates increase when they are moved to regions with long, cold winters. Honey bees in these regions may require extra insulation, food, and protection from predators to survive winter. In these hostile landscapes, honey bees are more dependent on humans and less able to exercise autonomy.

With the rapid spread of pests and pathogens, largely due to this movement across space, even feral honey bees face some of the complications of domesticity. One of the most universally harmful effects of domesticity is the rapid spread of pests and pathogens, which are then treated by humans in ways that may cause further problems for the domesticated animals (Farrell and Davies

2019). Even though honey bees retain a higher level of agency and autonomy from humans than other domesticated animals, they have not escaped this fate. Although honey bees in the wild encountered pests and pathogens, they were sometimes able to co-exist with them within regional boundaries. The bees could adapt to the threat posed by the pest over time, and many pests could not move across landscapes rapidly enough to devastate populations on a large scale (Seeley 2019). This adaptation has happened in species of honey bees that have not as domesticable as *Apis mellifera* but who are managed by humans such as the Asian honey bee (Thiessen-Jones and Bienefeld 2017).[2] As will be discussed in Chapter 3, when discussing the embeddedness of beekeeping within capitalist agriculture, the varroa mites' devastating effect on *Apis mellifera* populations both managed and feral, is an example of the problems of honey bee domestication.

What is abundantly clear about *Apis mellifera*, which for the rest of this book will be referred to simply as honey bees, is that they are deeply and intricately intertwined with human agricultural systems. Their semi-domestication occurred in the same period and among the same people who established grain-based agrarian societies (Crane 1999). In many parts of the world, human agricultural systems have included honey bees, especially agricultural systems that are large-scale and less biodiverse. While other species of bees engage in crucial pollination work within agricultural landscapes, the honey bee has been intentionally integrated into those landscapes for thousands of years.

Human agriculture and bee flourishing

Honey bees have played a special role in human agriculture for thousands of years and yet it is hard to concretely determine if it is mutually beneficial. Certainly, the keeping of honey bees benefits humans providing honey, wax, and other products (some people consumed the gathered pollen as well as larvae) (Crane 1999). Honey has a wide range of uses including as a sweetener; fermented into mead (possibly the first alcoholic beverage intentionally created by people), and as a medicine (Crane 1999). Wax also had a wide variety of uses including as the base of candles, salves and lotions, with many practical household uses, and as a medium in art. Managed honey bees would have also provided pollination for a variety of crops, although this pollination work was not needed due to the abundance of wild bees. It is important to consider how honey bees benefited from their initial semi-domestication and early integration into human agriculture. To an extent, beekeepers may have protected colonies from predators, the most damaging of which are bears, and the elements such as rainstorms, high winds, and excessive sun. Beekeepers in the past, as they do in the present, probably chose hive locations that were sunny, with some afternoon shade; contained wind breaks; and were protected from extreme weather hazards such as flooding. However, wild honey bees are usually quite adept at finding good nest location on their own without human intervention.

The most beneficial aspect that semi-domestication brought to honey bees was that it enabled them to flourish in regions in which they may not have thrived, or even been present without human intervention. Part of the reason for this thriving is that they were integrated into polycultural agricultural systems. Honey bees are generalist bees who find forage from a variety of flowering plants, but they have, in a sense, co-evolved with the plants cultivated by humans. Their integration into polycultural agricultural systems that featured a wide variety of plants flowering throughout the growing season was so beneficial for honey bees that they continue to seek out and prefer those plants (Urbanowicz et al. 2020). Although non-agricultural ecosystems may have experienced occasional dearth in terms of nectar and pollen, polycultural agriculture providing food, mostly to be directly consumed by the people who lived nearby, had continuous forage available for honey bees. As Crane (1999) describes in meticulous detail, the keeping of bees was an activity undertaken by numerous human societies using a wide diversity of practices and guided by dynamic and varied beekeeping philosophies with some early practices of beekeeping apparently designed to cause as little disruption to the colonies as possible. This can be seen in innovate early hive design, such as hives that closely mimic the preferred nesting site of wild honey bees, the hollowed-out portion of a tree trunk or a crevice in a rock face. The presence of calming tools such as smokers and entrances designed to cause little agitation to bees are other indications of beekeeping philosophies designed to minimally disrupt honey bees. Some beekeeping practices did include the seasonal killing of bees to get honey and wax, but this seems to not be the norm in the human history of beekeeping.

Wild bees and human agriculture

While honey bees have long been celebrated and integrated in many human societies, much less is known about the historical relationship between people and the thousands of bee species that do not produce honey. Human diets both before and after the establishment of agrarian societies have been highly dependent on the pollination work of wild bees, most of which do not produce honey consumed by people. While it is impossible to assess, it is reasonable to assume that the pollination work of wild bees would have been noticed by people whose everyday lives involved foraging for or cultivating plant-based foods. Among agricultural societies in which diversified polycultures were managed, human-created landscapes would have been quite beneficial for wild bees as they provided ideal forage conditions (e.g., flowering plants producing nectar and/or pollen); nesting locations (e.g., bare ground, pithy stems, decaying wood); and nesting materials (e.g., leaves, mud). These landscapes, particularly before the expansion of capitalist agriculture, would have been filled with wild bees and other pollinators.

The cultural and spiritual importance of bees

Within the agrarian societies in which honey bees were managed, bees often held a place of importance not only in relation to agriculture and food but also within artistic, philosophical, and spiritual life. Among the Ancient Greece, the Melissae, the Greek word for bee, are referred to in many myths as being bee-maidens, nymphs, priestesses of Artemis, or sometimes represented by the goddess Melissa (Ransome 2004). The oracle at Delphi was referred to as the Bee Oracle and both honey and bees played an important part in the rituals of the priestesses at the site (Ransome 2004). The Ancient Greek philosopher Aristotle wrote about the behaviour and social organization of bees, including providing scientific insights, some of which are correct and some of which are not but were nonetheless based on careful and frequent observation of honey bees. In fact, Aristotle integrated his understandings of the social relationships of honey bees into some of his ideas about human democracy and political organizing (Abbate 2016). As Abbate (2016) recalls, "Aristotle observed that both bees and ants engage in complex forms of interaction and cooperation and that they are able to adapt to changes in the environment in order to maintain good social order, leading him to conclude that they, too, are 'political animals'" (p. 56).

Honey bees were held in high esteem within North Africa and West Asia and are mentioned several times in the Koran and other religious texts. In Arabic and Muslim texts, honey was often discussed as medicine as well as food. As the writer Ibn Magih, a medieval scholar of hadith wrote, "Honey is a remedy for every illness, and the Koran is a remedy for all illnesses of the mind, therefore I recommend both remedies to you, the Koran and Honey" (Ransome 2004, p. 73). In parts of Europe various customs developed around the keeping of bees. Some of these customs were directly brought to the Americas by European settlers, including the custom of *the telling of the bees*, a practice reported in several European countries as well as the Northeastern US, in which beekeepers tell bees about notable things that have happened in their life since the last hive check, most importantly births and deaths (Burnside 2015). In some places, this practice also involved including bee hives in the mourning when family members of the beekeeper died, or of the beekeeper him or herself, by telling the bees about the death and covering the hive(s) in a mourning cloak (Morley 1899). These customs, stories, poems, and musings, although diverse, varied, and dynamic illustrate that many of the humans who lived among honey bees saw themselves as being in a meaningful relationship with bees that sparked curiosity, interest, and a sense of enchantment.

Capitalist agriculture and the global pollinator crisis

According to many scientists and environmentalists the Earth is in the midst of a mass extinction event, sometimes referred to as the 6th mass extinction[3] (Barnosky et al. 2011). Although the Earth has experienced five mass extinction events in its history, this is the first event triggered by the actions of one species – humans – and the only one to occur since the evolution of humans (Barnosky et al. 2011). A mass extinction event is deemed to have occurred (or be occurring) when the rate of extinction is accelerating much quicker than the background rate.[4] In the history of the Earth, mass extinctions have been caused by catastrophic events that cause global climatic changes and occur over short geologic times (but very large spans of time in human terms) of one to a few million years (Barnosky et al. 2011). The 6th mass extinction event, thus far, includes extinctions and endangerments of small numbers of species, but it also includes defaunation of *many* species. Defaunation is an important, but sometimes overlooked, concept in understanding the global biodiversity crisis because it signals that in addition to some species facing extinction, many species who do not risk extinction or endangerment are, nevertheless, experiencing a decline in their overall population (Weis 2018). This mass defaunation of animal species is coupled with a sharp increase in numbers of livestock animals, who are numerous but unhealthy, living overwhelmingly miserable lives (Weis 2018). When examining the biodiversity crisis, it is important to understand that the presence of large populations of domesticated animals, in the billions for pigs and chickens (Weis 2018), is not an indication that these animals are flourishing. The global pollinator crisis must be situated in the context of this larger crisis in biodiversity.

The global pollinator crisis occurs in the context of a widespread defaunation of insect populations (Wagner et al. 2021), that influential environmental writer George Monbiot refers to as an "insectageddon" (2017). Although many scientists have argued that this term, and some studies about insect decline, are alarmist, other scientists are highlighting the seriousness and uncertainty of insect decline. As Jereoen van der Sluijs, a professor of theory of science and ethics of natural sciences at Bergen University points out,

> Although this term has been criticized as being overly alarmist and unsubstantiated by data, entomologists warn that insects are indeed disappearing before we even have data. Of the approximately 5.5 million insect species, about 90% has not even been named, nor have their roles in ecosystems been mapped. *No global scientific monitoring of insect abundance in the past and present exists and there are no plans for systematic global monitoring in the near future.*
>
> (2020, emphasis added)

This uncertainty about actual insect populations makes insect decline especially troubling. The extent to which their numbers are dwindling is relatively unknown, and for some species will remain unknowable. While some species of insects, especially those that live in eusocial colonies such as honey bees, termites, and ants, are relatively well-studied and well-understood by scientists, most species of insects are unstudied. Adding to this complication is that there are many species of insects who have never been classified by scientists, especially those that live in tropical areas of the world (van der Sluijs 2020). If a baseline population has not been established for some insect species, then it is difficult to know the extent to which their numbers are dwindling.

Despite this limitation there have been some troubling longitudinal and review studies that indicate that populations of insects are in steep decline

(Habel et al. 2019; Sánchez-Bayo and Wyckuys 2019; Lister and Garcia 2018; Hallmann et al. 2017). A longitudinal survey in Germany (Hallmann et al. 2017) was conducted in a nature reserve located amongst landscapes of capitalist agriculture, and may indicate how capitalist agriculture affects species of insects in terms of both the diversity of species and the abundance within species (Hallman et al. 2017). The researchers posited that the estimated 76% flying insect biomass decline over almost 30 years was a result of the practices of capitalist agriculture, especially the use of systemic pesticides (Hallman et al. 2017). Sánchez-Bayo and Wyckuys (2019) likewise argue that the main driver of widespread insect declines is the intensification of agriculture. Another longitudinal survey conducted in Puerto Rico at a nature reserve not located near intensively managed agricultural landscapes, indicated that a decline in arthropod biomass, which they estimated had fallen 10 to 30 times since the 1970s, was possibly due to human-caused climate change (Lister and Garcia 2018). Both studies are contested among scientists with some arguing that longitudinal surveys were not as rigorous as they should be and that the claims being made were unnecessarily alarmist (Schowalter et al. 2021; Saunders et al. 2020). Some scientists have called for a cautious approach to proclaiming a widespread decline in insect populations, arguing that better funded scientific studies are needed. However, with lack of a baseline for most species of insects, there are few ways to truly know whether insect populations are in decline, if not through imperfect longitudinal studies. It should be noted that the decline of insect populations, like biodiversity loss more generally and the risk of climate change, is not an issue of mere scientific interest. Insect decline, biodiversity loss, and climate change dramatically affect all life on earth, including all humans. Ecological destruction, manifested in climate change and biodiversity loss, requires political action as well as massive societal transformations. In order for massive societal transformations to occur on the necessary scale there must be a sense of urgency about the multiple, intersecting crises faced by all life on Earth.

Like other insects, most species of wild bees are not widely studied, and their population numbers and health statuses are unknown (Siviter et al. 2021). This is partly because bee species are numerous, with 20,000 species worldwide. Most bees are solitary and not as easily studied by scientists as eusocial bees. As semi-domesticated animals heavily used within agricultural systems, honey bees are very well-studied and, although their populations are managed by humans, their decline in health and their general vulnerability to environmental degradation indicates that other species of bees may also be in trouble. Bumble bees, of which there are hundreds of species worldwide especially in temperate regions, are also widely studied by researchers because they are eusocial, living in colonies of several hundred members, depending on the species. The nests of eusocial bees are large enough to accommodate the adult and larval members of the colony and because of this, the wax and other materials used to construct the nest can be dismantled and thoroughly studied. Wax in particular gives scientists important information about exposure to pesticides and other toxins because it is a fatty substance in which many toxins accumulate. Bumble bees are also managed by humans for agricultural purposes, albeit on a much smaller scale than honey bees, which gives scientists easier access to nests and colonies. Although there are problems with extrapolating from the results of studies on bumble bees and highly managed honey bees, when discussing solitary, wild bees, it can give some insight into the multiple environmental problems faced by other insects. Indeed, research from studies on both honey bees and bumble bees indicates that bee populations face serious declines in health and, for some, species of wild bees, population (Woodcock et al. 2017; Goulson et al. 2015).

The long-standing interconnection between people and bees of all species becomes starkly apparent when grappling with the realities of the current decline in the health of honey bees and the health and populations of wild bees. While the global, capitalist food system seems to be powerful and well-established it is, in fact, extremely vulnerable. A steep decline in bee health and populations would cause a crisis for agriculture on a global scale, especially in the cultivation of many species of vegetables, fruit, and nuts (FAO 2018). It would also lead to a decline in some of the plants that pastured livestock consume such as alfalfa. There is no viable alternative to animal pollinators for plants that rely on their work. The dystopian imaginaries of robo-bees and genetically modified super bees have not yet left the realm of high-tech tinkering (Nimmo 2021). Engineers and scientists working on these projects have not found a viable alternative to bees as pollinators. Exploring these fake bees as a solution to the global pollinator crisis is a deeply cynical act when tens of thousands of bee species currently exist in a wide variety of landscapes around the world. The things that bees need to flourish are known and understood and, on the surface, extremely simple: they need ample forage in the form of nectar and pollen-rich plants, they need good nesting sites and they need adequate sources of nesting materials. Bees of all species need landscapes that are free from extensive pesticide usage, in the form of both insecticides *and* herbicides. Additionally, as I will argue in Chapters 6 and 7, honey bees need mindful beekeepers who engage in practices in which the preferences and physiological needs of bees are centred. While the needs of bees are relatively straightforward, these needs are in direct conflict with capitalist agriculture. Capitalist agriculture is not simply any form of agriculture that operates within the capitalist system. There are many forms of subsistence, smallholder agricultural operations that are only partially integrated into the global capitalist system (Wittman 2009). Capitalist agriculture is agriculture focused on the accumulation of wealth and capital through the simplifying and standardizing of landscapes for the purposes of the cultivation of crops, and raising of animals whose bodies and bodily products will be turned into commodities. Capitalist agriculture commoditizes food and this commodification is embedded within a global system of exchange in which the production of crops and livestock is often, but not always, intended for export.

Capitalist agriculture causes suffering to both wild animals and domesticated animals, albeit in different ways. For wild animals, the suffering largely occurs through their defaunation or removal from landscapes. For domesticated animals, their suffering occurs in the ways in which they are moved across and integrated, in large numbers, into capitalist landscapes. Attempts to decouple defaunation of wild animals and the suffering of domesticated "livestock" animals creates a fragmented and incomplete understanding of how capitalist agriculture deeply harms both groups of animals, causing suffering, misery, and death. The reasons for declining *health* in honey bees and other managed bee species, and declining *populations* in many species of wild bees are similar: simplified and standardized agricultural landscapes enabled by widespread use of pesticides, and climate change which is exacerbated by capitalist agriculture. To cast the vulnerabilities of honey bees and defaunation of wild bees as separate, unrelated issues, as some native bee advocates have attempted to do, is to obfuscate the role played by capitalist agriculture in both of these serious global problems.

The conflict between the needs of bees and the dominant practices of capitalist agriculture is at the heart of the global pollinator crisis. While there are many causes of the pollinator crisis, some quite specific to certain species, the incompatibility of capitalist agriculture with pollinator flourishing is the main overarching cause of recent declines of wild bee populations and managed bee health. A radical transformation of agriculture, enabling a move away from monocultured, pesticide-soaked landscapes is one of the most urgently needed solutions to the pollinator crisis. This is especially true as the impacts of climate change on populations of wild bees are in the beginning stages of being researched and understood by scientists. Emerging research suggests that some species of bees will not be able to adapt to changes in climate and will be harmed by extreme weather events (Soroye et al. 2020; Faleiro et al. 2018; Kerr et al. 2015). While struggles against climate change are crucial and urgent, even a steep and immediate reduction in fossil fuels use and atmospheric gas emission will not undo the process of climate change that has already begun. The effects of climate change that are being felt today are a result of past emissions, and the cascading effects of current emissions are yet to be truly realized in the global environment. With the knowledge that there will be *some* irreversible harm to bee species due to climate change, it is even more imperative that capitalist agriculture be radically transformed. As Nimmo (2015, pp. 185–186) argues, the problems of pollinator loss ultimately lie with the "industrial-capitalist political economic structure of the system".

Conclusion

There is a global decline in the health of honey bees and a decline in the health and populations of many species of wild bees. This is very troubling because of the important role that bees play in pollinating most species of plants. As Packer and colleagues (2007) state, a decline in bee species could lead to unprecedented collapse of terrestrial ecosystems. In many ways bee species are the canary in the coal mine when it comes to the impacts of capitalist agricultural systems on insects and other wildlife. The long entanglement of human diets with bees means that bee vulnerability will also cause vulnerability for humans and our food system. This is not a call to action to save the global capitalist agricultural system but instead to ensure the current and future ability of humans to cultivate food that leads to nutritionally sound and diverse diets that are culturally appropriate. Essentially the global pollinator decline requires humans to confront the dominant practices of capitalist agriculture so the intricate, complex, and long-standing relationship humans have with bees and other pollinators can be protected. The human relationship with bees of all species existed before and will hopefully exist after capitalism. This call to action becomes even more urgent when also considering the impact of climate breakdown on wild bee populations. The time to act on behalf of all species of bees is *now*.

Notes

1 Stingless bees form a large tribe *Meliponini*, of which there are many genera. The genus *Melipona* is the genus of stingless bees in which there are social, honey-producing bees who are actively managed by people in tropical and sub-tropical regions of the world.
2 The Asian honey bee, *Apis cerana*, is managed by beekeepers in many parts of Asia. However, they are not as easily moveable or retained as *Apis mellifera*, largely due to their tendency to swarm and abscond far more often (Thiessen-Jones and Bienefeld 2017). They are not as willing to live in human-created hive boxes and are kept in conditions that mimic their wild conditions. Even then, colonies are likely to leave within a year or two.
3 The 5th mass extinction event occurred around 65 million years ago (over a period of 1 to 2.5 million years) and involved the extinction of the dinosaurs (Barnosky et al. 2011).
4 The background rate is the rate in which a small number of species go extinct under normal conditions (Barnosky et al. 2011).

References

Abbate, C. (2016). "Higher" and "lower" political animals: A critical analysis of Aristotle's account of the political animal. *Journal of Animal Ethics*, 6 (1), 54–66. https://doi.org/10.5406/janimalethics.6.1.0054.

Barnosky, A., Matzke, N., Tomiya, S., Wogan, G. O. U., Swartz, B., Quental, T. B. … & Ferrar, E.A. (2011). Has the Earth's sixth mass extinction already arrived? *Nature*, 471, 51–57. https://doi.org/10.1038/nature09678.

Burnside, J. (2015). Apiculture: Telling the bees. *Nature*, 521, 30–31. https://doi.org/10.1038/521029a.

Crane, E. (1999). *The World History of Beekeeping and Honey Hunting*. New York: Routledge.

Dance, C., Botias, C., & Goulson, D. (2017). The combined effects of a monotonous diet and exposure to thiamethoxam on the performance of bumblebee micro-colonies. *Ecotoxicology and Environmental Safety*, 139, 194–201.

Ellis, R., Weis, T., Suryanarayanan, S., & Beilin, K. (2020). From a free gift of nature to a precarious commodity: Bees, pollination services, and industrial agriculture. *Journal of Agrarian Change*, 20 (3), 437–459. https://doi.org/10.1111/joac.12360.

Faleiro, F. V., Nemesio, A., & Loyolo, R. (2018). Climate change likely to reduce orchid bee abundance even in climatic suitable sites. *Global Change Biology*, 24 (6), 2272–2283. https://doi.org/10.1111/gcb.14112.

Farrell, M. J. & Davies, T. J. (2019). Disease mortality in domesticated animals is predicted by host evolutionary relationships. *Proceedings of the National Academy of Sciences*, 116 (16), 7911–7915. doi:10.1073/pnas.1817323116.

Food and Agriculture Organization (FAO). (2018). Bees matter: The importance of bees and other pollinators for food and agriculture. Food and Agriculture Organization of the United Nations, May 20. https://www.fao.org/3/i9527en/i9527en.pdf.

Food and Agriculture Organization (FAO). (2008). Pollination services for sustainable agriculture. Food and Agriculture Organization of the United Nations. https://www.fao.org/3/i1046e/i1046e.pdf.

Gill, R. J. & Raine, N. E. (2014). Chronic impairment of bumblebee natural foraging behaviour induced by sublethal pesticide exposure. *Functional Ecology*, 28, 1459–1471.

Goulson, D., Nicholls, E., Botias, C., & Rotheray, E. L. (2015). Bee declines driven by combined stress from parasites, pesticides, and lack of flowers. *Science*, 347 (6229). 10.1126/science.1255957.

Habel, J. C., Samways, M. J., & Schmitt, T. (2019). Mitigating the precipitous decline of terrestrial European insects: Requirements for a new strategy. *Biodiversity Conservation*, 28, 1343–1360. https://doi.org/10.1007/s10531-019-01741-8.

Hallmann C. A., Sorg, M., Jongejans, E., Siepel, H., Hofland, N...de Kroon, H. (2017). More than 75 percent decline over 27 years in total flying insect biomass in protected areas. *PLoS ONE*, 12 (10), e0185809. https://doi.org/10.1371/journal.pone.0185809.

Hill, D. B., & Webster, T. C. (1995). Apiculture and forestry (bees and trees). *Agroforest Systems*, 29, 313–320. https://doi.org/10.1007/BF00704877.

Kerr, J. Y., Pindar, A., Galpern, P., Packer, L., Potts, S. G., Roberts, S. M...& Pantoja, A. (2015). Climate change impacts on bumblebees converge across continents. *Science*, 649 (6244), 177–180. doi:10.1126/science.aaa7031.

Larson, G., Piperno, D. R., Allaby, R. G., Purugganan, M. D., Andersson, L., Arroyo-Kalin, M. ... & Fuller, D. Q. (2014). Present and future of domestication studies. *Proceedings of the National Academy of Sciences*, 111 (17), 6139–6146. doi:10.1073/pnas.1323964111.

Lister, B. C. & Garcia, A. (2018). Climate-driven declines in arthropod abundance restructure a rainforest food web. *PNAS*, 115 (44), https://doi.org/10.1073/pnas.1722477115.

Monbiot, G. (2017). Insectageddon: Farming is more catastrophic than climate breakdown. *Guardian*, October 20. https://www.theguardian.com/commentisfree/2017/oct/20/insectageddon-farming-catastrophe-climate-breakdown-insect-populations.

Morley, M. W. (1899). *The Honey-Makers*. Chicago: A. C. McClurg.

Nimmo, R. (2021). Replacing cheap nature? Sustainability, capitalist future-making and political ecologies of robotic pollination. *Environment and Planning E: Nature and Space*, 5 (1), 426–446, https://doi.org/10.1177/2514848620987368.

Nimmo, R. (2015). Apiculture in the Anthropocene. In Human Animal Research Network Editorial Collective (ed.), *Animals in the Anthropocene: Critical Perspectives on Non-human Futures*. Sydney: Sydney University Press, pp. 177–199.

Packer, L., Genaro, J. A., & Sheffield, C. S. (2007). The bee genera of Eastern Canada. *Canadian Journal of Arthropod Identification*, 3, 1–32.
Packer, L. (2011). *Keeping the Bees: Why All Bees Are at Risk and What We Can Do to Save Them*. New York: HarperCollins.
Ransome, H. M. (2004). *The Sacred Bee in Ancient Times and Folklore*. Mineola: New York.
Sánchez-Bayo, F. & Wyckhuys, K. A. G. (2019). Worldwide decline of the entomofauna: A review of its drivers, *Biological Conservation*, 232, 8–27, https://doi.org/10.1016/j.biocon.2019.01.020.
Saunders, M. E., Janes, J. K., & O'Hanlon, J. C. (2020). Moving on from the insect apocalypse narrative: Engaging with evidence-based insect conservation, *BioScience*, 70 (1), 80–89, https://doi.org/10.1093/biosci/biz143.
Schowalter, T. D., Pandey, M., Presley, S. J., Willig, M. R. & Zimmerman, J. K. (2021). Arthropods are not declining but are responsive to disturbance in the Luquillo Experimental Forest, Puerto Rico. *Proceedings of the National Academy of Sciences*, 118 (2) e2002556117; doi:10.1073/pnas.2002556117.
Scott, J. C. (2017). *Against the Grain: A Deep History of the Earliest States*. New Haven: Yale University Press.
Seeley, T. D. (2019). *The Lives of Bees: The Untold Story of the Honey Bee in the Wild*. Princeton: Princeton University Press.
Seeley, T. D. (2011). *Honeybee Democracy*. Princeton: Princeton University Press.
Siviter, H., Richman, S. K., & Muth, F. (2021). Field-realistic neonicotinoid exposure has sub-lethal effects on non-*Apis* bees: A meta-analysis. *Ecology Letters*, 24 (12), 2586–2597.
Smith, K. M., Loh, E. H., Rostal, M. K., Zambrana-Torrelio, C. M., Mendiola, L., & Daszak, P. (2013). Pathogens, pests, and economics: Drivers of honey bee colony declines and losses. *EcoHealth*, 10, 434–445.
Soroye, P., Newbold, T., & Kerr, J. (2020). Climate change contributes to widespread declines among bumble bees across continents. *Science*, 367 (678), 685–688.
Steinhauer, N., Kulhanek, K., Antunez, K., Human, H., Chatawannakul, P., Chauzat, M. P., & van Englesdrop, D. (2018). Drivers of colony losses. *Current Opinion in Insect Science*, 26, 142–148.
Theisen-Jones, H. & Bienefeld, K. (2016). The Asian honey bee (*Apis cerana*) is significantly in decline. *Bee World*, 93 (4), 90–97, doi:10.1080/0005772X.2017.1284973.
Tsing, A. (2003). Cultivating the wild: Honey hunting and forest management in Southeastern Kalimantan. In Zerner, C. (ed.) *Culture and the Question of Rights: Forests, Coasts, and Seas in Southeast Asia*. Durham: Duke University Press, pp. 25–55.
Tsvetkov, N., Samson-Robert, O., Sood, K., Patel, H. S., Malena, D. A., Gajiwala, P. H., Maciukiewicz, P.... & Zayed, A. (2017). Chronic exposure to neonicotinoids reduces honey bee health near corn crops. *Science*, 356 (June 30), 1395–1397.
Urbanowicz, C., Muniz, P. A., & McArt, S. A. (2020). Honey bees and wild pollinators differ in their preference for and use of introduced floral resources. *Ecology and Evolution*, 10 (13), 6741–6751. https://doi.org/10.1002/ece3.6417.
van der Sluijs, J. P. (2020). Insect decline, an emerging global environmental risk. *Opinion in Environmental Sustainability*, 46, 39–42, https://doi.org/10.1016/j.cosust.2020.08.012.
Wagner, D. L., Grames, E. M., Forister, M. L., Berenbaum, M. R., & Stopak, D. (2021). Insect decline in the Anthropocene: Death by a thousand cuts. *Proceedings of the National Academy of Sciences*, 118 (2). doi:10.1073/pnas.2023989118.

Weis, T. (2018). Ghosts and things: Agriculture and animal life. *Global Environmental Politics*, 18 (2), 134–142.

Wittman, H. (2009) Reworking the metabolic rift: La Vía Campesina, agrarian citizenship, and food sovereignty, *The Journal of Peasant Studies*, 36 (4), 805826, doi:10.1080/03066150903353991.

Woodcock, B. A., Bullock, J. M., Shore, R. F., Heard, M. S., Pereira, M. G., Redhead, J, & Pywell, R. F. (2017). Country-specific effects of neonicotinoid pesticides on honey bees and wild bees. *Science*, 356 (June 30), 1393–1395.

2 Bees in the Capitalocene

The idea that there is a human-caused 6th mass extinction of life on Earth (Barnosky et al. 2011) is often coupled with the assertion that Earth has entered a new geologic phase, the Anthropocene (Crutzen and Stoermer 2021). In this chapter I will argue that the Earth is indeed in the process of ecological destruction on a planetary scale that is more accurately understood as the Capitalocene as it is caused, not by humanity as a whole, but by a particular socioeconomic system that ultimately benefits only a small group of people. For bees of all species the Capitalocene, in the form of capitalist agriculture, threatens their health and, for some species, their existence, which will have serious, even irreparable, impacts on the functioning of all terrestrial ecological lifeworlds.

Capitalocene: the age of capital

The concept of the Anthropocene has received widespread attention from within and outside of academia. The concept was originally coined by biologist Eugene Stoermer and chemist Paul Crutzen in 2000 to highlight the profound, negative impact that humans have on the functioning of planetary systems and cycles (Crutzen and Stoermer 2021). The term is meant to highlight that the effect of human activity on planetary systems is significant enough to seriously and, in some cases, permanently, affect the functioning of those systems, with potentially disastrous results especially for the future existence of most species of animals and plants on Earth (Steffen et al. 2011). Although the concept is used by many scientists and social scientists, it is not widely accepted within the discipline of geology given the difficulties of determining if human activity has affected the functioning of the Earth's planetary systems enough to be recorded on the geological strata of the Earth. Nevertheless, the Anthropocene has captured the zeitgeist, conceptualizing the profound and devastating impact of humans on non-human nature.

However, the Anthropocene concept is problematic in several ways. First, there is no agreed upon baseline for determining when the Anthropocene, the geological age of humans, began (Steffen et al. 2011). The act of determining when the Anthropocene began is, a highly political act that indicates what

DOI: 10.4324/9781003142294-2

aspect of human activity the person making the claim believes is most harmful to the functioning of the planetary systems of Earth. Some scientists have proposed that the Anthropocene began with the establishment of the permanent, sedentary, large-scale agrarian societies which required the clearing of great swaths of land, accelerated the domestication of several species of animals, and led to the accumulation of wealth and capital amongst a small elite in those societies. Others argue that it began with the rise of the industrial revolution, marked by the invention of the steam engine and the widespread burning of coal, which allowed for the intensification and steeply increased scale of industrialization. Still others argue that the Anthropocene began with the Great Acceleration of industrial capitalism beginning after World War II with the explosion of fossil fuel-driven industry, energy use, and product creation (i.e., plastics). Lastly, some argue that it began with the rise of the Nuclear Age, also following World War II (Steffen et al. 2077), which has the potential to create large amounts of extremely toxic waste with no safe way to store it, and to cause a catastrophic global disaster.

The concept of the Anthropocene may be useful but it has the dangerous potential to homogenize human societies in ways that are ahistorical and inaccurate, erasing the ways in which certain socioeconomic systems harm the Earth more than others. It also hides the ways in which individual people are not equally implicated in this destruction of the Earth. Indeed, in popular and media usage, the term Anthropocene is often explicitly used to implicate humanity in the destruction of the Earth without addressing the destructive impacts of socioeconomic systems, most crucially, colonialism and capitalism. As a recent article in *Discover* states, "Welcome to the Anthropocene, a proposed new epoch in Earth history, in which *Homo sapiens are blindly steering the ship*" (Alex 2021, emphasis added). Another article, in the *New York Times*, about the multiple crises facing humanity post-COVID-19, asks, "How do we react to the *self-made devastation* of the Anthropocene?" (Nagamatsu 2022, emphasis added). An article in *Nature*'s online news website is simply titled "Humans vs Earth: the quest to define the Anthropocene" (Subramanian 2019). Even in academic use by scientific researchers, humanity as a whole is blamed for the multiple, intersecting crises facing the Earth. Steffen and colleagues (2007) clearly express this sentiment,

> Global warming and many other human-driven changes to the environment are raising concerns about the future of Earth's environment and *its ability to provide the services required to maintain viable human civilizations. The consequences of this unintended experiment of humankind* on its own life support system are hotly debated, but worst-case scenarios paint a gloomy picture for the future of contemporary societies
>
> (p. 614, emphasis added).

Activists and critical researchers have pointed out that blaming humanity as a whole for the devastating crises facing the Earth is inaccurate, unjust, and ineffective because it ignores the socioeconomic system (capitalism) that has shaped, extracted, polluted, and destroyed the ecological lifeworlds of the Earth to allow a small group of people to accumulate wealth (Moore 2015). As environmental historian Jason W. Moore argues the Anthropocene is an easy concept because "it does not challenge the naturalized inequalities, alienation, and violence inscribed in modernity's strategic relations of power and production" (2015, p. 82). Critical scholars and activists have proposed other ways of understanding the current epoch in which humanity finds itself. These alternatives to the Anthropocene are not necessarily replacements of the concept, partly because its use is ubiquitous. Rather, these alternatives are meant to disrupt the ways in which the concept is used and understood, highlighting the considerable problems and gaps.

The concept of the Capitalocene can provide an alternative way of understanding the dramatic effects humans have had on the planetary systems of the Earth. The term, originally coined by Andreas Malm and later developed by Moore (2015), helps to make visible the ways in which global capitalism organizes and disciplines nature, within which humans are embedded, for the benefit of a small group of people. The term provides an easily understandable critique of the Anthropocene, highlighting that it is capitalism, not humanity, that is disrupting the functioning of the Earth's systems in devastating and potentially permanent ways.

Moore (2015) argues that European colonialism in the Americas starting in 1492, marks the beginning of the Capitalocene, a world-making project in which the whole world, including all living beings and things, is subjected to extraction and plunder so that a small group of people can accumulate wealth, capital, and power. In Moore's view, the establishment of European colonialism in the Americas and the development of an economy based on plantation slavery were co-constitutive of one another. On plantation agricultural systems Indigenous people were forced off, killed, or enslaved; while people from West Africa were enslaved and forced to work in the fields, containing a small number of crops being grown in large amounts in order to be exported to Europe. These crops contributed to the rapid urbanization and industrialization of early capitalism in Europe, which required masses of workers to move to populous cities to work in factories (Mintz 1986). The central organizing logic of capitalism is that there must be continuous economic growth, which requires the constant search for new frontiers from which to plunder land, extract resources, and enclose commons.

Moore argues that there are several ways in which the ecological and human devastation caused by the Capitalocene can be traced to the beginning of European colonization of the Americas. One is through the massive loss of life of people in the Americas after the initial invasion of European colonialists. This loss of life was extreme, with researchers estimating that 90% of the Indigenous population of the Americas, about 55 million people. died within the first 100 years following the arrival of Columbus to the Americas due to direct genocide and, most dramatically, the spread of deadly pathogens to which people living in the Americas had no immunity (Koch et al. 2019).[1] This massive and unprecedented loss of human life over two of the Earth's continents resulted in a dramatic and rapid change in ecological lifeworlds as sophisticated agricultural systems collapsed, leading to rapid reforestation. This rapid shift in landscapes caused a shift in the CO^2 in the atmosphere, may have contributed to the Little Ice Age in the 17th century (Koch et al. 2019), and can be seen in the ecological record of the Earth. Other changes during the early stages of colonialism and capitalism include the devastation caused by the massive, forced movement of about 12 million people from West Africa to the Americas and Caribbean as part of the transatlantic slave trade (Lovejoy 1989) significantly and permanently disrupting societies in sub-Saharan Africa. The early processes associated with colonial-capitalism were also responsible for the massive, previously impossible, and large-scale movement of non-human animals, plants, and pathogens between Europe, Africa, and Asia and the Americas. Although movement of plants, pathogens, non-human animals, and humans had previously occurred, the scale and rapidity of the so-called Columbian Exchange far eclipsed anything that had previously occurred. Crosby (2004) describes this movement as ecological imperialism and argues it had a permanent and devastating impact on the people, societies, and ecological lifeworlds of the entire world.

The concept of the Capitalocene is useful for understanding the ways in which bees are embedded within and harmed by capitalist agriculture through the biological simplification and standardization of landscapes, plants, and non-human animals (Weis 2013). The simplification of landscapes occurs when biological diversity and complexity, including relationships that exist within ecological lifeworlds are diminished, intentionally or not. In the context of capitalist agriculture, it also refers to the simplification of the variety of crops being grown and animals raised, including of different breeds, and to the simplification of uses of crops and animals on farms. Standardization refers to the ways that landscapes are disciplined into standardized systems of operation, replicated across space. Wild spaces can exist, but only for specific purposes and in places where they are deemed acceptable. In terms of capitalist agriculture, standardization refers to the design and operation of agricultural landscapes, including a regimentation of the bodies of workers and non-human animals. In these simplified and standardized landscapes, human and non-human workers – such as honey bees – are enrolled as exploited labour, often moving across landscapes as the needs of the system necessitate. The humans, non-human animals, and plants that cannot exist in these landscapes are forcibly and violently removed or driven away by inhospitable living conditions such as, in the case of wild bees, a loss of forage, habitat sites, and adequate nesting materials. The concept of the Capitalocene provides a tangible way of understanding how monocultured agricultural landscapes have reworked large swaths of the Earth, while also highlighting the relationships of exploitation of both people and non-human nature upon which these landscapes are built and maintained.

The concept of the Capitalocene makes clear that it is not just that diverse, vibrant, and dynamic landscapes have been simplified and standardized but that those landscapes are part of a labour regime that involves disciplining the lives and bodies of living beings who are embedded or entrapped within those landscapes, making visible the relationships of exploitation and forced labour that exist within capitalist agriculture.

Settler-colonialism and honey bees in North America

Honey-producing bees existed in the Americas before the western honey bee. Stingless bees, native to parts of Central and South America, produce honey, and have been stewarded by the Mayan people for thousands of years (Jones 2012) but do not live outside of tropical regions. While there is evidence that honey bees were present in the Caribbean as early as 1617, the arrival of honey bees on mainland North America is documented to have occurred in 1622 having been brought to what is now Virginia by settler-colonialists (Crane 1999). Honey bees are part of the Columbian Exchange, the massive and rapid movement of species from Europe, Asia, and Africa to the Americas due to colonial capitalism that disrupted, changed, and destroyed landscapes and interspecies relationships. As such, honey bees should be understood as part of ecological imperialism (Crosby 2004). However, the individual species of animals and plants intentionally moved across continents were not in and of themselves necessarily a problem for the new ecological lifeworlds in which they inhabited. The problem partly arose due to the pace and scale through which they were moved, something that they would not be able to do on their own accord. The main reason ecological imperialism was so destructive to ecological lifeworlds is that these plants and animals were embedded within systems of colonial-capitalism. The crops and domesticated livestock animals moved as part of the Columbian Exchange were deployed within colonial-capitalism systems of agriculture, including but not only plantation agriculture, and, later, within the agricultural systems of settler-colonialists.

North America pre-1492 contained diverse permanent and semi-permanent settlements established by many different Indigenous nations. It is important to note that precolonial ecological lifeworlds were neither static nor 'pristine' in the sense of being absent of human intervention. Indigenous societies lived, foraged, cultivated crops, stewarded forests, fished, and hunted in North American landscapes for thousands of years before the arrival of Europeans. Indigenous societies consciously altered the landscapes, including nurturing certain plants such as fruit and nut trees in forested areas, and managing grasslands, meadows, and forest succession through fire (Kimmerer 2013). In the landscapes of eastern North America, for instance, there were relatively permanent human settlements that utilized regenerative agricultural landscapes. The romantic ideal of a pristine, untouched wilderness is a colonialist fantasy intended to hide the realities of attempted genocide of

Indigenous people and capitalist destruction of abundant ecological lifeworlds (Youdelis et al. 2020; Cronon 1995). In terms of procuring food, Indigenous nations of North America organized themselves in a variety of ways which included agriculture, foraging, fishing, food forestry, and hunting. The devastating loss of life that occurred after colonialism led to the collapse of some large settlements, a decrease in human-stewarded agricultural landscapes, and a loss of systems of ecological stewardship. In most regions of what is now Canada and the United States this rapid decrease in human population and dramatic change in land use happened many decades before the arrival of settler-colonialists.

The 17th century marked the violent arrival of settler-colonialism to the Eastern coast of North American and was the period during which many domesticated animals were brought to central and eastern North America, including honey bees. Due to their swarming behaviour and tendency to go feral, honey bees often preceded European settler-farmers who were slashing and burning their way through the forested landscapes of eastern North America during the 1600s. The arrival of these feral honey bees into a landscape through swarming may have given important information to Indigenous people. An 18th-century French settler writer wrote that

> The Indians [sic] look upon them [honey bees] with an evil eye, and consider their progress into the interior of the continent as an omen of the white man's approach: thus, as they discover the bees, the news of the event, passing from mouth to mouth, spreads sadness and consternation on all sides.
>
> (quoted in Crosby 2004, p. 109)

It is important to be critical and sceptical of settler accounts of Indigenous practices, feelings, and knowledges (Geniusz 2015), however this account highlights that the arrival of honey bees to a landscape may have served as a warning that settler-colonialists would soon follow.

Honey bees in North America likely played a complicated role as settler bees, a term suggested to me by Terrylynn Brant 'Sera:sera', the owner of Mohawk Seedkeeper Gardens at Six Nations of the Grand River (Brant, Turtle clan, Mohawk. Personal communication, 27 October 2018), embedded in but also somewhat autonomous from settler-colonial agriculture. Conceptualizing honey bees as settler bees is a much more accurate way of understating their complicated role in agricultural and ecological systems in Canada and the United States than considering them to be invasive species, something I will address in more detail in Chapter 6. Based on the historical records, the initial spread of honey bees across United States and Canada was slow. Although honey bees spread on their own due to swarming, this would have occurred in small increments distance-wise of only a few kilometres with each swarm.[2] Settler farmers kept honey bee hives as part of their larger agricultural operations, mostly for the wax and honey (Crane 1999). In the 1600s to 1900s, large beekeeping operations in North America were uncommon and migratory beekeeping for so-called pollination services was non-existent. Evidence of honey bees in Southern Ontario, about 1000 km from Virginia, for example, does not appear in historical records until 1776 (Crane 1999). Honey bees were first recorded on the west coast of the United States and Canada beginning in California in 1853 (Crane 1999).

It is impossible to know how the initial introduction of honey bees to North America affected wild bees. While the introduction of honey bees cannot be viewed as benign on wild bee populations, it is also important to keep focused on colonial-capitalism, the driver of the destructive changes of which they were one small part. The rapid spread of settler-colonial agricultural systems beginning in the 17th and 18th centuries brought multiple devastating waves of destruction to both Indigenous societies and non-human animals, and the honey bee was a small but integral part of the advancing colonial system of agriculture. As settler-colonialists cleared the forests, tore up grasslands, drained wetlands, and enclosed commonly stewarded land to implement private property regimes, most tied directly to settler agriculture at various scales, ecological landscapes were transformed along with human settlement patterns, agricultural systems, and interspecies relationships (Daschuk 2013).

The processes of enclosure and 'clearing' of the North American landscape took different forms, but two common features were that Indigenous people were targets of genocide, which included their forced removal from the land, and non-human nature was extirpated to smaller spaces and thoroughly controlled. As historian John Douglas-Belshaw argues, control of non-human nature is a central component of settler-colonialism in Canada:

> You see that river there? We can dam that. We can organize that water, we can make that water work for us. It's essentially the same mindset. I can reorganize this landscape, flatten it, plant lawn, find a non-indigenous species of plant, of grass, and completely extract anything that's not homogenous, that doesn't fit with this green pattern and control it ... A backyard with a big lawn is like a classroom for colonialism and environmental hostility
>
> (quoted in Bein 2020).

The development of capitalist agriculture regimes across the United States and Canada differs greatly depending on the region. It is not in the scope of this chapter to provide a detailed description of the varied, uneven, and dynamic development of capitalist agriculture in North America. However, it is important to note some key patterns. Systems of export-based, monocultured cash crops were in development with the planation economy soon after the earliest days of colonialist invasion. The plantation slavery system in the Americas was practised largely in the tropical and subtropical regions: the Caribbean, some parts of South and Central America, and, later, southern parts of North America and was integral to the development of not only capitalist agriculture but the entire system of global capitalism including the urban industrialization that occurred in Europe (Moore 2005). Other parts of the Americas, notably much of North America, were not sites of settler-colonialism or capitalist agriculture until the 1600s, beginning in the Northeastern United States, and did not intensify in many regions, especially in the west, until the 1800s and into the early 1900s.

In eastern North America, the establishment of small-scale settler-colonial farms reduced the flourishing of non-human nature, but small farms would nevertheless have provided some forage, habitat sites, and nesting materials to many species of native and wild bees. Small-scale settler farmers in the Northeastern United States, the Great Lakes region, and Southern Canada, were integrated into capitalist agriculture in that they produced some crops for market and for export, however, they also typically grew some subsistence crops, leading to relatively diverse plantings of crops. The small scale of these farms would have allowed for some areas of uncultivated forests and meadows. Although some wild bee species likely declined in abundance and diversity with the destruction of pre-colonial agricultural and forest ecosystems, those that survived evidently co-existed with introduced honey bees in forests and agricultural landscapes for hundreds of years in the northeastern regions of the United States. It is very difficult, almost impossible, to know how wild bees were affected by colonial invasion, settler-colonial agriculture, early capitalist agriculture, and the introduction of honey bees. There was no systematic research, at this time, into wild bee populations and many accounts of what existed in the landscape are anecdotical and recorded by settler-colonialists, some of whom were amateur naturalists. These accounts rarely included the perspectives of Indigenous people and, when they did, often distorted or diminished these perspectives (Genuisz 2009). What is known is that the initial ecological imperialism that occurred after invasion caused a massive loss of life throughout the Americas. The attempted genocide and forced removal of Indigenous people, widespread establishment of settler agriculture of varying scales, creation of large, industrialized cities, and continent-wide railway systems (later, highways) caused many other waves of destruction to non-human nature, likely including some species of bees.

The Capitalocene and the simplified and standardized landscapes of North America

The industrialization of capitalist agriculture intensified considerably in the 20th century and heralded a new wave of ecological destruction. Capitalist agricultural systems involve two central transformations that are devastating for wild and honey bees (and ecological lifeworlds in general): the creation of extensive monocultures and a dependence upon pesticides and other chemical inputs. Both transformations cause and require the simplification and standardization of landscapes which has harmful effects on non-human nature (Weis 2018). As the global capitalist agricultural system intensified across the Americas, and the world into the

20th and 21st century, the relationship between humans, honey bees, and wild bees was dramatically altered. The intensification of global, capitalist agriculture in North America in the 20th century was an uneven process, that is, it did not happen at the same time, scale, or pace throughout the continent. For this section, I will focus on how the industrialization and intensification of mixed crop and 'livestock' agriculture that saw the replacement of relatively small farms with large agribusiness harms bees of all species.

Over the course of the 20th and 21st century in agricultural regions of Canada and the United States, diversified small farms were rapidly replaced with large-scale agribusinesses producing cash crops including canola, wheat, corn, and soy. In Canada there has been a dramatic increase in average farm size alongside a dramatic decrease in the number of farms. While farming revenues continue to grow, the number of farmers in Canada is falling. According to Statistics Canada (2017a), from 1966 to 2016 the *number* of farms halved (from 430,000 down to 193,492) while the *size* of farms doubled from about 400 to 820 acres per farm. Currently, the highest proportion (32.9%) of Canadian agricultural operations grow oilseed and grains, a category that includes corn and soy grown primarily as livestock feed (Statistics Canada 2017a).

In Canada as well as the United States, farmers have faced government and corporate pressure for decades to "get big or get out", in the famous words of Earl Butz, secretary of the USDA. Farmers faced competitive pressure to specialize, often on as little as one or two cash crops. The same pressure was put on livestock farmers, with farmers compelled to specialize in one or two species of animals, who were increasingly concentrated into large barns and feedlots. The result was the creation of biologically simplified industrial landscapes that resemble 'oceans' of monocultures with 'islands' of concentrated animals (Weis 2013). This massive transformation has led to a new wave of destruction of ecological lifeworlds in these regions. The simplification and standardization of agricultural landscapes is created and maintained in co-constitutive ways. Farmers were increasingly encouraged to specialize in growing one or two cash crops, often for export. These grain or oilseed crops are increasingly to be turned into food for livestock embedded in intensive animal agriculture. Hybrid seeds were developed and marketed to farmers as being easier to grow, or more resistant to various pests and pathogens, although with the downside that they cannot be saved and used for the next season's crop. Hybrid seeds, often bred to be more productive, also represented a simplification and standardization of crop varieties with less diversity among domesticated plant species and little connection to the bioregions in which they are intended to be grown. Genetically engineered (GE) seeds in which DNA of plants (or animals) is modified, marking a sharp departure from the plant breeding done by farmers for thousands of years, were developed and patented by agrochemical corporations. These GE seeds represent a break from the long tradition of farmers breeding, saving, and stewarding seeds. Domesticated livestock animals were narrowed to a handful of livestock species, mainly pigs, chickens, and cows, and within these species, only a small number of breeds were encouraged. Heritage breeds of farmed animals became increasingly rare, to the extent that some risk endangerment and extirpation (Hall 2004).

The standardization and simplification of landscapes requires a war to be waged upon wild plants deemed to be 'weeds' and wild animals, especially insects. Agribusinesses focused on the growing of one or two main crops, making the crops and the agricultural operations highly vulnerable to pests and pathogens, and to competition from wild plants. The main way in which this war on wild non-human nature occurs is through utilizing a large array of herbicides, insecticides, and fungicides. This large-scale and widespread use of pesticides represents a collusion between governments and agrochemical corporations, particularly after World War II (Robbins 2007), something explored in more detail in Chapters 4 and 5. Often these pesticides are infused into the hybrid and GE seeds of cash crops further entrenching corporate control over farmers and agricultural systems.

This standardization and simplification of agricultural landscapes is a radical departure from the long relationship between people and bees. This disruption occurs largely through the destruction of landscapes that provide habitat sites and materials for wild bees and the increasing lack of adequate forage, potentially causing nutritional deficiencies in all bee species, including managed honey bees. As a result of this lack of habitat and forage, many species of wild bees are unable to thrive in agricultural landscapes (Goulson et al. 2015) and honey bees are increasingly sickly. The destruction of the long-standing and mutually beneficial human and bee relationship also occurs through the widespread use of insecticides and other pesticides. In response to the decreasing abundance and diversity of wild bees, managed honey bees and, in smaller numbers, bumble bees are brought into landscapes in which crops need animal pollination at ever-increasing numbers. Yet these landscapes, due to their lack of diverse forage and high presence of pesticides, harm managed bees leading to a severe decline in health (Durant 2019).

Monocultures of soy and corn

Throughout North America, and the world, there are several crops that are monocultured on a large scale. However, two crops, corn, and soy, dominate the rural landscapes of eastern and central North America and increasingly other parts of the world such as Argentina and Brazil. A critical examination of these crops is important to understanding the way in which monocultures negatively affect the health of bees and other insect pollinators, serving as a warning to other parts of the world in which these two crops have not yet become dominant. Although wheat is the main crop, per acreage, in Canada, it is closely followed by canola (Statistics Canada 2021). Soy and corn are the main crops grown in Ontario, the most populous province in Canada (Statistics Canada 2021), and corn is the main crop grown in the United States (USDA

2022). What is striking about the fact that soy and corn dominate huge parts of North America is that, unlike wheat, they are not being grown to directly feed humans. Instead, they are being grown to feed livestock and, in the case of corn in the United States, as a source of biodiesel (Veljković et al. 2018).

Oceans of corn and soy

The rise of monocultured corn and soy in Ontario illustrates the dramatic shift in agricultural land use and scale that has occurred in the 20th and 21st century in many places throughout the world, changes that directly and negatively impact pollinators, especially wild bees. Ontario is one of the largest and most important crop-producing regions of Canada and its capitalist monoculture production is heavily focused upon corn and soy, grown for feed production (Hamel and Dorf 2014). As Weis (2013) argues, a meatification of the human diet has occurred over the past few decades, leading to the creation of concentrated animal feeding operations (CAFOs) in which large amounts of livestock animals are raised, many whose bodies will be turned into 'cheap meat' products. This intensification of livestock agriculture requires the intensification of grain-oilseed monocultures to feed the billions of animals, mainly pigs and chickens, that will pass through CAFOs on a global scale.

Most of the corn production in Ontario occurs in Southern Ontario, which is where most of the human population of the province resides (Government of Ontario 2021). Across Ontario as a whole, corn and soy occupied a little over 2 million hectares in 2016 (Statistics Canada 2017b), and both crops require heavy inputs of fertilizer, pesticides, and water. Although both crops are self-pollinating, bee species do sometimes collect pollen and nectar from them if they cannot find other food sources and some solitary bees nest in soy and corn fields (Wheelock et al. 2016). Nevertheless, oceans of corn and soy provide far from ideal nutritional conditions for bees, which is made worse by the removal of once-common patches of wildflowers and hedgerows of trees on farms (Durant 2019), reducing forage for wild bees. In such landscapes, wild specialist bees are most vulnerable as they do not fly far from their nesting site to find forage (Kim et al. 2006). Although generalist bees such as honey bees and native bumble bees can often still find forage in biologically degraded landscapes, in places like weedy ditches and among the 'weeds' in fields, the nature of industrial production poses other complications for their health. One of the biggest threats is the treatment of fields with systemic insecticides, especially since traces of these chemicals are often found in surrounding wildflowers (Mogren and Lundgren 2016).

Corn and soybean are some of the handfuls of crops that are commercially grown using GE seeds. These seeds, patented by agrochemical companies, are also often infused with systemic pesticides. Corn, in particular, is one of the main crops on which neonicotinoids, a class of systemic pesticides that have been the target of anti-pesticide activism and scientific investigation over the past decade and half, is used. In Ontario, 95% of corn crops are treated with neonicotinoids usually in the form of infused seeds (Ontario Bee Health Working Group 2014). According to Statistics Canada, corn accounted for 61.7% of seeded area in 2011 in Ontario and ranks as the number one crop in the province and number three crop in the country (Hamel and Dorf 2014). Even though bees do very little pollination of corn, neonicotinoids have been found in high amounts in bee-loving wildflowers near treated corn crops (David et al. 2016). A study by Tsvetkov and colleagues (2017) of bee exposure to neonicotinoids through proximity to corn crops in Ontario, Quebec, and Indiana, found that "honey bee colonies near corn are ... chronically exposed to NNIs [neonicotinoid insecticides] for a substantial proportion of the active season in temperate North America". Soy seeds are also often patented GE seeds commonly infused with neonicotinoids, with 55–60% of soy crops in Ontario treated with neonicotinoids (Ontario Bee Health Working Group 2014). The vast monocultures of corn and soy in Ontario and much of eastern and central United States poses a great risk to wild bees and managed honey bees.

Corn and soy monocultures starkly demonstrate the way in which the interests of small-scale, diversified farmers are intertwined with wild and honey bee health. The farming of soy and corn as a grain crop destined for CAFOs requires farming on a large scale, and is a manifestation of the latest push for farmers to "get big or get out". Following this trajectory there has been a decrease in the number of corn farms (although less so in sweetcorn) and an increase in size of these farms in Canada. Hamel and Dorf triumphantly state in a report for Statistics Canada that:

> This crop's story continues to unfold. Foremost, corn's productivity has increased significantly with the evolution of agricultural practices, the development of hybrid varieties, and new advancements in the field of biotechnology that transfer a gene from one organism to another (e.g., technologies using recombinant DNA). The versatility of this crop, combined with the breeding advances made by plant scientists, make it a popular commodity for the feed, livestock, and industrial sectors. Thus, the future of corn appears to be sweet, and with ongoing research and development it seems that the sky – or rather, the farm field – is the limit.
>
> (Hamel and Dorf 2014)

For advocates of pollinator health and small-scale farmers, innovation and advancement in corn cultivation is not cause for celebration but is highly problematic given that corn is one of the dominant monocultured crops in the world and corn seeds are one of the main sources of neonicotinoids in the world. In addition to high inputs of pesticides, monocultured corn also requires high inputs of artificial fertilizers and water, the overuse of both have harmful impacts on the ecosystem (Hamel and Dorf 2014). Corn grown in Ontario is intimately connected to agrochemical corporations from the seed to the final product. Around the world corn, long used as an essential and diverse food for people in the Americas, is now primarily grown to feed livestock in CAFOs or to be turned into ethanol. And yet, as Robin Wall Kimmerer (2018) reminds us, it is not corn, itself, that is the problem, a plant with an entangled and meaningful relationship with many Indigenous peoples in the Americas. She says,

> This remarkable plant has been known by as many names as the peoples who have grown it: The Seed of Seeds, Our Daily Bread, Wife of the Sun, and Mother of All Things. In my own Potawatomi language, we say *mandamin*, or the Wonderful Seed. The scientific name is *Zea mays*, "mays" referring to the Taino name that Columbus recorded in his journal when first tasting "a sort of grain which they call *mahiz*, which very well tasted when boiled, roasted, or made into porridge." *Mahiz*, meaning the "Bringer of Life," became the word maize in English. These indigenous names honor maize as the center of culture and reflect a deeply respectful relationship between people and the one who sustains them.
>
> The term used for the modern crop carries none of this feeling and is rooted in intentional blindness to the original meaning of the plant. Rather than adopt the reverent indigenous name, English settlers simply called it corn, a term applied to any grain—from barleycorn to wheat. And so it began, the colonization of corn.

Like honey bees, it is the way in which corn has been embedded within colonialism and the capitalist agriculture that causes it to be part of a harmful system.

Landscapes of scarcity in the Capitalocene

The expansion of capitalist landscapes and the gradual disappearance of small-scale mixed-crop farms and pasture adversely affects the flourishing of all bee species. To flourish, bees, and other pollinators need forage (nectar and/or pollen rich flowers) and habitat (both nesting sites and materials). While the monocultured landscapes of crops described above may have high yields of corn and soy they are, in fact, landscapes of scarcity for bees and other non-human animals. Although many of the world's fruit and vegetable crops are still grown by small-scale farmers and peasants (FAO 2022), the trajectory towards increasingly industrialized agricultural landscapes that meet the demands of global capitalism continues to intensify in scale and pace. Wild bees have a particularly hard time thriving in landscapes of scarcity due to a lack of nesting materials, adequate nesting sites, and a lack of forage. For example, several studies on bumble bees, who as eusocial bees tend to be more widely studied than other species of wild bees, indicate that some species are facing defaunation (Siviter et al. 2021; Soroye et al. 2020) while others are at more serious risk of endangerment and extirpation (Cameron et al. 2011; Government of Ontario n.d.).

It is estimated that about 70% of wild bees in the world nest in the ground, many within a few hundred metres of foraging sites (Zurbuchen et al. 2010). Wild bees suffer when land use changes make it difficult or impossible for them to find adequate habitat. Bee species also need a diversity of materials to build their nests, including clay and the leaves of specific species of plants. In monocultured landscapes in which hedgerows and wildflowers are increasingly scarce, a handful of crops dominate, and the soil is tilled or drenched in pesticides, it is very difficult for many species of bees to find safe spaces to build nests, which can have serious consequences, particularly more vulnerable species of bees.

Another problem capitalist agriculture poses for wild bees is that some species of solitary bees do not travel far from their nest to find forage. This means that good sites for building a nest must be near abundant sites of forage. Although some species of bumble bees will fly up to 1 km from their nest in search of food (Osborne et al. 2008), most other species of wild bees will only fly a few hundred metres. Furthermore, some wild bees need specific species of flowering plants from which to forage. While some bees, including most species of bumble bees and honey bees, are generalists, gathering pollen and nectar from a wide variety of plants, many solitary species of bees are specialists, having evolved to have symbiotic relationships with certain types of plants. For example, squash bees such as *Peponapis pruinosa* exclusively gather pollen and nectar from plants in the *Cucurbita* genus (Chan et al. 2019). In order for squash bees to survive, their nests must be near squash, melons, and cucumber plants (or their wild counterparts). Although, this may be easy for squash bees, since some of their preferred species of plants are commercially grown (although the soil may be drenched in pesticides and fertilizers, and their nests risk being tilled), this can be difficult for species of bees that have symbiotic relationships with wild plants that are not commercially cultivated.

It is increasingly common for farmers to remove hedgerows, which were often comprised of the types of shrubs and perennials that are ideal nesting sites for these species of bees (Durant 2019). Removing hedgerows increases the amount of land available to be cultivated and makes it easier for large machinery to work the fields. Another troubling trend in some parts of North America is for farmers to clear cut stands of forests near their agricultural fields. While governments may enact bylaws against this, farmers sometimes defy or oppose these bylaws. For example, the Ontario municipality of Chatham-Kent is a largely agricultural area that is also one of the most ecologically significant and sensitive bioregions in Ontario, the Carolinian bioregion. The municipality has one of the lowest tree cover rates in the province at 6% (Campbell 2019) and when the municipal government proposed a bylaw to disallow the clear cutting of woodlots larger than 1.25 acres, farmer opposition to the bylaw was fierce and reportedly included farmers pre-emptively clearcutting woodlots on their land (Ontario Grain Farmer 2014).

The loss of pastureland is also an important contributor to forage loss for bees and other insect pollinators, although it is important to note that pasturelands are very contradictory in terms of their environmental impacts. Not all pasturelands are beneficial to ecological lifeworlds. Some pasturelands feature monocultures of mostly invasive grasses and are overgrazed to the point of having very little ecological benefit (Dorrough et al. 2004). Further, the largescale grazing of rudimentary animals is a contributor to climate change (Grossi et al. 2019). However, in areas of the world in which grassland prairies, featuring mostly perennial grasses and herbaceous flowering plants, are the dominant ecosystem, pastureland can play an important ecological role, particularly when a polyculture of mostly native plants is allowed to flourish (Engle et al. 2008). As livestock agriculture intensifies, with farmed animals often crammed into large buildings or CAFOs, much of North America has lost pastureland, which would have been valuable nesting sites for both ground and cavity nesting species of bees as well as forage sites, where wild flowers are allowed to bloom.

The encroachment of agricultural land onto forested areas, even relatively small pockets of forests such as shrubby hedgerows and woodlots, can pose significant problems for wild bees. While many bees gather nectar from flowering herbaceous plants and woody shrubs, some of the best sources of pollen, which is essential to the diet of all bees, are found in trees (Hill and Webster 1995). This is especially true in the spring when many of the most abundant herbaceous sources of nectar and pollen have yet to flower. Trees can be essential for survival of bees in the spring and early summer because pollen is crucial for the rearing of larvae. Even for managed honey bees, trees are an essential source of spring pollen that allows them to feed larvae and build their colony's population for the busy summer months.

The importance of scale in bee flourishing within agriculture

The ways in which bees are harmed within monocultured landscapes is not only due to a scarcity of nesting sites and forage or the high use of pesticides, it is also directly due to the scaling up of agribusiness. As Weis (2010) argues, when farmers increase the scale of their operations, they are forced onto the "accelerating treadmill" of capitalist agriculture. For example, they typically invest in larger machinery, as human or animal labour is no longer practical or economically viable. As mentioned earlier, the use of large machinery can necessitate that hedgerows and flower strips are removed for the very practical reason that these machines need to easily manoeuvre on the landscape. The disappearance of farms that are diversified and include raising farm animals for multifunctional uses including labour, alongside growing a variety of crops, creates the need for artificial fertilizer as onsite manure may no longer be present. Growing one or two dominant crops necessitates the use of pesticides because the entire operation is extremely vulnerable to pests, pathogens, and competitive 'weeds'. In a diversified, small-scale farming operation, the farmer may be able to recover easily if one of the crops suffers due to a disease, an insect infestation, or a particularly virulent 'weed'. In a high-capital agricultural enterprise in which only one or two crops are being grown losing a crop can mean the growing season is effectively over which is a financial disaster for the farmer. For a large-scale agribusiness this capital investment takes many forms including the land, the machinery (often millions of dollars), the farm buildings, the seeds (which need to be purchased every year from an agrochemical corporation and often include complicated contracts that lock farmers into continued usage), the pesticides, and the artificial fertilizers. Even if these types of farmers want to decrease use of pesticides or allow some diversified plantings, they often are not able to get off this accelerating treadmill of capitalist agriculture due to the amount of capital they have already invested in their operation and the amount of debt they are carrying as a result of that investment. Scaling up agriculture often entails locking farmers, and beekeepers, into the global capitalist system in ways that seem unescapable.

Conclusion

The simplification and standardization of landscapes requires a high use of pesticides including insecticides, herbicides, fungicides, and miticides which have been demonstrated to be harmful to bees and many other non-human animals. Rachel Carson's seminal book *Silent Spring* (1962) first drew popular attention to the effects that some common pesticides at the time were having upon wildlife, and the long-term risks of bioaccumulation. Her book was a catalyst for the establishment of environmental regulatory agencies, as well as helping to inspire popular interest in ecological agriculture and organic gardening. Carson famously described pesticides as a part of a broader war against non-human nature associated with industrialization, which had a literal dimension, as several of the most used pesticides in the 20th century were originally created for use in war (Robbins 2007; Daniel 2005). In Chapter 4, I will explore in depth the effects of pesticides on wild bees and managed honey bees, as well as the complications and uncertainties that arise when trying to determine the harm caused by pesticides in ecological lifeworlds, as opposed to controlled lab settings. In Chapter 5 I will examine how agrochemical companies have wielded power to influence governmental policy on pesticide regulation.

Before exploring the role of pesticides in the pollinator crisis it is important to critically examine the ways in which honey bees have become embedded in capitalist agriculture through the rise of the commercial, migratory beekeeping industry. The rise of the commercial, migratory beekeeping industry in the 20th century is directly related to the inhospitable environment that monocultured landscapes create for wild bees because, as discussed, some species of wild bees simply cannot flourish in monocultured landscapes. When agricultural landscapes require insect pollination, especially when this pollination is needed en masse at a very specific blooming time, the scarcity of wild pollinators becomes a serious problem. Instead of solving this problem by increasing hedgerows, engaging in some ecological restoration, and planting polycultures, the response from agribusinesses has been to bring in the 'services' of managed bees, mainly honey bees. In many ways the beekeeping industry has mimicked the 'go big or get out' trend that has occurred in other agricultural industries. This has caused the beekeeping industry to pivot away from the production of 'products of the hive' to the provision of pollinator services within the simplified and standardized landscapes we have discussed in this chapter. The landscapes of scarcity created in the Capitalocene in which honey bees are now embedded directly harms honey bees and indirectly harms beekeepers and wild bees.

Notes

1 Pests and pathogens also caused devastation in Central and South America and the Caribbean. However, in the first 200 years of invasion, this was accompanied by explicit acts of genocide.
2 Typically, a strong honey bee colony swarms one or more times in the late spring, often in May and June in the northern hemisphere.

References

Alex, B. (2021). The human epoch: When did the Anthropocene begin? *Discover*, June 19. https://www.discovermagazine.com/environment/the-human-epoch-when-did-the-anthropocene-begin.

Barnosky, A., Matzke, N., Tomiya, S., Wogan, G. O. U., Swartz, B., Quental, T.B... & Ferrar, E. A. (2011). Has the Earth's sixth mass extinction already arrived? *Nature*, 471, 51–57, https://doi.org/10.1038/nature09678.

Bein, S. (2020). Is it time to decolonize your lawn? The traditional lawn – manicured, verdant, under control – now finds itself at the confluence of two hot-button issues: Climate change and Indigenous rights. *The Globe and Mail*, September 5. https://www.theglobeandmail.com/canada/article-is-it-time-to-decolonize-your-lawn/.

Cameron, S. A., Lozier, J. D., Strange, J. P., Koch, J. P., Cordes, N., Solter, L. F., & Griswold, T. L. (2011). Patterns of widespread decline in North American bumble bees. *PNAS*, 108 (2), 662–667, https://doi.org/10.1073/pnas.1014743108.

Campbell, C. (2019). Chatham-Kent gets $1 million to increase tree cover. *CTV News Windsor*, November 22. https://windsor.ctvnews.ca/chatham-kent-gets-1m-to-increase-tree-cover-1.4698163.

Carson, R. (1962). *Silent Spring*. Boston: Houghton Mifflin.

Chan, D. W., Prosser, R. S., Rodríguez-Gil, J. L., & Raine, N. E. (2019). Risks of exposure to systemic insecticides in agricultural soil in Ontario, Canada for the hoary squash bee (*Peponapis pruinosa*) and other ground-nesting bee species. *Scientific Reports*, 9, 11870.

Crane, E. (1999). *The World History of Beekeeping and Honey Hunting*. New York: Routledge.

Cronon, W. (1995). The trouble with wilderness; Or, getting back to the wrong nature. In Cronon, W. (ed.), *Uncommon Ground: Rethinking the Human Place in Nature*. New York: W. W. Norton, pp. 69–90.

Crosby, A. W. (2004). *Ecological Imperialism: The Biological Expansion of Europe 900–1900*. Cambridge: Cambridge University Press, 2nd ed.

Crutzen, P. J. & Stoermer, E. F. (2021) The "*Anthropocene*" *(2000)*. In Benner, S., Lax, G., Crutzen, P. J., Pöschl, U., Lelieveld, J., & Brauch, H. G. (eds.), *Paul J. Crutzen and the Anthropocene: A New Epoch in Earth's History*. The Anthropocene: Politik – Economics – Society – Science, vol 1. Cham: Springer. https://doi.org/10.1007/978-3-030-82202-6_2.

Daniel, P. (2005). *Toxic Drift: Pesticides and Health in the Post-World War II South*. Baton Rouge: Louisiana State University Press in association with Smithsonian Institution, Washington, DC.

Daschuk, J. W. (2013). *Clearing the Plains: Disease, Politics of Starvation, and the Loss of Aboriginal Life*. Regina: University of Regina Press.

David, A., Botias, C., Abdul-Sada, A., Nicholls, E., Rotheray, E. L., Hill, E. M., & Goulson, D. (2016). Widespread contamination of wildflower and bee-collected pollen with complex mixtures of neonicotinoids and fungicides commonly applied to crops. *Environment International*, 88 (3), 169–178.

Dorrough, J., Yen, A., Turner, V., Clark, S. G., Crosthwaite, J., & Hirth, J. R. (2004). Livestock grazing management and biodiversity conservation in Australian temperate grassy landscapes. *Australian Journal of Agricultural Research*, 55, 279–295. https://doi.org/10.1071/AR03024.

Durant, J. (2019). Where have all the flowers gone? Honey bee declines and exclusions from floral resources. *Journal of Rural Studies*, 65 (1), 0.1016/j.jrurstud.2018.10.007.

Engle, D. M., Fuhlendorf, S. D., Roper, A., & Leslie, D. M. (2008). Invertebrate community response to a shifting mosaic of habitat. *Rangeland Ecology & Management*, 61(1), 55–62, https://doi.org/10.2111/06-149R2.1.

FAO. (2022). FAO's global action on pollination services for sustainable agriculture. https://www.fao.org/pollination/background/bees-and-other-pollinators/en/, accessed January 25, 2022.

Geniusz, M. S. (2015). *Plants Have So Much to Give Us, All We Have to Do Is Ask: Anishinaabe Botanical Teachings*. Minneapolis, University of Minnesota Press.

Goulson, D., Nicholls, E., Botias, C., & Rotheray, E. L. (2015). Bee declines driven by combined stress from parasites, pesticides, and lack of flowers. *Science*, 347 (6229). doi:10.1126/science.1255957.

Government of Ontario. (2021). About Ontario. Accessed January 24, 2022. https://www.ontario.ca/page/about-ontario.

Government of Ontario. (n.d.) *Rusty-patched bumble bee*. Accessed October 2020. https://www.ontario.ca/page/rusty-patched-bumble-bee.

Grossi, G., Goglio, P., Vitali, A., & Williams, A. G. (2019). Livestock and climate change: Impact of livestock on climate and mitigation strategies. *Animal Frontiers*, 9 (1), 69–76, https://doi.org/10.1093/af/vfy034.

Hall, S. J. G. (2004). *Livestock Biodiversity: Genetic Resources for the Farming of the Future*. Hoboken: Blackwell Publishing.

Hamel, M.-A. & Dorf, E. (2014). Corn: Canada's third most valuable crop. *Statistics Canada*. http://www.statcan.gc.ca/pub/96-325-x/2014001/article/11913-eng.htm.

Hill, D. B. & Webster, T. C. (1995). Apiculture and forestry (bees and trees). *Agroforest Systems*, 29, 313–320. https://doi.org/10.1007/BF00704877.

Jones, J. (2012). Stingless bees: A historical perspective. In Vit, P., Pedro, S. R. M, & Roubik, D. (eds.), *Pot-Honey: A Legacy of Stingless Bees*. New York City: Springer, pp. 219–227.

Kim, J., Williams, N., & Kreman, C. (2006). Effects of cultivation and proximity to natural habitat on ground-nesting native bees in California sunflower fields. *Journal of the Kansas Entomological Society*, 79 (4), 309–320.

Kimmerer, R. W. (2018). Corn tastes better on the honour system. *Emergence*. https://emergencemagazine.org/feature/corn-tastes-better/.

Kimmerer, R.W. (2013). *Braiding Sweetgrass: Indigenous Wisdom, Scientific Knowledge and the Teaching of Plants*. Minneapolis: Milkweed Editions.

Koch, A., Brierley, C., Maslin, M. M., & Lewis, S. L. (2019). Earth system impacts of the European arrival and Great Dying in the Americas after 1492. *Quaternary Science Reviews*, 207, 13–36, https://doi.org/10.1016/j.quascirev.2018.12.004.

Lovejoy, P. (1989). The impact of the atlantic slave trade on Africa: A review of the literature. *The Journal of African History*, 30 (3), 365–394. doi:10.1017/S0021853700024439.

Mintz, S. (1986). *Sweetness and Power: The Place of Sugar in Modern History*. New York: Penguin Books.

Mogren, C. L. & Lundgren, J. G. (2016). Neonicotinoid-contaminated pollinator strips adjacent to cropland reduce honey bee nutritional status. *Scientific Reports*, 6. https://doi.org/10.1038/srep29608.

Moore, J. W. (ed.). (2015). *Anthropocene or Capitalocene? Nature, History, and the Crisis of Capitalism*. Oakland, PM Press.

Nagamatsu, S. (2022). In a virus-stricken future, humanity endures despite the grief. *New York Times*. January 18. https://www.nytimes.com/2022/01/18/books/review/sequoia-nagamatsu-how-high-we-go-in-the-dark.html.

Ontario Bee Health Working Group. (2014). Ontario Health Working Group report. *OMAFRA*. Accessed July 4. http://www.omafra.gov.on.ca/english/about/ beehealthworkinggroupreport.htm#neon.

Ontario Grain Farmer. (2014). The woodlot debate, April. https://ontariograinfarmer.ca/2014/04/01/the-woodlot-debate/.

Osborne, J. L., Martin, A. P., Carreck, N. L., Swain, J. L., Knight, M. E., Goulson, D., ... & Sanderson, R. A. (2008). Bumblebee flight distances in relation to the forage landscape. *Journal of Animal Ecology*, 77 (2), 406–415.

Robbins, P. (2007). *Lawn People: How Grasses, Weeds, and Chemicals Make Us Who We Are*. Philadelphia: Temple University Press.

Siviter, H., Richman, S.K., & Muth, F. (2021). Field-realistic neonicotinoid exposure has sub-lethal effects on non-*Apis* bees: A meta-analysis. *Ecology Letters*, 24 (12), 2586–2597.

Soroye, P., Newbold, T., & Kerr, J. (2020). Climate change contributes to widespread declines among bumble bees across continents. *Science*, 367 (678), 685–688.

Statistics Canada. (2021). Principal field crop areas, June 2021. *The Daily Statistics Canada*. https://www150.statcan.gc.ca/n1/daily-quotidien/210629/dq210629b-eng.htm.

Statistics Canada. (2017a). A portrait of 21st-century agricultural operations. *Census2016*, May 17. http://www.statcan.gc.ca/pub/95-640-x/2016001/article/14811-eng.htm.

Statistics Canada. (2017b). Cropland in Ontario grows despite fewer farms. *Statistics Canada*. https://www150.statcan.gc.ca/n1/pub/95-640-x/2016001/article/14805-eng.htm.

Steffen W., Grinevald J., Crutzen P., & McNeill, J. (2011). The Anthropocene: Conceptual and historical perspectives. *Philosophical Transactions of the Royal Society A*. 369, 842–867, http://doi.org/10.1098/rsta.2010.0327.

Subramanian, M. (2019). Humans versus Earth: The quest to define the Anthropocene. *Nature*, 572, 168–170. doi:10.1038/d41586-019-02381-2.

Tsvetkov, N., Samson-Robert, O., Sood, K., Patel, H. S., Malena, D. A., Gajiwala, P. H., Maciukiewicz, P.... & Zayed, A. (2017). Chronic exposure to neonicotinoids reduces honey bee health near corn crops. *Science*, 356 (June 30), 1395–1397.

United States Department of Agriculture. (2022). Corn and other field grains. Economic Research Service USDA. https://www.ers.usda.gov/topics/crops/corn-and-other-feedgrains/.

Veljković, V. B., Biberdžić, M. O., Banković-Ilić, I. B., Djalović, I. G., Tasić, M. B., Nježić, Z. B., & Stamenković, O. Y. (2018). Biodiesel production from corn oil: A review. *Renewable and Sustainable Energy Reviews*, 91, 531–548. https://doi.org/10.1016/j.rser.2018.04.024.

Weis, T. (2010). The accelerating biophysical contradictions of industrial capitalist agriculture. *Journal of Agrarian Change*, 10 (3), 315–341.

Weis, T. (2013). *The Ecological Hoofprint: The Global Burden of Industrial Livestock*. London, Zed.

Weis, T. (2018). Ghosts and things: Agriculture and animal life. *Global Environmental Politics*, 18 (2), 134–142.

Wheelock, M. J., Rey, K. P., & O'Neal, M. E. (2016). Defining the insect pollinator community found in Iowa corn and soybean fields: Implications for pollinator conservation. *Environmental Entomology*, 45 (5), 1099–1106, https://doi.org/10.1093/ee/nvw087.

Youdelis, M., Nakoochee, R., O'Neil, O., Lunstrum, E., & Roth, R. (2020). "Wilderness" revisited: Is Canadian park management moving beyond the "wilderness" ethic? *The Canadian Geographer*, 64 (2), 232–249. https://doi.org/10.1111/cag.12600.

Zurbuchen, A., Landert, L., Klaiber, J., Müller, A., Hein, S., & Dorn, S. (2010). Maximum foraging ranges in solitary bees: Only few individuals have the capability to cover long foraging distances. *Biological Conservation*, 143 (3), 669–676, https://doi.org/10.1016/j.biocon.2009.12.003.aq.

3 The *Apis*-industrial complex

The commodification of the lives and work of honey bees

To understand the global pollinator crisis, it is crucial to analyze the ways in which honey bees, through the commercial beekeeping industry, are embedded into the global capitalist agriculture system. Building on the themes of Chapter 2, this chapter examines how commercial migratory beekeeping is used within capitalist agriculture as an override to the harm caused to wild bees. This type of beekeeping forces honey bees onto the treadmill of industrial agriculture, adopting many of the practices associated with industrial livestock agriculture including the simplification of diets, the use of prophylactic antibiotics, and the heavy use of miticides (Ellis et al. 2020). Although hobbyist beekeepers are often blamed for the spread of pests and pathogens, most commonly the varroa mite (Andrews 2019), commercial migratory beekeeping has the unique potential to spread pests and pathogens *on a large-scale* between colonies and across vast distances, including across and between continents (Seeley 2019; Seeley and Visscher 2015). These practices result in *sickly yet numerous* animals, that are highly susceptible to stressors, as demonstrated by the crisis of colony collapse disorder in the mid-2000s and the mass infestation of varroa mites in North American bee colonies.

Managed honey bees play an important yet complicated role within capitalist agriculture. Like other species of bees, they are deeply harmed by the creation of the simplified and standardized landscapes of the Capitalocene but they are also embedded within those agricultural landscapes and, in fact, necessary for its functioning. Honey, the main reason why honey bees were domesticated by humans, is an important global agricultural product. In 2020 the global honey market yielded USD 7.84 billion and is expected to increase to USD 11.88 billion in 2028 (Fortune Business Insights 2021). According to the FAO the worldwide production of honey was close to 1.8 million tonnes with an estimated 94 million bee hives under management (FAOSTAT 2022), although the actual amount of honey and number of beehives is likely greater due to underreporting. The work of honey bees as pollinators is even more important to the global capitalist agricultural system. The FAO estimates that the work of pollinators affects yields on 35% of the global agricultural land and is essential to the development of 87 crops (FAO 2022). The value of the global crops that rely on the work of pollinators is between USD 235 billion to USD 577 billion

DOI: 10.4324/9781003142294-3

per year (FAO 2022). The work of honey bees as pollinators is required by vegetable, nut, and fruit farmers due to the defaunation of wild bees and has spurred the development of a pollination services industry. This industry is mostly concentrated in North America, with the biggest concentration of revenue in the California almond industry (Goodrich and Durant 2021). While the pollination services industry is expected to grow in North America, there is also forecasted to be significant growth in the Asia Pacific region (Knowledge Sourcing Intelligence 2021[1]).

The integration of honey bees into human agricultural systems has meant that beekeeping as an industry has also experienced pressure to increase scale and intensify operations. The intensification of agriculture necessitated the creation of a large-scale commercial beekeeping industry which mirrors many of the practices within industrial livestock agriculture (Ellis et al. 2020). Although products of the hive are commercially important within the global food system one of the main ways in which commercial beekeeping operations in North America create a profit is through providing pollination services to large-scale farmers. As agricultural landscapes intensified, creating increased biological standardization and simplification, so too did the need for pollination services from commercial beekeepers and their bees (Ellis et al. 2020). As outlined in Chapter 2, since some species of wild bees often do not thrive in monocultures, the crops that required animal pollination needed the work of managed bees. The defaunation of wild bees is directly related to the increase of honey bees being brought onto monocultured landscapes to provide pollination services. Used to pollinate monocropped fields in the wake of a native pollinator decline, honey bees are, as Watson and Stallins argue, a "rescue pollinator" (2016, p. 229), part of a biological override to mask the accelerating contradictions of capitalist agriculture (Weis 2010). In order to provide pollination services for farmers, migratory commercial beekeepers move across large distances, especially in the United States, to fulfil pollination contracts (Durant 2019). Honey bee hives are packed up at night when most of the foraging bees have returned to the hives, put onto transport trucks, and moved to new locations where they will pollinate a crop that is in bloom for about three to six weeks, depending on the crop, before being moved to a new location and a new crop. In North America, honey bees are commonly used to pollinate cranberries, blueberries, apples, stone fruit, and almonds (Sagili and Burgett 2011).

The rise of migratory, commercial beekeeping

As explored in Chapter 1, beekeeping using *Apis mellifera* has been an integral part of human agricultural systems, particularly those of North Africa, West Asia, and Europe, for thousands of years. Until the 19th century, beekeeping was largely done on a relatively small scale. While some people may have specialized as beekeepers, managing many colonies, and making a livelihood from the products of the hive, it was common for small farmers and peasants to manage a small number of colonies of bees to provide a source of honey and wax for their household or immediate community (Crane 1999). Migratory beekeeping did exist on a small scale, most notably in parts of Europe, but it did not intensify and increase in scale until the late 1800s and early 1900s (Crane 1999). As agriculture became more intensified and simplified in parts of the world, so did the beekeeping industry. The rise of commercial beekeeping and its embeddedness within the global, migratory industry occurred rapidly in the last century. There were several developments that were instrumental to enabling the scaling up of the commercial beekeeping industry. First, the development of hive bodies that allowed for easier manipulation of bee colonies by beekeepers combined with the creation of highways that eventually crisscrossed whole continents, allowing for easier movement of bee colonies. Second, the defaunation of wild bees in monocultured landscapes triggered the development of a large-scale commercial beekeeping industry based on the provision of so-called pollination services to farmers. Third, beekeeping using *Apis mellifera* was promoted as a way to integrate large-scale monoculture agricultural systems and, in some cases, as a development strategy in the Global South.

Hives, highways, and the manipulation of honey bee colonies

After their (semi)-domestication honey bee colonies were kept in a variety of different hive types intended to mimic their preference for living in tight, enclosed cavities, which in the wild would typically be the hollowed-out sections of large trees. Human-created hives took a variety of forms, including cut up and hollowed out logs, cavities in rocks, simple boxes, and straw skeps (Crane 1999). Although there were likely some advantages to these types of hives for the bees, they created a dilemma for beekeepers, namely, how to get the honey and wax out of the hive while minimizing bee deaths and stings to the beekeeper. Another dilemma for beekeepers was determining how much honey and wax to take from the colony if its size, the amount of honey and pollen, and the number of worker bees cannot be easily accessed. Commonly used traditional hive bodies didn't give an easy way for beekeepers to find or remove the queen, check on larvae, and move bees from one colony to another. While some beekeeping practices may have emphasized only taking a small portion of honey comb from each hive, leaving enough for the bees, it became common practice in some parts of Europe to kill the entire colony each year to obtain the honey and wax. Beekeepers would then replace the colony with a swarm in the spring, considerably shortening the lifespan of entire colonies, a practice which was replicated by some settler beekeepers in North America (Crane 1999).

The beekeeping practices common in certain parts of Europe were brought to North America by European settlers where, as mentioned earlier, beekeeping was integrated in and often preceded settler-colonial agriculture due to swarming behaviour and honey bee colonies' tendency to go feral. Beekeeping by settlers in Canada and the United States continued much the same way that it had occurred in Northern and Western Europe.[2] Hive boxes or skeps were used to house the bees with varying amounts of honey and wax taken by the beekeeper depending on the needs and scale of the beekeeping operation. Beekeeping operations at this time in Canada and the United States tended to be small in scale, either done to provide honey and wax to the household, or to provide honey and wax commercially to the community or region (Crane 1999).

A few key innovations in beekeeping allowed for changes to the human-honey bee relationship, and paved the way for beekeeping practices to intensify and increase in scale, alongside and intertwined with other forms of agriculture. In 1851 L. L. Langstroth, a Reverend in Pennsylvania, invented a hive now known as the Langstroth hive that had stackable rectangular boxes and removable frames (Crane 1999). As the bee colony in a Langstroth hive grows, filling up the hive boxes with brood, bees, and honey, beekeepers stack on new boxes with empty frames. This innovation allowed beekeepers to increase the amount of honey and wax produced by their colonies as honey bees naturally attempt to fill their nests with honey comb and will produce more honey than they need for their survival if given more room. It also allowed for easy manipulation of honey bee colonies by beekeepers. With Langstroth's hives, beekeepers could easily check on bees and remove frames and boxes of honey and bees. They could quickly create new honey bee colonies by removing the frames filled with bees and putting them in a new box ready to be transported. Perhaps most importantly, the Langstroth hives allowed beekeepers to easily find and, if they wanted, remove the queen. The invention of the Langstroth hive led to increased honey and wax production and a change to beekeeping practices, allowing for more manipulation of bee colonies (Ellis et al. 2020). The Langstroth hive, and other hives that featured removable frames, may have allowed for the development of the intensified breeding of honey bee colonies, which eventually led to an industry based on raising and selling honey bee queens and colonies, something which has become an international industry (Oertel 1980).

Langstroth hives are now the main type of beehive used in North America and Europe, and although not inherently harmful to bees, the initial advantages of the Langstroth were mostly to beekeepers not the bees. In some ways the Langstroth hive may have been an improvement for honey bees when compared to some of the hive cavities that were used by beekeepers because it allowed for the removal of honey and wax without destroying the colony. However, the initial disadvantage to honey bees, especially before the widespread advent of the now endemic varroa mite, is that it allows and creates the conditions for increased beekeeper manipulation of bee hives. Although a high level of manipulation of bee hives by beekeepers may be necessary to a degree due to serious pests and pathogens that plague honey bees, it is important to note that the invention of the Langstroth hive created the conditions for the development of a large commercial beekeeping industry that allowed for the exponential growth of those pests and pathogens in the first place.

One of the most important aspects of the development of the Langstroth hive is that its widespread adoption by beekeepers led to increased standardization of beekeeping. While different hive types are used by hobbyist and small-scale beekeepers,[3] once beekeepers reach a certain scale of operation in North America and other parts of the world, they tend to gravitate towards Langstroth hives almost exclusively. Since the Langstroth hive is widely used by commercial beekeepers, if a beekeeper uses an alternate hive type, they may have to build their own hive boxes and will not be able to easily install a nucleus colony. The beekeeping industry tends to cater toward beekeepers who use Langstroth bee hives, with a variety of useful products developed specifically for those hives. The straw skep, still an almost universal symbol of beekeeping, is used by very few beekeepers in Canada and the United States. In fact, in some provinces and states skeps are not permitted to be used for biosecurity reasons because they lack removable frames, something considered essential for monitoring and treating pests and pathogens.

Another significant development that changed many of the traditional practices of beekeeping was the rise of a sub-industry that transported mated queens to beekeepers (Oertel 1980). This is related to the development of the Langstroth hive, since queen bees could be easily found, removed, and then moved across space and place to form new colonies. This meant that beekeepers could more easily requeen colonies,[4] instead of waiting for the colony to produce a new queen, a process that can take several weeks. It also allowed for earlier splitting of hives in the spring to establish new colonies. In regions of the world with cold winters and cool springs, queens could be imported from warmer regions to create new colonies earlier in the spring. As highways and cheap fossil fuels made cars and trucks the dominant forms of transportation in North America, it became common for beekeepers to purchase 'packages' of bees as starter colonies or to purchase queen bees to establish new colonies (Oertel 1980). This allowed beekeepers to quickly establish larger apiaries than before since they were not limited by the reproduction of their colonies and the restrictions of their climate (Oertel 1980). Air travel to transport goods now allows for queen bees to be imported from all over the world, the only limitation being the biosecurity and importation rules of the countries and regions involved.[5] In Ontario, for instance, it is commonplace for queen bees to be imported in mid-spring from countries with warmer climates and large beekeeping industries including Chile and Southern USA (Malbeuf 2020).

The establishment of cross-continental highways, coupled with the creation of monocultures of crops, allowed for the commercial beekeeping industry to scale-up substantially by moving across the continents fulfilling pollination contracts (Ellis et al. 2020). As is true for other forms of agriculture, beekeeping has evolved into an industry in which operations have scaled up in size, with fewer operations maintaining larger apiaries. For example, in Canada, 80% of bee colonies are managed by 20% of beekeepers (Canadian Honey Council n. d.). While there has been a growing number of hobbyist beekeepers in Europe and North America who typically have less than ten hives, the number of *small-*

scale and medium-sized commercial beekeepers has not grown at the same rate. The beekeeping industry in Canada, the United States, and parts of Europe is increasingly stratified with a small number of commercial beekeeping operations owning most of the managed colonies on one end and hobbyist beekeepers managing very few bee colonies on the other (Ferrier et al. 2018). Beekeepers trying to create a viable livelihood out of a moderately-sized or small-scale beekeeping operation are increasingly forced out of the industry (Potts et al. 2010; Daberkow et al. 2009). This is largely because beekeeping in North America produces a significant amount of revenue by providing pollination services to farmers (Daberkow et al. 2009) with large beekeeping operations relying more heavily on revenues from pollination contracts than medium to small operations. As Cilia (2019) states, "commercial beekeepers in the United States comprise about twelve hundred people who, for the most part, were born and raised in beekeeping families" (p. 836). The ability to travel over distances to fulfil pollination contracts is possible only for larger enterprises who have a large number of honey bee colonies, staff, and trucks. Migratory, commercial beekeeping has transformed the long-standing, largely mutually beneficial relationship between honey bees and humans and has made the previously benign role of honey bees within human agriculture problematic for both honey bees and wild bees.

Pollination services and honey bee labour

Pollination services are more than a profitable livelihood stream for commercial beekeepers brought about due to the defaunation of wild bee species within the simplified and standardized landscapes of the Capitalocene. Pollination services represent the tendency of neo-liberal capitalism to seek to monetize all life and enterprise commoditize nature, partly through the concept of ecosystem services (Dempsey 2016). The concept of ecosystem services has been widely adopted by environmentalists, policymakers, and scholars attaching monetary value to the work done by non-human nature in healthy ecosystems. The concept of ecosystem services is deployed in discussions about the crises insects face from the combined effects of climate change and capitalist agriculture, and the grave scientific warnings given about the devastating effects the continuing declines of insects and other arthropods will have on both humans and non-human animals, not only as pollinators but also decomposers, predators, and prey (Lister and Garcia 2018; Hallmann et al. 2017). Patel and Moore (2017) argue that while the concept of 'ecosystem services' could conceivably be used to helpfully highlight the work of other-than-humans, it also risks essentializing and commodifying that work, and can obfuscate the ways in which animal bodies and lives are harmed and exploited.

Perhaps unsurprisingly in the Capitalocene the value of non-human nature is most often calculated in terms of monetary value to corporations, industries, and sectors within the capitalist economy. In this way, the concept of ecosystem services exists within and replicates the hegemony of a neo-liberal capitalist system that seeks to commodify all aspects of human and non-human life. Ecosystem services is an approach that continues to privilege human domination of non-human nature, leaving the colonial-capitalist framework intact. Non-human animals, plants, and ecological lifeworlds matter, under the ecosystem services concept, because they benefit humans or, more problematically, because they are essential to capitalist industries. A monetary value is put on the services, or labour provided by non-human life, which is meant to illustrate not only why these lifeforms and worlds matter, but also, apparently, to convince governments and institutions that make policies to protect them. The concept of ecosystem services cheapens the existence of non-human natures by reducing them and their lives to the ways in which they benefit capitalism.

Reducing bees to the ways in which they benefit capitalist agriculture is problematic because it denies the intrinsic value of their lives. Honey bees pollinate flowers in the process of gathering food for themselves and their larvae. By doing so, they benefit plants and many other animal species, and their work helps with the functioning of the ecological lifeworlds in which they live. But they gather the honey and pollen for their survival and the survival of their offspring, and, in the case of eusocial bees, their colonies. Although it remains highly controversial in animal rights theory to argue that insects should be given ethical consideration that acknowledges potential intelligence, preferences, or even the ability to feel pain[6] (although, confusingly, many vegans eschew honey), as a researcher who is also a beekeeper and gardener, I believe that bees have a clear set of preferences for how they wish to live, recognizable to people who spend time observing them. While scientists have not determined whether insects have consciousness or feel pain, this retelling of a discussion about whether insects feel pain between a professor in the environmental humanities (who is also a hobbyist beekeeper) and Sainath Suryanarayanan, a trained entomologist, is illuminating with respect to both the challenges of knowledge in this regard, and the moral implications. Swan states:

> But could insects feel emotional angst? [We leaned] forward into our quiet voices and the small circle of intimacy created by our shared knowledge that many would find blasphemous. "I didn't prove it, *scientifically*," [Sainath] said, "but I could feel it. Of course, they suffer. Their long antennae caressing each other – their feet and tongues touching. Yes, they do. They suffer."
>
> I felt a tightness in my chest as I imagined my own honeybees, their bird-like faces, the soft yellow hair on their abdomens, the tentative way they explored my hands. The way they touched each other with so much tenderness. I could not imagine piercing the belly of a live bee with a scalpel, watching it struggle and flail its arms. Torturing insects was something I knew some children did, but I had not been one of them.
>
> (Swan 2014)

Bees play a crucial role in the functioning of ecological lifeworlds, including the ones in which human food systems are embedded, but they pollinate for their own reasons and this should be reason enough to not destroy their ability to exist. Their lives matter because they are living beings not because they benefit humans and they should be given ethical consideration in terms of how they are used and exploited by the industries in which they are put to work. Discussion about the importance of pollinators often includes a quantification of the monetary value of their work within capitalist agriculture, based on the production of honey but also on the 'work' of pollinating crops. In doing so, this conception of ecosystem, or pollination services reduces the work of bees to their embeddedness within capitalist agriculture, obfuscating how this embeddedness harms managed honey bees and wild bees. It naturalizes the use of bees within migratory, commercial beekeeping and makes invisible the ways in which honey bees have been made to be sickly, vulnerable animals.

There are at least 20,000 different species of bees in the world, and numerous species of bees can be found in every continent on Earth except for Antarctica. Although humans stewarded honey-producing bees throughout the world, including various species of honey bee and stingless bees, they were managed by humans for their honey and wax not their pollination services. Wild bees and other pollinators provided the pollination needs of human agriculture as well as most terrestrial ecosystems on Earth without the need of semi-domesticated honey bees. It is important to consider why managed honey bees are now so widely used to pollinate crops, including small-scale farms that have diversified plantings of crops. It is tempting to argue that it was the innovation of the beekeeping industry, notably changes in hive bodies that allowed for movement across space, that led directly to the pollination services industry. This explains how honey and wax production increased in scale and intensification, and explains why it was possible to create a migratory, commercial beekeeping industry. However, it does not explain why there was ever a need for pollination services in the first place and the way in the provision of these services became an essential component of fruit, nut, and vegetable production. As examined in Chapter 2, the standardization and simplification of landscapes on a large scale is a key feature of capitalist agriculture. Although wild bees are understudied, the rise of pollination services indicates the extent to which many species of wild bees simply cannot thrive in capitalist agricultural landscapes, or at least cannot thrive to the extent that they can provide the pollination needs of monocultures of fruit and nut trees, and fields of fruiting vegetables. Entomology is a relatively new discipline, initially created to classify and, later, control insects, and the extent to which the populations of wild bees declined in the early to mid-part of the 20th century, during which the latest wave of simplification and standardization of grain-oilseed landscapes was beginning is not well mapped. That the rise of pollination services, was preceded by the increasing use of pesticides, fertilizers, and large-scale machinery indicates that there was likely a rapid decrease of wild bee populations to the extent that it necessitated the rise of an industry that provided pollination services of managed honey bees, and to a lesser but still notable extent, managed bumble bees, mason bees, and orchard bees.

Even with defaunation of some wild bee species, pollination services are only necessary in systems of large-scale monocultures of crops that need insect pollination to produce fruit or seed. Corn, soy, wheat, and cottonseed, some of the main monocultured crops in the world, do not need insect pollination to produce fruit or seed. In a polycultural or small-scale monoculture system, there will likely be enough wild pollinators to pollinate the necessary crops, partly because those systems provide wild bees and stationery honey bees, with enough forage for the season and with a short distance from good forage sites to nesting sites and/or materials. It is the large-scale monocultures of fruit and nut-bearing trees, berries, and some vegetables that need insect pollination during the bloom which can occur for a relatively short period of time. If these crops go into bloom in a landscape in which hundreds or thousands of acres of land are inhospitable to many species of wild bees, the need arises for a commercial pollination services industry. As previously discussed, once farmers scale up their production, investing thousands or millions of dollars in machinery, removing wilder vegetation, and investing in the means to intensively produce one or two crops, it becomes very hard for them to scale down when they notice a problem such as lack of wild bees. It is much easier to introduce a human-managed pollinator for the duration of the bloom for a nominal fee.

Honey bees are relatively easy to move over great distances, due to a combination of easy to manipulate hive bodies, highways, and transport trucks, have become the solution to the problem of a lack of wild pollinators for large-scale monocultures. Although honey bees have been integral to human agriculture for thousands of years in many regions of the world, commercial, migratory beekeeping is now embedded within capitalist agriculture and is indispensable for monocultured fruit, nut, berry, and vegetable crops that require insect pollination to produce fruit and seeds. It is unsurprising then, that this type of beekeeping is promoted, alongside increasingly intensified, large-scale agricultural systems in the Global South, even in regions in which other species of honey bees already exist, alongside local beekeeping or honey hunting practices (Theisen-Jones and Bienefeld 2016).

Migratory, commercial beekeeping and honey bee vulnerability

While the rise of migratory, commercial beekeeping may be a concern to small-scale beekeepers, threatening traditional beekeeping practices and livelihoods with the same 'get big or get out' mentality that has driven many small-scale farmers out of agriculture, it is most harmful to honey bees, whose labour is exploited to provide these pollination services. Migratory, commercial beekeeping, which Nimmo (2015), calls the "*Apis*-industrial complex" (p. 185) creates sickly, yet numerous honey bees and, by doing so, may also harm wild bees through the spread of pathogens. The body of evidence on harm caused to honey bees by their embeddedness in capitalist agriculture as pollinators is small but significant. It is important to note that it is often difficult for scientists and, perhaps even more so, social scientists to critically analyze the practices and outcomes of commercial beekeeping. Like other forms of so-called livestock agriculture, the commercial beekeeping industry does not want to be scrutinized in ways that might affect their operations. Also, like other livestock industries commercial beekeepers have been openly hostile to government programs that regulate their practices to ensure increased animal health. For example, when the Ontario government passed legislation that would require veterinarian approval to use antibiotics, beekeepers were in strong opposition, particularly commercial beekeepers who use prophylactic antibiotics to prevent a very serious bacterial honey bee disease, American Foulbrood (AFB) (OMAFRA n.d.).

Yet, while the body of evidence is small the multiple threats to honey bee health, most dramatically seen in the crisis of Colony Collapse Disorder (CCD) in the United States, but also evident in increasing winter mortality of honey bees in temperate climates require a serious examination of how honey bees are harmed by the role they play within capitalist agriculture. As Durant (2019) argues, honey bees are vulnerable animals. Common practices within commercial beekeeping that may harm honey bees include the movement of bee colonies over vast distances; the keeping of hundreds or even thousands of colonies of bees in close proximity to one another which may increase the spread of pests and pathogens; the use of miticides to kill varroa mites (Johnson 2015; Martin 2004); the use of prophylactic antibiotics to protect against AFB (OMAFRA n.d.); and the routine feeding of sugar syrup and artificial pollen patties.

Movement across space and honey bee stress

Migratory, commercial beekeeping involves beekeepers and their employees travelling in transport trucks with hundreds or even thousands of colonies of bees across vast areas to fulfil pollination contracts for monoculture crops within large-scale agricultural operations (Cilia 2019). In both Canada and the United States, a small number of commercial beekeeping enterprises manage the great majority of honey bee colonies. In Canada, approximately 20% of the country's 7,000 beekeepers manage 80% of all 600,000 honey bee colonies, with the main commercially pollinated crops being canola, blueberries, and apples (Canadian Honey Council, n.d.). In the United States, the commercial beekeeping industry is one of the most migratory in the world, with beekeepers criss-crossing the country in an annual circuit to pollinate almonds, blueberries, cranberries, and other high-value crops (Ellis et al., 2020). In blooming periods of commercial crops that depend on animal pollination, there are thousands or even millions of bee colonies from multiple beekeepers bought to the area. The almond industry in California is the most extreme example of this, as 1.2 million acres of almond trees need cross-pollination in the blooming season in February (Goodrich and Durant 2021). In 2020, over 88% of all the honey bee colonies in the United States, amounting to about 2.4 million colonies, were brought to the almond-growing regions in California for about six weeks of pollination (Goodrich and Durant 2021). The almond pollination industry is big business with farmers paying anywhere from $150–200 per hive. A survey of beekeepers who provide pollination services during the almond harvest found that 28% of respondents used an almond pollination broker to secure pollination contracts (Goodrich and Durant 2021).

The movement of bee colonies over long distances in a relatively short period of time can have detrimental effects on the bees and the ecological lifeworlds in which they are placed. The bees are transported to a different bioregion with a novel set of environmental conditions, including different flowers in bloom, and this may cause some harm to both individual bees and the colony as a whole. Honey bees, unlike fully domesticated farm animals, leave human-created shelters to forage and, in doing so, foster their own relationship with the landscapes in which they forage. Scientists have demonstrated that bees navigate partly by remembering structures in the landscape including trees and buildings (Kheradmand and Nieh 2019), and that they remember the locations of patches of good forage (Menzel et al. 2005). The constant movement from one monocultured landscape to another interrupts the ways that they navigate and move around landscapes. Of course, this may be advantageous to the beekeeper and farmer, keeping the honey bees close to the fields in which they have been brought to pollinate but it can interrupt the proper functioning of the colony.

A comparative study on the impacts of migratory beekeeping on the health of honey bees, conducted in the United States, found that the migratory adult bees had a significant decrease in lifespan and a change in oxidative stress levels (Simone-Finstrom et al. 2016). Another study, conducted in Turkey, found that in areas where migratory honey bees were brought, there was less genetic diversity of the bees in the area – migratory, stationary, and wild (Kükrer et al. 2021). This is concerning for several reasons. One is that in areas of the world with wild, native populations of honey bees, this could lead, over time, to an eclipsing of wild subspecies as semi-domesticated varieties of honey bees come to dominate. Two, this decrease in genetic diversity can be seen as part of the biological simplification and standardization that marks capitalist agriculture. Within capitalist agriculture species of crops and domesticated (or semi-domesticated) animals are standardized in terms of characteristics and traits, intentionally done to meet the needs of the industry in which they are embedded. In terms of honey bees, less genetic diversity could lead to less resilience as they encounter a variety of stressors in the environment including exposure to pesticides; pests and pathogens; climate-change caused extreme weather events; and lack of diversity of forage. In fact, in the face of unsustainable winter colony losses, several agricultural ministries have intervened to encourage beekeepers to breed more resilient bees (Ontario Beekeeping Association n.d.).

Pesticide exposure during pollination

Although large-scale, often monocultured organic farms also use the pollination services of honey bees, most of the farms on which honey bees are used to pollinate treat their crops with a combination of pesticides including herbicides, insecticides, and fungicides. Pollinating honey bees encounter thousands of acres of fields with only one type of plant in bloom, and, potentially, a toxic soup of chemicals used on that crop, the combination of which can put immense stress on their bodies. The use of pesticides on landscapes in which honey bees are brought to pollinate has been an issue of contention and conflict between beekeepers and farmers. This conflict is not often over the use of pesticides, as the commercial beekeepers who are fulfilling pollination contracts know whether they are working with conventional or organic farms, but about the timing of pesticide use in relation to the arrival of bees to the space and the combinations of pesticides being used. For example, some commercial beekeepers who provided pollination services for blueberry farms in the Fraser Valley in British Columbia refused to bring their honey bees to pollinate in the summer of 2018 due to long-simmering concerns about the use of harmful pesticides, particularly fungicide, that could harm the bees (Cruickshank 2018). Similar concerns have been raised about the combination of insecticide and fungicide use and negative impacts on bees during the California almond industry (Wade et al. 2019).

There is a strong body of evidence that the synergistic effects of pesticides in combination with one another, and with other agrochemicals present in rural landscapes, may cause more harm to honey (and other) bees than if they had encountered only one type of pesticide (Wang et al. 2020; Tosi and Nieh 2019; Zhu et al. 2017; Thompson et al. 2014). While herbicides and fungicides may not have been formulated to harm insects, there are indications that they do cause harm, especially in combination with insecticides, something common in the landscapes of the Capitalocene. There is increasing evidence that honey bees used for pollination services have nutritionally deficient diets (Arien et al. 2018; Wright et al. 2018; Sharpe and Heyden 2009) which, when combined with pesticide exposure may cause an amplification of harm to honey bee colonies (Tosi et al. 2017; Schmel et al. 2014).

Lack of adequate nutrition and artificial feeding

Although honey bees are used within agricultural landscapes for their so-called pollination services, honey bees embedded in capitalist agricultural systems can experience a lack of adequate nutrition. Honey bees moved to standardized and simplified landscapes to provide pollination services may be placed on fields of blooming plants that provide them with ample sources of pollen and nectar. However, they may have deficiencies since the pollen and nectar is typically only from one crop for a period of several weeks. Several studies have demonstrated that honey bees face nutritional deficiencies when placed in intensive agricultural landscapes that feature monocultured crops (Dolezal et al. 2019; Dolezal and Toth 2018; Alaux et al. 2017; Tosi et al. 2017; Smart et al. 2016; Donkersley et al. 2014). The monocultured landscapes of capitalist agriculture are, in many ways, "green deserts" for honey bees, and other pollinators

(Dolezal et al. 2019). As Dolezal and colleagues conclude, "Intensively farmed agriculture can provide a short-term feast that cannot sustain the long-term nutritional health of colonies." Studies have consistently shown that honey bees have better health when placed on landscapes that feature a diversity of flowering plants throughout the growing seasons, potentially resulting in have lower infestations of mites, more brood, and better overwintering success (Smart et al. 2016).

Nutritional health in honey bees may be important in helping them to deal with multiple stresses they encounter in the agricultural landscapes on which they are placed to forage. There is some evidence that nutritional stress and exposure to neonicotinoids may work synergistically to cause health declines in honey bee colonies (Tosi et al. 2017). Poor nutrition may make honey bees more susceptible to pests and pathogens and, conversely, pathogens may make honey bees more likely to suffer from nutritional stress (Dolezal and Toth 2018). Further, honey bees may need different food sources for different purposes, for example a different diet may be needed to combat viruses than to raise brood. If their nutritional sources are only one crop, they may not have a diverse enough diet to thrive.

The spread of pests and pathogens

There are many pests and pathogens that affect the health of honey bees, the spread of which is likely intensified by the commercial, migratory beekeeping industry. This is a complicated issue in which blame has been placed on all types of beekeepers and scales of beekeeping operations. While some bee researchers and beekeepers argue that the focus should be simply on combatting pests and pathogens, and not assigning blame, I believe that understanding the geopolitics of the spread of pests and pathogens is crucial to combatting out-of-control infestations, such as the one that exists with the varroa mite. To understand the threat that pests and pathogens poses to honey bees, we must situate the beekeeping industry within the global capitalist agricultural system.

The most serious pest threat to honey bees in the United States and Canada is the varroa mite (*Varroa destructor*). The mass infestation of varroa mites among honey bees is a topic of contestation and conflict between beekeepers about the best beekeeping approaches and practices. Varroa mites were originally only found on the Asian honeybee, *Apis cerana*, a species of honey bee that has developed a tolerance to the mites and is able to co-exist with them (OMAFRA n.d.). The varroa mite spread to *Apis mellifera*, as the Western honey bee was introduced to parts of Asia such as Japan and Thailand due to the expansion of commercial beekeeping[7] (Roth et al. 2020). The mite was detected on honey bees in Europe in the 1970s and rapidly began to infest bee colonies in Asia and Europe (Roth et al. 2020). The mite first appeared in the United States in 1987 and although Canada quickly closed its border to the importation of bees from the United States, was detected in Canada in 1989 (OMAFRA n.d.). Since then, varroa mites have spread to affect virtually 100%

of all colonies in North America and Europe. The only country in the world that does not have a varroa mite infestation in honey bees is Australia (Roth et al. 2020).

The varroa mite attaches to the bodies of bees, usually their thorax, and sucks their body fat (OMAFRA n.d.) The gestation of young mites occurs on the bee larvae and they develop when the brood cells are capped and the bee larvae pupates. The adult mites are present on the young adult bees when they emerge from their cells and can easily spread amongst bees within colonies and to bees in other colonies when foraging on the same flower. Honey bees also spread mites to other colonies when they rob weaker colonies of their honey supplies, and when adult male bees, or drones, 'drift' into other colonies. The drifting behaviour of drone bees, who have no role within the colony other than reproduction, coupled with the preference of adult mites to feed and hatch young on drone larvae, who are fatter and have a longer development period than worker bees, makes drones a significant spreader of mites within and between honey bee colonies (OMAFRA n.d.). The varroa mite's parasitic behaviour harms individual bees, but mites do the most damage to honey bees by spreading viruses, such as the deformed wing virus, within colonies (Wilfert et al. 2016). Although the varroa mite does not have a parasitic relationship with non-*Apis* bees, there is a high degree of concern among native bee scientists that the pathogens it spreads may infect other species of bees (Nanetti et al. 2021).

It is important to consider how commercial, migratory beekeeping may have helped to spread the varroa mite, not to blame individual beekeepers or beekeeping operations, but to understand the ways in which the embeddedness of honey bees within capitalist agriculture may create the conditions in which pests and pathogens can flourish. Although the mites can spread quickly between colonies through bee interactions on flowers and the drift of drone bees to neighbouring hives, commercial beekeeping has potentially accelerated this spread in two ways. One, commercial apiaries keep hundreds of colonies together in a relatively small space. When being brought to pollinate regions in which there are thousands or millions of acres of a crop in bloom at the same time, such as the almond boom in California, thousands of honey bee colonies from all over the continent can be in very close proximity to one another for a period of several weeks. From his studies on feral bees, Seeley (2019) argues that feral honey bee colonies prefer to be about 1 km apart. It is important to note that he is studying honey bees in a forested area and this pattern may be different in other types of landscapes. However, it is notable that feral bees seem to prefer to be distant from one another, something only possible in a one-hive apiary, with no neighbouring apiaries.

The second way that commercial beekeeping potentially accelerated the spread of varroa mites is in the movement over vast distances and geographic landscapes. Through commercial, migratory beekeeping, viruses can spread quickly to hundreds or thousands of colonies, who are then transported to different parts of the continent. In the United States, commercial migratory honey bees criss-cross the country in a typical season, spreading whatever pathogen or parasite they are carrying to the migratory, stationary, and feral honey bees in each location. Although hobbyist beekeepers are sometimes blamed for the varroa mite infestation due to their perceived lack of adequate treatment for mites, the effects of migratory commercial beekeeping on the initial spread of honey bees should not be ignored. Honey bees cannot move more than a few kilometres their own. They forage within 3–5 km of their hive (8 to 12 km if there is a dearth of flowering plants) and typically only swarm within a few kilometres of the origin colony. If honey bee colonies were mostly stationary, only moved for emergency reasons such as being predated on by bears, or in the path of potential climate disasters, and the selling of queen bees and nucleus colonies was kept very local, their spread across landscapes through swarming would be slow and incremental, as would the movement of honey bee pests and pathogens. While some honey bee parasites move independent of honey bees such as the small hive beetle, varroa mites move on and with honey bees.

While varroa mites are the most widespread honey bee pest, the most feared pathogen among beekeepers in North America is American Foulbrood, a bacterium that spreads quickly through an apiary, rotting the brood when it infects a colony (OMAFRA n.d.). American Foulbrood can easily and quickly decimate several apiaries as sickly bees interact with uninfected bees on flowers or rob one another's hives. The only treatment allowed for AFB in some areas of North America, such as Ontario, is to burn all the hives in an apiary including the adult bees, the brood, and the woodenware. The burning of the hives in an apiary in which AFB has been found includes colonies that may be unaffected and is a huge loss for beekeepers and for bees. Both the disease itself and the treatment for the disease can decimate an apiary and AFB can quickly spread to neighbouring apiaries, threatening other beekeeping operations. Some beekeepers, particularly commercial ones, use prophylactic antibiotics to inhibit the occurrence of AFB. The use of antibiotics for AFB is not effective after the bacterium has been discovered in a colony. Instead, the use of antibiotics potentially prevents the occurrence of the disease, although critics argue that antibiotic use is not a solution to the problem of AFB as it only supresses the bacterium, which can stay dormant or suppressed in hive bodies and wax for many years. Some bee researchers and beekeepers argue that the prophylactic use of antibiotics in beehives can contribute to antibiotic resistance emerging over time, part of a more serious problem within livestock agriculture of an overuse of antibiotics for prophylactic reasons (Ontario Beekeepers' Association 2018).

Use of miticides in the hive

The prevalence of pests and pathogens among honey bees has led to a high level of pesticide and antibiotic use within beekeeping operations. The most widely used pesticides within beekeeping operations are miticides, used to control varroa mite populations. The use of miticides to control mites is a controversial, polarizing practice, as is, on the other side of the interventionist spectrum, the complete non-treatment for mites. Miticides have been shown to have detrimental effects on bee colonies, most concerningly queen bees (Ilyasov et al. 2021; Diep 2013). In honey bee colonies, the worker bees live short, busy lives of six weeks to three months, depending on the time of year, with overwintering worker bees living longer. A queen bee, in contrast, typically lives five to seven years overseeing many generations of worker bees within her colony. Due to multiple factors, including the overuse of miticides and the presence of pathogens, queen bees' lives have been shortened in the past few decades (McAfee et al. 2021; Amiri et al. 2017), with queen bees now living an average of three or fewer years in some parts of the world (Diep 2013). Not only does this serve another blow to the sustainability of the beekeeping industry – while also driving the shipping of mated queen bees over distances – it also increases the vulnerability of honey bees, as it indicates that colonies as a whole are sickly.

Some of the initial miticides used to treat varroa mites in North America and Europe have been banned because they proved to be harmful to bees, especially queen bees. However, years after these miticides were banned traces of them can still be found in honey bee wax (Mullin et al. 2010). Pesticides residue is often found in wax because it is a fat, and toxic chemicals tend to accumulate in fats. Wax foundations are typically used for years by beekeepers and are placed into multiple bee colonies (Mullin et al. 2010). Even when wax foundations are retired, wax residue remains on hive bodies and other beekeeping equipment and tools. Like other beings who are targeted with pesticides, varroa mites quickly developed resistance to some of the most widely used miticides, something which is expected to continue, causing agrochemical corporations to continuously develop new types of miticides (Martin 2004).

There are non-pesticide treatments approved for usage by beekeepers including the use of organic acids (formic and oxalic) and essential oil (thymol). The chemical composition of the organic acids and oils makes it unlikely for mites to develop resistance (Johnson 2015) but these organically derived treatments can also be hard on colonies and queen bees, especially formic acid (Johnson 2015). In terms of mite treatments, commercial beekeepers commonly use miticides and formic acids while hobbyist beekeepers are more likely to use the acids and essential oil, or to not treatment at all (Ellis 2021). Thomas Seeley (2019) argues that the honey bee in North America would have developed a natural immunity to the varroa mite if there had been no miticides available when varroa mites first arrived on the North American continent. He posits that the mites would have decimated most colonies in North America but the survivor colonies would have had some genetic immunity and over a few generations, honey bee populations would have been replenished. He argues that this has happened with other bee parasites, and possibly with varroa mites in *Apis cerana*, or the Asian honey bee, which has since adapted to co-existing with varroa mites. Although some beekeepers, including Seeley with his conception of Darwinian beekeeping, argue that this approach could work in regions in which all beekeepers agree to not treat for mites and let survivor honey bees replenish populations, it is unlikely to occur outside of very isolated geographic regions since honey bees move across landscapes (albeit only within several kilometres) and interact with honey bees from other colonies. This is also highly unlikely outside of isolated regions because all beekeepers would have to agree to not treat their bees and let most of their colonies die, and would not be able to bring in any bees outside of a strictly specified geographic range for a prolonged period. If beekeepers depend on beekeeping for their livelihood, they would have to essentially allow their livelihood to collapse for years, making this an unlikely option, especially within capitalism, but also within other systems of agriculture.

Pests and the scapegoating of hobbyist beekeepers

Hobbyist beekeepers are acutely aware that the commercial sector commonly blames them for the prevalence of mites in North American honey bee colonies (Andrews 2019), due to the perception that they do not sufficiently monitor their hives for mites and do not adequately treat their colonies. Negative perceptions of hobbyists are augmented by studies of honey bee colony loss which often show that small-scale beekeepers are more likely to have higher rates of overwintering hive loss than commercial beekeepers (Bruckner et al. 2020). However, here it should be noted that these studies are based on *voluntary* reporting of information given by beekeepers about mite treatments and winter mortality, and this is not necessarily accurate as some groups of beekeepers may be more willing than others to give factual accounts of what they perceive to be sensitive information. Further, winter mortality rates do not necessarily reflect the loss of colonies due to mite infestation as larger enterprises with thousands of hives and a large number of staff may use techniques such as eradicating or consolidating weak hives before winter begins (Steinhauer et al. 2018). It is notable that some large surveys of winter mortality of honey bee colonies such as those conducted by the Ontario Ministry of Agriculture, Farming, and Rural Affairs (OMAFRA) found little difference in mortality rates between commercial and small-scale beekeepers (OMAFRA 2018). There is uncertainty in understanding how much individual practices affect overall mite populations in a region versus larger dynamics of beekeeping as an industry within the larger capitalist agriculture system.

Several studies, including my own PhD dissertation have shown that some hobbyist beekeepers are reluctant to treat their bees for pests and pathogens with some beekeepers espousing 'treatment-free' beekeeping as the best method (Ellis 2021; Andrews 2019). Honey bees are semi-domesticated animals and they do require some human intervention, especially with respect to managing pests and pathogens, which relates to the fact that domestication entails some inherent risk for non-human animals. A beekeeper I spoke to for my dissertation, who co-founded an urban beekeeping operation in an Ontario city, suggested that there may have been a time when beekeepers could have been minimally interventionist, but this is no longer possible with the almost universal spread of varroa mites across North America. I concur with this perspective, and while I think it is important to recognize that hobbyist beekeepers are not *responsible* for the rapid spread of mites across North America, I also believe that in the present context, the reluctance of some to treat may lead to the unnecessary death of many colonies

Integrated pest management (IPM) is often promoted as a solution to mite infestations and is an approach which encourages beekeepers to begin with the gentlest, least invasive method to deal with infestations. An IPM approach can work with both organic and non-organic beekeeping practices. Yet however much IPM grows among hobbyist and small-scale beekeepers, it seems unlikely that varroa mites can be adequately controlled in North America given the current state of the beekeeping industry. As discussed earlier, the use of harsher miticides not only kills mites but also harms bees, most worryingly queen bees, and has already led to some resistance among mites (Johnson 2015). Further, the migratory nature of large-scale commercial beekeeping imposes chronic risks, as the continental-scale movement of huge populations of unhealthy honey bees is bound to spread pests and pathogens among them, though the specifics of the risk of these diseases is a severely understudied subject (Ellis et al. 2020; Steinhauer et al. 2018; Smith et al. 2013).

The common accusations that hobbyist beekeepers are a central cause of mite infestations serves to downplay the role that the migratory, commercial beekeeping industry – which is deeply embedded within capitalist agriculture – played in initially spreading varroa mites, and continues to play in creating 'super mites' that are resistant to treatments. Risks are further complicated by the case made by Giacobino and colleagues (2017) that environment may matter more for bee vulnerability than do beekeeper practices, which indicates that solutions need to be much bigger than individual beekeepers' practices. While varroa mites are a serious problem for honey bees and beekeepers, it is important to understand the problem of mites in the context of the commercial beekeeping industry, including how the viruses spread by mites might interact with colonies that are already weakened by other forces outside the control of individual beekeepers such as exposure to pesticides and poor nutrition.

The problems posed by mites to honey bees worldwide are severe and considerable effort and research has been put into solving them not only by beekeepers but, because it threatens to harm an entire agricultural industry, by scientists and governmental bodies. What is lacking in most of the proposed solutions is an understanding of this dilemma in the context of honey bees' role within the capitalist agriculture system. There is a reluctance to interrogate the practices of the commercial beekeeping industry and the embeddedness of the industry within landscapes of scarcity that harm honey bees. This has led to a situation in which the practices of individual beekeepers are blamed for the infestation of mites. While treatment-free beekeeping methods can seriously exacerbate regional mite populations within honey bee colonies, it is important to look at the ways in which the honey bees' role within the global capitalist agriculture system plays a significant part in the spreading of pests and pathogens, and in the development of mites and pathogens that are resistant to pesticides, a known and well-studied phenomena that occurs with other agricultural 'pests', pathogens, and weeds. While pathogens and parasitic animals exist and cause harm in all ecological lifeworlds, it is imperative to understand how capitalism working within nature (Moore 2005), especially within agricultural and extractive industries, spreads them far beyond their natural or possible range, seriously magnifying harm. Ecological imperialism (Crosby 2004), it seems, is still at work, although it has changed from the initial forces of European colonialism to the continued harm of capitalist industries that seek economic growth and wealth accumulation at all costs.

The global spread of *Apis mellifera* and large-scale commercial beekeeping

Migratory commercial beekeeping is big business in many parts of the world, essentially wherever there are vast monocultures of fruits, nuts, and fruiting vegetables. Although the industry is perhaps most intensified and embedded within agricultural systems in the United States, it is prominent in many other countries in the world including Canada, China, Argentina, the United Kingdom, and countries in the European Union. In parts of the world where other honey-producing species of honey bees and stingless bees are managed by humans, there has been a move, often promoted by the government or international development agencies, to implement beekeeping of *Apis mellifera*. In some of these instances, beekeeping is promoted as a regional agricultural activity that can provide a sustainable livelihood for local people largely through the production of honey and beeswax (Patel et al. 2021). This is especially appropriate in regions of the world such as sub-Saharan Africa, Northern Africa, and Eastern Europe where *Apis mellifera* has lived in both wild and managed forms for thousands of years. But it potentially becomes a problematic practice when it one, threatens traditional forms of beekeeping specific to that region, and two, promotes large-scale, migratory beekeeping which can damage the health of local honey bees and the local beekeeping industry (Buchori et al. 2022; Theisen-Jones and Bienefeld 2016). In some cases, the promotion of beekeeping as a livelihood or regional agricultural development strategy could see the expansion of migratory, commercial beekeeping (Requier et al. 2019). As demonstrated in this chapter, the ways in which honey bees are embedded and entangled in capitalist agriculture harms them, causing, among other things, increased exposure to pesticides, colony stress, and decline, and increased spread of pests and pathogens. A concern for advocates of small-scale beekeeping is that a push for beekeepers to scale up their enterprises may push them onto the treadmill of capitalist agriculture with its accelerating contradictions and crises. Traditional beekeeping practices in many parts of the world, including those of non-*Apis mellifera* bees such as the

Asian honey bee and multiple species of stingless bees, is infused with collective knowledge and practices that is specific to certain regions and communities. A loss of these practices and knowledges will potentially have negative repercussions for beekeepers, local small farmers, and the bees themselves.

Notes

1. It is important to note that information about the value of the pollination industry is difficult to obtain, which is why some of the sources are business forecasting firms. There is a significant knowledge gap in terms of the migratory commercial beekeeping industry.
2. Beekeeping practices in eastern and southern Europe tend to be distinctive from the practices of beekeepers in western European and the United Kingdom (Crane 1999). These practices were not brought to the Americas until waves of immigration from those regions. Some of the practices were not replicated in North America in any significant scale, partly due to geography and climate but also due to beekeeping already having been standardized and embedded within agriculture.
3. Even though the Langstroth is the mostly widely used in commercial operations, there are different hive types in use around the world especially among small-scale beekeepers. For example, the Warre hive uses smaller, square hive boxes than Langstroth hives and is typically made from thicker wood with removable bars or frames (not foundations) on which honey bees build honey or brood comb. The top bar hive, used by some hobbyist beekeepers in North America, and small-scale commercial beekeepers in the Global South, is a long rectangular box in which wooden bars are placed on top of the hive body under the lid. The bees build down from the top bar and beekeepers expand the hive horizontally not vertically. In theory the top bars, from which comb is built, can be removed although in practice bees tend to build in ways that do not allow for easy removal of honey comb in this hive type.
4. This is commonly done for several reasons: if the queen is not laying properly; if the queen has died; and if the hive is aggressive, which is often attributed to the genetics of the queen.
5. Some countries, such as Australia, restrict the importation of bee colonies and queen bee to stop the flow of pests and pathogens. For Australia this has resulted in one of the few populations of honeys bees that are not infested with varroa mites.
6. Some prominent animal rights theorists argue against giving insects ethical consideration (Gruen 2015; Donaldson and Kymlicka 2010), although they presumably do not eat products from insects such as honey.
7. *Apis cerana*, the Asian honey bee, does produce honey and is the focus of a small-scale beekeeping industry, particularly in Japan. Several characteristics of the Asian honey bee do not make it easy to manage to the same degree as *Apis mellifera*.

References

Alaux, C., Allier, F., Decourtye, A., Odoux, J. F., Tamic, T., Chabirand, M., ... & Henry, M. (2017). A 'landscape physiology' approach for assessing bee health highlights the benefits of floral landscape enrichment and semi-natural habitats. *Scientific Reports*, 7(1), 1–10. https://www.nature.com/articles/srep40568?origin=ppub.

Amiri, E., Strand, M. K., Rueppell, O., & Tarpy, D. R. (2017). Queen quality and the impact of honey bee diseases on queen health: Potential for interactions between two major threats to colony health. *Insects*, 8(2), 48. https://doi.org/10.3390/insects8020048.

Andrews, E. (2019). To save the bees or not to save the bees: Honey bee health in the Anthropocene. *Agriculture and Human Values*, 36, 891–902. https://doi.org/10.1007/s10460-019-09946-x.

Arien, Y., Dag, A., & Shafir, S. (2018). Omega-6:3 ratio more than absolute lipid level in diet affects associative learning in honey bees. *Frontiers in Psychology*, https://doi.org/10.3389/fpsyg.2018.01001.

Bruckner, S., Steinhauer, N., Engelsma, J., Fauvel, A. M., Kulhanek, K., Malcolm, E, ... & Williams, G. (2020). 2019–2020 honey bee colony losses in the United States: Preliminary results, Bee-Informed Partnership. beeinformed.org.

Buchori, D., Rizali, A., Priawandiputra, W., Raffiudin, R., Sartiami, D., Pujiastuti, Y. ... & Johannis, M. (2022). Beekeeping and managed bee diversity in Indonesia: Perspective and preference of beekeepers. *Diversity*, 14 (1), 52. https://doi.org/10.3390/d14010052.

Canadian Honey Council. Industry overview. Accessed January 20, 2020. https://honeycouncil.ca/archive/honey_industry_overview.php.

Cilia, L. (2019). The plight of the honeybee: A socioecological analysis of large-scale beekeeping in the United States. *Sociologia Ruralis*, 59 (4), 831–849.

Crane, E. (1999). *The World History of Beekeeping and Honey Hunting*. New York: Routledge.

Crosby, A. W. (2004). *Ecological Imperialism: The Biological Expansion of Europe 900–1900*. Cambridge: Cambridge University Press, 2nd ed.

Cruickshank, A. (2018). BC beekeepers worry blueberries are making their bees sick. *The Toronto Star*, April 28. https://www.thestar.com/vancouver/2018/04/28/bc-beekeepers-worry-blueberries-are-making-their-bees-sick.html.

Daberkow, S., Korb, P., & Hoff, F. (2009). Structure of the US beekeeping industry: 1982–2002. *Journal of Economic Entomology*, 102 (3), 868–886. https://doi-org.proxy1.lib.uwo.ca/10.1603/029.102.0304.

Dempsey, J. (2016). *Enterprising Nature: Economics, Markets and Finance in Global Biodiversity Politics*. Hoboken: John Wiley.

Diep, F. (2013). Royal pains: Why queen honeybees are living shorter, less productive lives. *Scientific American*, September 16. https://www.scientificamerican.com/article/royal-pains-why-queen-honeybees-are-living-shorter-less-productive-lives/.

Dolezal, A. G. & Toth, A. L. (2018). Feedbacks between nutrition and disease in honey bee health. *Current Opinion in Insect Science*, 26, 114–119. https://doi.org/10.1016/j.cois.2018.02.006.

Dolezal, A. G., Clair, A. L. S., Zhang, G., Toth, A. L., & O'Neal, M. E. (2019). Native habitat mitigates feast–famine conditions faced by honey bees in an agricultural landscape. *Proceedings of the National Academy of Sciences*, 116 (50), 25147–25155. https://doi.org/10.1073/pnas.1912801116.

Donaldson, S. & Kymlicka, W. (2010). *Zoopolis: A Political Theory of Animal Rights*. Oxford: Oxford University Press.

Donkersley, P., Rhodes, G., Pickup, R. W., Jones, K. C., & Wilson, K. (2014). Honeybee nutrition is linked to landscape composition. *Ecology and Evolution*, 4 (21), 4195–4206. https://doi.org/10.1002/ece3.1293.

Durant, J. (2019). Where have all the flowers gone? Honey bee declines and exclusions from floral resources. *Journal of Rural Studies*, 65 (1), 0.1016/j.jrurstud.2018.10.007.

Ellis, R. (2021). Pollinator people: An ethnography of bees, bee advocates and possibilities for multispecies commoning in Toronto and London, ON. [Doctoral dissertation, University of Western Ontario]. Electronic Thesis and Dissertation Repository. 7796. https://ir.lib.uwo.ca/etd/7796.

Ellis, R., Weis, T., Suryanarayanan, S., & Beilin, K. (2020). From a free gift of nature to a precarious commodity: Bees, pollination services, and industrial agriculture. *Journal of Agrarian Change*, 20 (3), 437–459, https://doi.org/10.1111/joac.12360.
FAO. (2022). FAO's global action on pollination services for sustainable agriculture. https://www.fao.org/pollination/background/bees-and-other-pollinators/en/, accessed January 25, 2022.
FAOSTAT. (2022). Crops and livestock products. https://www.fao.org/faostat/en/#data/QCL.
Ferrier, P. M., Rucker, R. R., Thurman, W. N., & Burgett, M. (2018). Economic effects and responses to changes in honey bee health, ERR-246, U.S. Department of Agriculture, Economic Research Service.
Fortune Business Insights. (2021). The global honey market is forecasted to grow from $8.17 billion in 2021 to $11.88 billion in 2028 at a CAGR of 5.5% in forecast period, 2021-2028. https://www.fortunebusinessinsights.com/industry-reports/honey-market-100551.
Giacobino, A., Pacini, A., Molineri, A., Cagnolo, N.B., Merke, J., Orellano, E. ... & Signorini, M. (2017). Environment or beekeeping management: What explains better the prevalence of honey bee colonies with high levels of Varroa destructor? *Research in Veterinary Science*, 112, 1–6.
Goodrich, B. K. & Durant, J. L. (2020). 2021 Almond pollination outlook: Economic outlook and other considerations. *West Coast Nut*, 12–18.
Gruen, L. (2015). *Entangled Empathy: An Alternative Ethic for Our Relationships with Animals.* Brooklyn, Lantern Books.
Hallmann C.A., Sorg, M., Jongejans, E., Siepel, H., Hofland, N. ... & de Kroon, H. (2017). More than 75 percent decline over 27 years in total flying insect biomass in protected areas. *PLoS ONE* 12 (10), e0185809. https://doi.org/10.1371/journal.pone.0185809.
Ilyasov, R., Lim, S., Lee, M. L., Kwon, H. W. & Nikolenko, A. (2021). Effect of miticides Amitraz and Fluvalinate on reproduction and productivity of honey bee *Apis mellifera*. *Uludağ Arıcılık Dergisi*, 21 (1), 21–30. doi:10.31467/uluaricilik.883775.
Johnson, R. M. (2015). Honey bee toxicology. *Annual Review of Entomology*, 60, 415–434.
Kheradmand, B. & Nieh, J. C. (2019). The role of landscapes and landmarks in bee navigation: A review. *Insects*, 10 (10), 342. https://doi.org/10.3390/insects10100342.
Knowledge Sourcing Intelligence. (2021). Global pollination market size, share, opportunities, COVID 19 impact, and trends by type (self-pollination, cross-pollination), by crop type (almond, sunflower, canola, others), by end-users (agricultural companies, farmers, gardeners), and by geography – forecasts from 2021 to 2026. https://www.knowledge-sourcing.com/report/global-pollination-market.
Kükrer, M., Kence, M., & Kence, A. (2021). Honey bee diversity is swayed by migratory beekeeping and trade despite conservation practices: Genetic evidence for the impact of anthropogenic factors on population structure. *Frontiers in Ecology and Evolution*, 9. 10.3389/fevo.2021.556816.
Lister, B. C. & Garcia, A. (2018). Climate-driven declines in arthropod abundance restructure a rainforest food web. *PNAS*, 115 (44), https://doi.org/10.1073/pnas.1722477115.
Malbeuf, J. (2020). Honeybee farmers facing 'desperate situation' as bee imports slow. *CBC News*, April 2, https://www.cbc.ca/news/canada/edmonton/honeybee-alberta-canada-import-1.5515575.

Martin, S. J. (2004). Acaricide (pyrethroid) resistance in Varroa destructor. *Bee World*, 85 (4), 67–69.

McAfee, A., Chapman, A., Pettis, J. S., Foster, L. J., & Tarpy, D. R. (2021). Trade-offs between sperm viability and immune protein expression in honey bee queens (*Apis mellifera*). *Communications Biology*, 4 (48) https://doi.org/10.1038/s42003-020-01586-w.

Menzel, R., Greggers, U., Smith, A., Berger, S., Brandt, R., Brunke, S. ... Watzl, S. (2005). Honey bees navigate according to a map-like spatial memory. *Proceedings of the National Academy of Sciences*, 102 (8) 3040–3045; doi:10.1073/pnas.0408550102.

Moore, J. W. (2005). *Capitalism in the Web of Life: Ecology and the Accumulation of Capital*. New York: Verso.

Mullin, C. A., Frazier, M., Frazier, J. L., Ashcraft, S., Simonds, R., van Engelsdorp, D., & Pettis, J. S. (2010). High levels of miticides and agrochemicals in North American apiaries: Implications for honey bee health. *Plos ONE*. https://doi.org/10.1371/journal.pone.0009754.

Nanetti, A., Bortolotti, L., & Cilia, G. (2021). Pathogens spillover from honey bees to other arthropods. *Pathogens*, 10 (8), 1044. https://doi.org/10.3390/pathogens10081044.

Nimmo, R. (2015). Apiculture in the Anthropocene. In Human Animal Research Network Editorial Collective (eds.), *Animals in the Anthropocene: Critical Perspectives on Non-Human Futures*. Sydney: University of Sydney Press, pp. 177–199.

Oertel, E. (1980). History of beekeeping in the United States. In *Agriculture Handbook 335*. Washington, DC: United States Department of Agriculture, pp. 2–9.

Ontario Beekeepers' Association. (2018). Antibiotic access working group bulletin. https://www.ontariobee.com/sites/ontariobee.com/files/document/OBA_%20Antibiotic_Progress_Bulletin_November_2018.pdf.

Ontario Beekeeping Association. (n.d.). Ontario resistant honey bee selection program. https://www.ontariobee.com/ORHBS.

Ontario Ministry of Agriculture and Rural Affairs. (2018). 2018 Ontario Apiculture Winter Loss Survey. http://www.omafra.gov.on.ca/english/food/inspection/bees/2018winterloss.htm#results.

Ontario Ministry of Agriculture and Rural Affairs. (n.d.). Varroa mite: biology and diagnosis. http://www.omafra.gov.on.ca/english/food/inspection/bees/varroa-biology.htm.

Ontario Ministry of Agriculture and Rural Affairs. (n.d.). American foulbrood: Prevention and management. http://www.omafra.gov.on.ca/english/food/inspection/bees/afb-mgmt.htm.

Patel, R. & Moore, J. W. (2017). *A History of the World in Seven Cheap Things: A Guide to Capitalism, Nature, and the Future of the Planet*. Berkeley: University of California Press.

Patel, V., Pauli, N., Biggs, E., Barbour, L., & Boruff, B. (2021). Why bees are critical for achieving sustainable development. *Ambio* 50, 49–59. https://doi.org/10.1007/s13280-020-01333-9.

Potts, S. G., Roberts, S. P. M., Dean, R., Marris, G., Brown, M. A., Jones, R., Neumann, P., & Settele, J. (2010). Declines of managed honey bees and beekeepers in Europe. *Journal of Apicultural Research*, 49 (1), 15–22. https://doi.org/10.3896/IBRA.1.49.1.02.

Requier, F., Garnery, L., Kohl, P. L., Njovu, H. K., Pirk, C. W. W., Crewe, R. M., & Steffan-Dewenter, I. (2019). The conservation of native honey bees is crucial. *Trends in Ecology & Evolution*, 34 (9), 789–798. https://doi.org/10.1016/j.tree.2019.04.008.

Roth, M. A., Wilson, J. M., Tignor, K. R., & Gross, A. D. (2020). Biology and management of Varroa destructor (Mesostigmata: Varroidae) in *Apis mellifera* (Hymenoptera: Apidae) colonies. *Journal of Integrated Pest Management*, 11(1), 1. https://doi.org/10.1093/jipm/pmz036.

Sagili, R. R. & Burgett, D. M. (2011). Evaluating honey bee colonies for pollination: A guide for commercial growers and beekeepers. A Pacific Northwest Extension Publication, 623. https://catalog.extension.oregonstate.edu/sites/catalog/files/project/pdf/pnw623.pdf.

Schmel, D. R., Teal, P. E. A., Frazier, J. L., & Grozinger, C. M. (2014). Genomic analysis of the interaction between pesticide exposure and nutrition in honey bees (Apis mellifera). *Journal of Insect Physiology*, 71 (Dec.), 177–190.

Seeley, T. D. (2019). *The Lives of Bees: The Untold Story of the Honey Bee in the Wild*. Princeton: Princeton University Press.

Seeley, T. D. & Visscher. M. L. (2015). Crowding honeybee colonies in apiaries can increase their vulnerability to the deadly ectoparasite Varroa destructor. *Apidologie*, 46 (6), 716–727.

Sharpe, R. J., & Heyden, L. C. (2009). Honey bee colony collapse disorder is possibly caused by a dietary pyrethrum deficiency. *Bioscience Hypotheses*, 2(6), 439–440. https://doi.org/10.1016/j.bihy.2009.01.004.

Simone-Finstrom, M., Li-Byarlay, H., Huang, M. H., Strand, M. K., Rueppell, O., & Tarpy, D. R. (2016). Migratory management and environmental conditions affect lifespan and oxidative stress in honey bees. *Scientific Reports*, 6. https://www.nature.com/articles/srep32023.

Smart, M., Pettis, J., Rice, N., Browning, Z., & Spivak, M. (2016). Linking measures of colony and individual honey bee health to survival among apiaries exposed to varying agricultural land use. *PloS One*, 11 (3), e0152685. https://doi.org/10.1371/journal.pone.0152685.

Smith, K. M., Loh, E. H., Rostal, M. K., Zambrana-Torrelio, C. M, Mendiola, L., & Daszak, P. (2013). Pathogens, pests, and economics: Drivers of honey bee colony declines and losses. *EcoHealth*, 10, 434–445.

Steinhauer, N., Kulhanek, K., Antunez, K., Human, H., Chatawannakul, P., Chauzat, M. P., & van Englesdrop, D. (2018). Drivers of colony losses. *Current Opinion in Insect Science*, 26, 142–148.

Swan, H. (2014). The sorrow of bees. *Aeon*, November 26. https://aeon.co/essays/bees-have-feelings-too-and-scientists-should-respect-them.

Theisen-Jones, H. & Bienefeld, K. (2016). The Asian honey bee (*Apis cerana*) is significantly in decline. *Bee World*, 93(4), 90–97, doi:10.1080/0005772X.2017.1284973.

Thompson, H. M., Fryday, S., Harkin, S., & Milner, S. (2014). Potential impacts of synergism in honeybees (Apis mellifera) of exposure to neonicotinoids and sprayed fungicides in crops. *Apidologie*, 45 (5), 545–553. doi:10.1007/s13592-014-0273-6.

Tosi, S. & Nieh, J. C. (2019). Lethal and sublethal synergistic effects of a new systemic pesticide, flupyradifurone (Sivanto®), on honeybees. *Proceedings of the Royal Society B*, 286 (1900). https://doi.org/10.1098/rspb.2019.0433.

Tosi, S., Nieh, J. C., Sgolastra, F., Cabbri, R. & Medrzycki, P. (2017). Neonicotinoid pesticides and nutritional stress synergistically reduce survival in honey bees. *Proceedings of the Royal Society B: Biological Sciences*, 284. http://dx.doi.org/10.1098/rspb.2017.1711.

Wade, A., Lin, C. H., Kurkul, C., Regan, E. R., & Johnson, R. M. (2019). Combined toxicity of insecticides and fungicides applied to California almond orchards to honey bee larvae and adults. *Insects*, 10 (1), 20. https://doi.org/10.3390/insects10010020.

Wang, Y., Zhu, Y. C., & Li, W. (2020). Interaction patterns and combined toxic effects of acetamiprid in combination with seven pesticides on honey bee (*Apis mellifera* L.). *Ecotoxicology and Environmental Safety*, 190, 1. https://doi.org/10.1016/j.ecoenv.2019.110100.

Watson, K., & Stallins, J. A. (2016). Honey bees and Colony Collapse Disorder: A pluralistic reframing. *Geography Compass*, 10 (5), 222–236.

Weis, T. (2010). The accelerating biophysical contradictions of industrial capitalist agriculture. *Journal of Agrarian Change*, 10 (3), 315-341.

Wilfert, L., Long, G., Leggett, H. C., Schmid-Hempel, P., Butlin, R., Martin, S. J., & Boots, M. (2016). Deformed wing virus is a recent global epidemic in honeybees driven by Varroa mites. *Science*, 351 (6273), 594–597. doi:10.1126/science.aac9976.

Wright, G. A., Nicolson, S. W., & Shafir, S. (2018). Nutritional physiology and ecology of honey bees. *Annual Review of Entomology*, 63 (1), 327–344. https://doi.org/10.1146/annurev-ento-020117-043423.

Zhu, Y. C., Yao, J., Adamczyk, J., & Luttrell, R. (2017). Synergistic toxicity and physiological impact of imidacloprid alone and binary mixtures with seven representative pesticides on honey bee (Apis mellifera). *PLoS ONE*, 12 (5). doi:10.1371/journal.pone.0176837.

4 Toxic flowers and uncertain science
Pesticides and bees

Bees of all species derive their food from flowers. They drink the nectar of flowers and, depending on species, bring it to their nests to make honey. They gather pollen, something that makes them excellent pollinators because their hairy bodies evolved to gather as much pollen as possible. This pollen is mixed with honey to make bee bread, or eaten directly and pollen is especially important as a protein source for developing larvae. Their flower foraging is what makes bees the world's most efficient and important pollinators. However, their foraging not only provides bees with food but also with a toxic soup of chemicals that causes serious harm. In the United States, there are 500 different pesticide compounds licensed for use including insecticides, herbicides, miticides, arachnicides, and fungicides (Goulson 2020). Pesticide use is on the rise, for example in the United Kingdom the number of insecticide and herbicide applications nearly doubled between 1990 and 2016 (Goulson 2020), and it can be common that pesticides that are banned in the Global North for causing harm to people or ecological lifeworlds are still heavily marketed to governments and farmers in the Global South (Goulson 2020).[1]

This chapter examines the large body of research about the impacts of pesticides, including insecticides, herbicides, and fungicides, on bees (Cressey 2017; Woodcock et al. 2017; Brandt et al. 2016; Gill and Raine 2014). The landscapes in which bees of all species forage and the habitats in which native bees make their home are increasingly filled with pesticides that, scientists suggest, work synergistically to harm bees (David et al. 2016). While a growing number of people are concerned with the impacts of pesticides on bees, there are questions about both the reliability of the science and the corporatization of scientific research (Conner 2020; Fang 2020; Suryanarayanan and Kleinman 2017).

Pesticides: war, agriculture, and entomology

To describe pesticides as a powerful tool in the war against non-human nature may seem hyperbolic, but the development of pesticides and the explosion of use of certain pesticides is directly related to the development of biochemical warfare. This is well-illustrated with the histories of dichlorodiphenyltrichloroethane

DOI: 10.4324/9781003142294-4

(DDT) and Agent Orange, among other pesticides. The first pesticide made of synthetic chemicals was DDT; before its invention, lead arsenic was primarily used for insect control (Robbins 2007). During World War II, DDT was widely produced and used for the control of lice and mosquitos in the trenches. As Robbins (2007) argues, by the end of World War II DDT was hailed as a "war hero" (p. 52). Its production had also increased during this time and, without the pest-producing conditions of war, chemical corporations looked to agriculture as a recipient of surplus DDT. It was largely thought of as a relatively safe and even benign chemical, especially compared to lead arsenic which had several very serious effects on people (Robbins 2007). However, Rachel Carson, in her book *Silent Spring*, first published in 1962, warned of the very serious harmful effects of DDT on non-human natures (Carson 1962).

Another pesticide developed for war was Agent Orange, a combination of two herbicides the dioxin-based 2,4,5-T and 2,4-D.[2] Developed by the US Army in the 1940s, these herbicides were used in various combinations during the Vietnam War[3] to defoliate trees and shrubs behind which fighters from the National Liberation Front of South Vietnam might hide and to kill crops en masse to starve the Vietnamese population. The US Air Force sprayed nearly 19 million gallons of herbicides on the Vietnamese countryside, 11 million gallons of which was Agent Orange (Institute of Medicine 1994). Both Vietnam's Ministry of Health and the US Department of Veteran Affairs (USDVA) have compiled lists of diseases and conditions presumed to be related to Agent Orange and other dioxin herbicides used in the Vietnam War (Martin 2015). The USDVA's list includes several cancers, type 2 diabetes, and numerous birth defects in children of veterans, especially female veterans, including congenital heart disease and spina bifida (Martin 2015). The Vietnamese Red Cross estimates that 1 million Vietnamese people have health problems related to Agent Orange and other herbicides used by the US military and the USDVA believes that 2.6 million military personnel were exposed (King 2012). Agent Orange and other herbicides used in the Vietnam War were produced for the US military in large quantities by US chemical corporations including Dow and Monsanto (Dow n.d.). Dow's website describes the corporation as being "compelled" to produce these herbicides by the US military, denies there are any ill-health effects in people, and claims that Dow has no moral responsibility for the use of these herbicides in the Vietnam War (Dow n.d.).

As the histories of DDT and dioxin-based herbicides illustrate, the technological development and manufacturing capacity for biological and chemical warfare dramatically accelerated during World War II (Robbins 2007). Although the United States has been more or less continually at war to some degree since the end of World War II, the massive build up during that time nevertheless left surplus capacity and some of the leading chemical weapons manufacturers increasingly turned this technology towards agriculture and lawncare (Robbins 2007). In the 1950s and 1960s, chemical manufacturers began to aggressively research, develop, and market new insecticides and herbicides based on synthetic chemicals (Robbins 2007). There are multiple reasons why Rachel Carson famously described industrial agriculture as being at war with insects and undesired plants regarded as 'weeds', including the fact that the main tool that emerged to fight these 'pests' literally emerged out of the military industrial complex. Animal advocates who critically study livestock agriculture make similar connections between humans' treatment of animals within capitalism and war (Wadiwel 2015). Wadiwel expands on this idea through an exposition of the violence enacted on the bodies and lives of domesticated livestock. The chronic applications and bioaccumulation of chemical pesticides are how this war manifests for insects and other invertebrates.

Entomology and the science of killing

Scientific research about insects is a relatively new discipline although scientific curiosity about and interest in insects, was something that people engaged in for hundreds of years. Insects were classified by naturalists and early scientists and the behaviours and lifecycles of honey bees were often first described by observant beekeepers, among which was Aristotle (Ransome 2004). But the science of insects, entomology; bees, melittology; and the related sub-discipline of pollination and conservation biology, fully developed in the 20th century. The discipline of entomology originally advanced within academic institutions and industry to assist with controlling insects who act as pests in agricultural systems, and insects who are parasitic towards humans or spread disease, such as mosquitos. Although the discipline has evolved considerably since its development and institutionalization, its origins are in insect control, not insect flourishing. It is important to understand the origins of the discipline because it continues to affect the ways in which research into bees and other insects is conducted. One, the newness of the discipline, especially scientific inquiry into insect population stability and health, is one of the reasons why there is not population baseline data for many species of bees, and why many species of insects have not and will not be studied in any depth (van der Sluijs 2020). Two, the origins of the discipline in insect control continues to drive some of the science being done about insects because there remains an integration between some sub-disciplines of entomology and the agrochemical and agribusiness industry (Fang 2020). This is especially true in the study of honey bees, and may put constraints on the type of research being done about honey bee pests and pathogens; the impacts of certain types of beekeeping on honey bee health; and the negative effects of pesticides on bees and other insects. Like other academic disciplines, the sciences have entangled, contradictory, and sometimes problematic relationships with capitalism and colonialism (Conner 2020). For example, the study of insects came into its own as a formalized subdiscipline of biology, entomology, in large part through the search for effective insecticides (Robbins 2007). Scientists, including entomologists, need funding for labs and equipment and often find it in corporations, even more so with widespread government cutbacks to higher education throughout the neoliberal era which can cause a dependence on corporate funding of research (Fang 2020), and clearly this risks reducing the willingness to engage in overtly political debates especially those that challenge agrochemical corporations.

It is important to understand these critiques of entomology and other scientific disciplines in the context of the neoliberalization of academia and knowledge more generally. Neoliberalization of knowledge has occurred in different ways all over the world, partly depending on the extent to which universities are publicly funded. In countries in which universities are largely publicly funded, the neo-liberalization of knowledge has occurred through cutbacks to funding, or targeted funding or removal of funding for political purposes (Mintz 2021; Troiani and Dutson 2021). Due to these cutbacks, universities began to lean heavily towards philanthropist and corporate funding, although government funding is still the primary source of research funding for most academics in these countries. In the United States and other countries in which many universities are private institutions, the neo-liberalization of the academy has occurred in more intense ways through philanthropic and corporate funding. Although academia remains committed to rigorous, peer-reviewed research, university priorities are shaped by donor priorities particularly on politically controversial topics.

It is important to remember that insecticides are developed by scientists who, to some extent, are experts on insects. Scientists who design insecticides have to have some knowledge about insect bodies, lifecycles, and social organization. Pesticides are as much an artifact of science as the empirical research into harm caused by these pesticides, and agroecological research into practices that promote on-farm biodiversity. The point here is to emphasize that within capitalism science can both uphold destructive ecological and oppressive systems or seek to dismantle them. Agrochemical corporations, and the military industrial complex, rely heavily on the STEM disciplines, often hiring scientists and academics from leading research universities (Conner 2020). Science is political, and scientists, like all humans, are political actors. When defending science, we must always ask what type of science we are defending and acknowledge that science is complex, contested, dynamic, and uncertain. In terms of the flourishing of insects, it is important to ask who funds scientific research and what views scientists may have about capitalism, corporate funding of science, and capitalist agriculture. This is not an attack on science but an argument for critical engagement with scientific disciplines and, most importantly, a call to action for public funding of scientific research.

Just as scientific research leads to the development of pesticides, there has been some important scientific research into the harms caused by pesticides. There is now a very large body of rigorous scientific evidence about the harm neonicotinoids, a class of pesticides that will be extensively discussed in this chapter, cause to bees. This research was partly propelled by the alarms raised by beekeepers about honey bee health (Suryanarayanan and Kleinman 2017) which led to coalitions of activists including beekeepers and environmentalists collectively pressuring individual governments, the European Union, and international institutions associated with the United Nations to fund scientific research about neonicotinoids. Scientists who study insects are now being compelled to take a position on pesticides and participate in policymaking and advocacy about insect flourishing. Some scientists are answering this call by advocating for restrictions or even bans on certain classes of neonicotinoids (Goulson 2018).

The harm, complexity, and uncertainty of neonicotinoids

Neonicotinoids are a class of systemic pesticides that has exploded in use on a global scale over the past two decades. In this section I will examine what neonicotinoids are, how they harm bees, and how they became so ubiquitous in agriculture. Since the early 1990s, neonicotinoids have gone from not being used at all, to being extensively used on many commercial crops globally. It is important to note when discussing neonicotinoids that there are other types of systemic pesticides that have similar actions as this class of pesticides, and will replicate most of the same problems within agricultural and ecological landscapes. While this is sometimes used to discourage anti-pesticide activists from pursuing bans on pesticide use, it can also serve to draw attention to the larger problem which is capitalist agriculture and its attempts to standardize and simplify diverse ecological lifeworlds, of which pesticides is one particularly egregious tool.

Neonicotinoids are synthetic neurotoxins that are structurally similar to nicotine (Hladik et al. 2018). There are eight different types of neonicotinoids that are commercially available, under various brand names: imidacloprid, thiacloprid, clothianidin, thiamethoxam, acetamiprid, nitenpyram, dinotefuran, and sulfoxaflor (Pollinator Network @ Cornell n.d.). Worldwide there are six agrochemical corporations that produce commercially available neonicotinoids: Bayer (imidacloprid, thiacloprid, and clothianidin), Syngenta (thiamethoxam), Corteva (sulfoxaflor), Nippon Soda (acetamiprid), Mitsui Chemicals (dinotefuran), and Sumitomo Chemicals (nitenpyram). Neonicotinoids affect insects by causing abnormal behavior, immobility, and death (Brandt et al. 2016). The neonicotinoid class of pesticides are distinctive in that they are both systemic and persistent. In this context the word 'systemic' refers to the fact that they spread to all plant tissues via the vascular system, including the pollen, nectar, and guttation fluid (Brandt et al. 2016). 'Persistent', in turn, means that neonicotinoids are present and accumulate in the environment through various pathways rather than quickly dissipating. Even when they are delivered as a seed coating, they can be found in soil, waterways, and nearby plants (Brandt et al. 2016; Mogren and Lundgren 2016; Fairbrother et al. 2014; Krupke et al. 2012). Neonicotinoids are water-soluble and can easily be absorbed by plants through both their roots and leaves (Goulson 2013). Research has indicated that neonicotinoids persist and accumulate in the soil for much longer than previously thought (Goulson 2013).

Neonicotinoids were developed in the 1980s, first appearing on the market in the early 1990s (Borsuah et al. 2020). They were approved for use in the

United States in 1994, followed by Canada in 1995, and are now the most widely used class of insecticides in the world (Borsuah et al. 2020). Currently neonicotinoids are registered for use in 120 countries, and account for 25% of global insecticide sales (Borsuah et al. 2020). Imidacloprid was the first neonicotinoid that was approved for use (Borsuah et al. 2020) and so tends to be the most heavily researched neonicotinoid, and the one most often implicated in harming pollinators and other animals. For example, it is the only neonicotinoid that the Canadian federal government recently considered (but decided against) restricting due to the harm it causes to aquatic animals and waterways (Pesticide Management Regulatory Agency 2016). Neonicotinoids are not only used in field-based agriculture. They are also used in urban and forested areas, commonly as tree injections to protect against insects such as the emerald ash borer, which has seriously damaged ash trees in North America. They are also widely used in the greenhouse industry as foliar sprays, soil drenches, and granular applications, including for ornamental flowering plants. Some of these ornamental plants are marketed as pollinator-friendly plants, even though all aspects of the plant (nectar, pollen, guttation fluid) can potentially harm insects, including bees. Another common use of neonicotinoids is at the household level, against parasitic insects such as fleas and bed bugs (Hladik et al. 2018).

The use of neonicotinoids in industrial agriculture

In less than three decades neonicotinoids have come to dominate the capitalist agriculture landscape. For example, in Canada they are used on about 95% of corn crops and 55–60% of soy bean crops (Ontario Bee Health Working Group 2014), with a similar trajectory in the United States (Hladik et al. 2018). These crops are mostly grown to produce livestock feed, not to directly feed people (Hamel and Dorf 2014). Although initially applied through both foliage spray and seed coating, 80% of neonicotinoids currently used in agriculture globally are delivered as a seed coating (Borsuah et al. 2020). Seed coatings are used on almost 100% of corn planted in the United States and canola planted in Canada and are common on many other crops grown on a large scale around the world including soybeans, oilseed rape, cereals, rice, cotton, and sunflowers (Furlan et al. 2021). A recent study by Tsvetkov and colleagues (2017) of bee exposure to neonicotinoids through proximity to corn crops in Ontario, Quebec, and Indiana found that "honey bee colonies near corn are ... chronically exposed to [neonicotinoids] for a substantial proportion of the active season in temperate North America" (p. 1395). Originally thought to be less harmful to surrounding ecological lifeworlds based on the assumption that the crop will absorb most of the pesticide, the widespread availability of neonicotinoid coated seeds has increased the use of these pesticides globally (Furlan et al. 2021). Seeds coated with neonicotinoids have also created a situation in which these pesticides are used prophylactically and not as part of an integrated pest management plan (Furlan et al. 2021), even though claims are often made by farmers to the contrary.

Evidence of harm

In France in 1996, beekeepers noticed that there was an increase in the mortality of honey bee colonies near fields in which farmers were applying imidacloprid, a new product at the time (Hladik et al. 2018). This was the beginning of what became a global movement raising concern about neonicotinoids and bees, and placing pressure on countries and international bodies to institute bans and moratoriums. This also led to what became a large body of evidence interrogating whether, and how, neonicotinoids harm bees. Currently, there is a strong body of evidence indicating that both honey and wild bees are negatively affected by neonicotinoid pesticides. While there have been some reports of immediate poisonings of bee colonies with neonicotinoids (Fairbrother et al. 2014), most of the effects of neonicotinoids on bees, are thought to be sublethal, cumulating over time, with some researchers suggesting that toxic amounts of pesticide exposure could be reached in the field within days or weeks (Goulson 2013). Research has shown that cumulative neonicotinoid exposure causes a variety of health problems in honey bees including affecting their learning, foraging, and homing abilities (Tison et al. 2019; Goulson 2013), interrupting their sleeping patterns and circadian rhythms (Tackenberg et al. 2020), causing poor foraging patterns (Colin et al. 2019); and weakening queens (Vergara Amado et al. 2020). Lab experiments have also demonstrated that neonicotinoid pesticides have a negative impact on the functioning of the immune systems of worker bees (Tarek et al. 2018; Brandt et al. 2016).

One of the largest studies conducted on the effects of neonicotinoids on both honey and wild bees found that exposure to low levels of neonicotinoids may cause reductions in hive fitness when combined with a number of local environmental factors (Woodcock et al. 2017), such as exposure to fungicides and miticides; parasites; lack of diverse flowers for foraging; and extreme or unpredictable weather due to climate change. In honey bees, neonicotinoids have frequently been detected in bee bread (a mixture of pollen and honey) and honey (Brandt et al. 2016). Research in the United States on the wax and pollen of honey bee hives detected the presence of at least one pesticide and 120 other agrochemicals in each hive (David et al. 2016). This indicates that honey bees in the field are chronically exposed to a complex mixture of pesticides and agrichemicals (David et al. 2016). In fact, a recent study on honey bee exposure to neonicotinoids from corn crops found that "acute toxicity of neonicotinoids to honey bees doubles in the presence of a commonly encountered fungicide" (Tsvetkov et al. 2017). The study also found that most neonicotinoid-positive pollen sampled in honey bee hives was from non-target plants, and not pollen from treated corn, indicating that neonicotinoids accumulate in the environment through drift as well as persistence in soil and waterways.

Neonicotinoids and wild bees

There is widespread agreement that defaunation is occurring among wild bees throughout North America and Europe, with neonicotinoids being pinpointed as one of several potential causes. Information about the effects of neonicotinoids on wild bees is somewhat uncertain, although there has been some research done on wild bumble bees. Bumble bees are social insects like honey bees, maintaining small colonies of a few hundred bees, depending on species. Most other wild bees are solitary and tend to have more specialized foraging patterns. For example, most wild bees forage over shorter distances than honey bees and bumble bees (Packer et al. 2007). It is important to note that in the research about neonicotinoids the honey bee is often substituted for other types of bees (van der Sluijs 2020), which some experts argue is inappropriate. Wild bees provide a high amount of pollination, but they are not under the management of humans. There are some indications that wild bees are more vulnerable to the effects of pesticides and other factors, such as climate change, than honey bees (Goulson 2013). There have also been suggestions by some entomologists that the complexity of honey bee colonies may protect them from the negative effects of pesticides (Suryanarayanan 2015). Several studies conducted in Europe have indicated that managed honey bees are at less risk of harm by neonicotinoids than other species of bees. Field studies conducted in Sweden, the United Kingdom, Hungary, and Germany have indicated that bumble bee colonies and solitary mason bees performed poorly when exposed to neonicotinoids whereas they had variable impacts on honey bee colonies (Hladik et al. 2018). These studies are concerning because they indicate that wild bees, often unstudied, could have high levels of negative impacts due to pesticide exposure, particularly in regions in which honey bees have been found to be struggling due to high use of pesticides. In other words, these studies indicate that if honey bees are struggling due to pesticide exposure, wild bees are probably doing even worse.

One study found that bumble bees who foraged wildflowers near treated crops had higher levels of pesticide contamination in their hives than nearby honey bees, mostly due to the shorter foraging distances of the former (David et al. 2016). Other studies have shown that neonicotinoid exposure has chronic and acute effects on the foraging activities of bumble bees which could be detrimental, over time, to colonies and species (Gill and Raine 2014). A study recently conducted by Woodcock and colleagues (2017) found that the negative impact of neonicotinoids on several species of wild bees were associated with the residues found in nests, which points to the problem with the persistence of neonicotinoids in the environment. A study on bumble bees found that bumble queens exposed to thiamethoxam, a widely used neonicotinoid pesticide, are less likely to initiate a new colony, with a 26% reduction (Baron et al. 2017). Baron and colleagues (2017) postulated that this reduction could, over time, dramatically increase the likelihood of population extinction. A comprehensive review of 53 studies on neonicotinoid effects on wild species of bees found that neonicotinoid exposure impaired bumble bee colony growth; negatively impacted reproductive output across all bees studied; had negative effects on bumble bee foraging; and reduced the size of *Bombus* species (Siviter et al. 2021). The authors of the review pointed out that most studies on wild bees and neonicotinoid exposure were conducted on two genera, *Bombus* and *Osmia*, indicating a serious knowledge gap about other genera (Siviter et al. 2021).

Although the impact of neonicotinoids on wild bees is not fully understood and has not been fully addressed by many of the stakeholders, it is perhaps a more pressing and troubling issue than the impact on honey bees. Honey bees are managed by humans who breed them and ensure their survival. It is hard (but not impossible) to imagine circumstances in which the domesticated honey bees will be made extinct.[4] A mass reduction in the population of honey bees would have to coincide with a collapse of the global beekeeping industry, something that would likely only happen during a large-scale agricultural crisis. Wild bees are not managed by humans (with a few exceptions) and are much more vulnerable to forage and habitat loss. Wild bees are not only essential for so-called ecosystem services due to their pollination work but they are also a vital part of ecosystems on every continent on Earth, except Antarctica. The loss of wild bees could cause ecosystem collapse to an extent which we cannot comprehend (Packer 2011). The protection of wild bees should be at the forefront of discussions about bans or moratoriums on neonicotinoids.

Impacts on other animals

A large body of evidence indicates that honey bees and wild bees are adversely impacted by neonicotinoids and evidence is now accruing that this class of pesticides is also negatively affecting other types of animals (Campbell et al. 2022; Gibbons et al. 2015; van der Sluijs et al. 2015). As persistent and systemic pesticides, neonicotinoids move through the landscape and make their way into waterways, non-target wildflowers, and animal bodies. In a comprehensive review of the impacts of neonicotinoids, van der Sluijs and colleagues (2015, pp. 48–49) state that:

> The present scale of use, combined with the properties of these compounds, has resulted in widespread contamination of agricultural soils, freshwater resources, wetlands, non-target vegetation and estuarine and coastal marine systems, which means that many organisms inhabiting these habitats are being repeatedly and chronically exposed to effective concentrations of these insecticides.

As this statement indicates, there have been recent studies conducted about harm caused by neonicotinoids to aquatic insects due to these pesticides easily leaching into ground water and waterways. Studies indicate that approximately 20% to 75% of neonicotinoids that are applied as seed coatings or as foliage sprays can be transported to surface waters by runoff and leached into groundwater (Borsuah et al. 2020). In waterways, neonicotinoids can persist for days to weeks and are believed to harm aquatic invertebrates, impacting aquatic food webs (Borsuah et al. 2020). Species of flies such as mayflies, caddisflies, and midges, were found to be the most sensitive aquatic taxa to neonicotinoids in a review study that examined 214 acute and chronic toxicity tests. These insects are essential food to birds, fish, and amphibians (Hladik et al. 2018). Scientists have also raised the alarm that neonicotinoids may harm birds. While there is some concern that birds may be harmed by eating neonicotinoid-coated seeds, studies indicate that birds avoid these seeds if they have other food sources, which they may not in heavily monocultured landscapes. Most harm being done to birds by neonicotinoids is through the depleting of populations of insects that are consumed in great qualities by insectivores (Hladik et al. 2018).

Surprisingly for a pesticide that is systemic, persistent, and has been widely used around the world for decades, there are very few studies done on potential effects on humans. A small number of studies indicate that humans are ingesting neonicotinoids, for example studies conducted on children in China and Japan found neonicotinoids present in urine samples (Lu et al. 2018). In a small study conducted by Lu and colleagues (2018) looking at neonicotinoid residues in fruit purchased in China and in the United States, researchers found 100% of fruit sampled had at least one residue from neonicotinoids. Although a relatively small study, humans are likely consuming small amounts of neonicotinoids, whether this will culminate over time to cause health problems is unknown.

Neonicotinoid resistance

Like other widely used pesticides, the targeted pests have developed resistance to neonicotinoids. Resistance to neonicotinoids has developed in some targeted insects relatively quickly following their introduction, with a case of resistance first being reported in 1996 (Furlan et al. 2021). In fact, one of the first targeted insects in North America, the basis of which neonicotinoids were approved to use in Canada, the Colorado potato beetle (*Leptinotarsa decemlineata*) developed resistance to imidacloprid 10 years after its introduction (Furlan et al. 2021). By 2009, resistance to neonicotinoids was present in 95% of Colorado potato beetles in Northeastern and Midwestern USA (Szendrei et al. 2012). Other insects have developed resistance to neonicotinoids, including the brown planthopper (*Nilaparvata lugens* Stål) which affects rice crops in Thailand, Japan, Vietnam, and China (Matsumura et al. 2008) and tobacco thrips (*Frankliniella fusca* Hinds), which affect cotton crops in the Southern USA (Furlan et al. 2021). When resistance to pesticides occurs among targeted pests, farmers tend to use more of the pesticide, or a combination of pesticides, both of which can increase the problem. As Weis argues, "the chemical fix for industrial agriculture has routinely led to a treadmill of dependence as resistance develops, natural controls diminish and more or new inputs are applied" (2010, p. 320). Resistance also propels agrochemical companies to develop new varieties of pesticides which may be even more harmful. Development of resistance of insects and plants to pesticides is one of the most striking examples of the accelerating treadmill of capitalist agriculture (Weis 2013), as insects and plants will always evolve resistance to widely used pesticides propelling the devlopment and use of novel, and potentially more harmful, pesticides.

The toxic flowers of the Capitalocene

Neonicotinoids and other systemic insecticides are not the only agricultural chemicals that cause harm to bees, fungicides and herbicides also do so. It is a common misconception to assume that only insecticides kill insects. In fact, scientific evidence demonstrates that the synergistic effects of multiple toxins encountered by bees when foraging causes more harm than exposure to only one pesticide, especially the combination of neonicotinoids and fungicides (Iverson et al. 2019; Sgolastra et al. 2017; Thompson et al. 2014). In some agricultural landscapes, plants that have been treated with herbicides are threatening the health of bees and other pollinators. To add to the problem, wildflowers that grow near fields containing neonicotinoid-treated crops have been shown to take up these insecticides due to their persistence in soil and waterways. This creates an almost wicked problem for modern-day agricultural systems: the lack of wildflowers is a problem for bees and can cause nutritional deficiency or starvation, but the presence of wildflowers near agricultural fields treated with pesticides harms bees by exposing them to a toxic soup of chemicals. In the Capitalocene, it seems, flowers near landscapes of capitalist agriculture have become toxic to bees. To understand the mix of toxins encountered by foraging bees, it is important to begin with an examination of one of the mostly widely used herbicides not only in agriculture but in ecological restoration and lawn care, a herbicide long thought to be relatively benign, glyphosate. I will then examine some of the evidence of harm caused by a synergy of toxins which includes insecticides, herbicides, fungicides, and miticides, as well as the non-active ingredients added to these solutions.

Is glyphosate harmless?

While neonicotinoids are the most widely used class of insecticides in current use globally, the most widely used herbicide in many parts of the world is glyphosate, which is frequently referred to by its most common brand name, Roundup©. Roundup is owned by Monsanto, which was acquired by Bayer Crop Science in 2018 (OECD 2018) to form the largest and most powerful agrochemical corporation in the world. Glyphosate is a broad-spectrum herbicide that was first introduced on the global market in 1974 (Benbrook 2016) to provide weed control of grasses and broad-leaf herbaceous plants. When applied to the foliage of plants, glyphosate is taken up by the plants, causing death within a few days after application (Van Bruggen et al. 2018). Within agriculture, glyphosate is commonly applied before planting a crop and, for genetically engineered (GE) glyphosate-resistance crops, after planting (Van

Bruggen et al. 2018). It is also commonly used in orchards to control wild plants growing between trees. The use of glyphosate has increased substantially since the mid-1990s, partly due to the development of GE seeds of major grain and oilseed crops (soybeans, canola, cotton, and corn) designed to be glyphosate-resistant, meaning that the crops can be withstand being sprayed with glyphosate.

While glyphosate is primarily used in agriculture (in terms of tonnage), it is also widely used in large-scale ecological restoration projects to destroy invasive plant species and on lawns to kill 'weeds.' Glyphosate believed to have minimal negative effects on non-human animals, humans, and ecological lifeworlds, with the exception of the targeted plants. In fact, the use of glyphosate is defended by many ecologists, conservation biologists, and some environmentalists as a relatively harmless herbicide that kills invasive species and is, therefore, an important tool in attempts to restore ecological landscapes and help plants native to regions to thrive. This argument may be especially prominent in restoration ecological and naturalist circles in North America where ecological landscapes have been decimated by colonialism and capitalist agriculture and so restoration can be seen as a form of decolonization (Mastnak et al. 2014). Glyphosate is also widely used throughout North America to maintain weed-free lawns in public spaces such as parks and schoolyards, and in private spaces such as the front and backyards of home owners. Although cosmetic pesticide use is banned in some places, for example cities in Ontario, people can often purchase glyphosate in most hardware stores.

Within capitalist agriculture the use of glyphosate is endemic. The agribusiness industry defends the use of glyphosate by similarly arguing that it is benign, but also with the argument that the alternatives to glyphosate were and are worse. Many governmental bodies around the world uphold glyphosate as a safe herbicide, for example the Environmental Protection Agency of the United States states that there are no health risks to humans when used properly (EPA 2021). In contrast, the World Health Organization's International Agency for Research on Cancer categorizes glyphosate as "probably carcinogenic to humans" (IARC n.d.). Roundup – along with Monsanto – has been the target of intense activist campaigns although activists have routinely been dismissed as being ill-informed leading them to mistakenly attack a useful and gentle herbicide (Berezow 2018). Berezow (2018) boldly states that, "glyphosate does not cause cancer because it does not harm humans. *It is an herbicide, so it is only toxic to plants*" (p. 204, emphasis added). This claim, in and of itself, is very weak as many pesticides have negative impacts on non-target plants and animals, including, in some cases, humans.

The reasons for the confusion, and limited empirical evidence about glyphosate became clear following a well-publicized US court case in California, in which Dewayne Johnson, a long-time landscape worker who contracted non-Hodgkin lymphoma which he believed was due to constant workplace exposure to glyphosate, sued Monsanto. During his court case, evidence was unearthed of a targeted campaign waged by Monsanto to silence and discredit critics (Goulson 2020; Richmond 2018). This campaign was not only aimed at activists but was also intended to discredit academic research critical of Monsanto's products and activities as the company not only produces glyphosate but other pesticides, and holds the patent to some genetically engineered seeds. The uncovering of Monsanto's strategic campaign to silence, target, and control academic research being conducted about potential harm of glyphosate towards humans and other animals is particularly concerning. Some researchers were found to have falsified results due to pressure from Monsanto which causes a distrust in the public about the independence of science from corporations (Goulson 2020; Richmond 2018). This case demonstrates the need for scientific research to be publicly funded; to be conducted in ways that are open and transparent; and to be subject to scrutiny from peers and public institutions, not private industry. It also points to a much bigger problem within the STEM disciplines in terms of how the research of scientists employed by or conducting research paid by corporations should be reviewed, critiqued, and analysed within academia, including by academic journals. The result of the strategic campaign waged by Monsanto on scientists and anti-pesticides activists is that there is a lack of rigorous studies on effects of glyphosate on humans and non-human nature.

In terms of the effects of glyphosate on bees, there is a small but growing body of scientific evidence demonstrating that glyphosate may be harmful to honey bees and wild bees (Battisti et al. 2021; Abraham et al. 2018; Seide et al. 2018). There is some evidence that glyphosate may harm the gut microbiota of honey bees (Motta and Moran 2020); disrupt sleep cycles (Vásquez et al. 2020), and negatively impact larval develop (Vásquez et al. 2018). Some evidence indicates that the mixture used to create the final product is a lethal combination for bees (and other insects) because of the effects of combining the non-active ingredients with glyphosate (Graffigna et al. 2021; Abraham et al. 2018). Even if glyphosate benignly works as it should and kills 'weeds,' without any other effects on non-human nature, it is still harmful to wild bees because it further reduces forage in landscapes that, as discussed, have largely been denuded of wildflowers (Florencia et al. 2017). The plants most often targeted with pesticides are not necessarily invasive, which poses problems for specialist bees. Many opportunistic plants that grow in disturbed soil are native plants that are essential for the flourishing of wild bees and other native pollinators. Common milkweed in Ontario is a good example, as this native plant that is essential for the flourishing of bees and many other pollinating insects in North America was, until 2014, on the Noxious Weeds List maintained by OMAFRA (Kaknevicius 2014). Common milkweed was on this list because it grows opportunistically and because the milky substance released from the stem can be harmful to cows and other pasturing livestock. This designation meant that milkweed could not be intentionally grown, and its seedlings and seeds could not be sold anywhere in the province, a rule that was clearly detrimental to bees and other pollinators, especially monarch butterflies who depend on it as a larval host. Because of this, milkweed was the target of a concerted campaign by conservationists to de-list it as a noxious weed, which was successful in Ontario as well as other Canadian provinces and US states.[5] While campaigns to de-list milkweed as a noxious weed have been successful in North America, many other wild plants that serve as important pollinator forage or larval hosts continue to be targeted across large swaths of agricultural landscapes and subjected to widespread pesticide use. In short, there is an inherent tension between the pervasive use of herbicides and the flourishing of bees and other pollinators.

One of the most well-documented and concerning impacts of the widespread use of glyphosate is that some particularly opportunist weeds are evolving to be glyphosate-resistant (Schafer et al. 2014; Shaner et al. 2012; Green and Owen 2011; Duke and Powles 2008). The presence of these so-called superweeds may propel farmers to use even more glyphosate on their crops or to combine glyphosate with other, more harmful pesticides. The agrochemical response to the development of these superweeds is the development of GE glyphosate-resistant seeds that are also resistant to other herbicides such as 2,4-D and dicamba (Van Bruggen et al. 2018). While this may solve the problem of superweeds by allowing farmers to use these pesticides on their crops, there is a high likelihood that weeds will develop resistance to multiple herbicides (Van Bruggen et al. 2018). This is another stark indication of how capitalist agriculture forces farmers onto a treadmill of accelerating contradictions, treating problems with solutions that cause even more serious problems, a seemingly never-ending process. For organic farmers, the presence of superweeds may cause considerable problems in their fields because they may not be as easily managed using manual methods. In terms of bee health, multiple studies have indicated that pesticides are most harmful in combination (Van Bruggen et al. 2018), so farmers using a combination of herbicides to combat superweeds in crops whose seeds were likely coated with systemic pesticides may cause an increase in harm to bees of all species. An examination of the potential harms caused to bees by glyphosate makes visible a very uncomfortable fact about the global agricultural system: monocultured fields of crops that require high inputs of pesticides are not landscapes in which bees can thrive. Capitalist agriculture creates landscapes of scarcity that threaten the diverse, dynamic ecological lifeworlds in which animals (including humans) and plants evolved and live.

Uncertain science and conflicting conceptions of expertise

Although entomology as a discipline is embedded within industrial agriculture, with its origins in understanding the behaviour and lifecycle of insects to better control them for agriculture, there is a growing number of entomologists and other scientists who are willing to make political critiques of industrial agriculture (Seeley 2019; Goulson 2018; Suryanarayanan 2015). These critical entomologists tend to also be interested in a serious engagement with beekeepers, bee advocates, and environmental activists as well as with social scientific researchers and are co-creating a body of work that is a crucial tool in efforts to change policy, especially around pesticide use and regulation. For example, Dave Goulson, a leading bumble bee researcher, has led research in the European Union about the effects of neonicotinoid pesticides on bees, particularly bumble bees. He was the architect of the call by 232 scientists to ban neonicotinoid pesticides and is centrally engaged in wild bee advocacy in the European Union and the UK (Goulson 2018).

Sainath Suryanarayanan, a trained entomologist who often collaborates with social scientists, offers a critique on the production of knowledge within the biological sciences, particularly in terms of the way that scientific research and experimentation inadequately examines complex ecological lifeworlds engaging in reductionist simplification of what is inherently complex (Suryanarayanan and Kleinman 2017; Suryanarayanan 2015). In his critiques of scientific research into pesticide impacts on honey bees, he argues against lab-based experiments that cannot understand synergistic relationships between bees, the mix of pesticides they encounter in fields, and the other factors that may interact with these pesticides. However, he acknowledges that field-based experiments may not establish direct causal relationships because of the complexity of the environment and the multiple stressors encountered by bees in landscapes. Suryanarayanan argues for a scientific approach that accepts and works with this complexity, is aware of the broader sociopolitical context, and is interested in the knowledge and expertise of other people who intimately know bees. Suryanarayanan (2015) recognizes that socioecological complexity is bound in uncertainty, which, he points out, "stems not only from the biological complexity of interactions between assemblages of plants and pollinators, but also from the multiplicity of values represented by those for whom and by whom the policy is made" (p. 150). Uncertainty is inherent in complex ecosystems, he concludes, and it must not hold us back from action, especially for issues in which a lack of action will potentially have more harmful results than acting incorrectly.

As Suryanarayanan and Kleinman (2017) point out, the essential factor in understanding the heavy influence of the agrochemical industry on the government regulation of pesticides is in how these corporations reinforce the idea that only one type of scientific evidence matters and, furthermore, that government action should only happen under conditions of *certainty*. The agrochemical industry conducts, funds, and otherwise supports scientific research that aims to find definitive evidence of harm – a direct cause and effect using scientific research in the field. One of the main critiques used to argue against bans and moratoriums on neonicotinoid pesticides is that there is scientific uncertainty about the harm caused by this class of pesticides. Those who make this claim argue that the science is too complex and incomplete and therefore should not be acted upon. In a review study funded by Bayer Crop Science, the authors state

> The available data indicate that there may be effects to individual honeybees housed under laboratory conditions and exposed to unrealistically high concentrations of the insecticides. However, under field conditions and

exposure levels, similar effects on honeybee colonies have not been documented. It is not reasonable, therefore, to conclude that crop-applied pesticides in general, or neonicotinoids in particular, are a major risk factor for honeybee colonies, given the current approved uses and beekeeping practices.

(Fairbrother et al. 2014, p. 729)

This claim demands a certainty about exposure *in the field* that simply is not possible due to the nature of complex ecosystems. As Suryanarayanan argues,

The practical challenges entailed in isolating the effects of the chemical in question from potentially confounding sources of environmental variability, require a high number of colonies, resources, and time to achieve sufficient statistical power. As a result, field experiments tend to be relegated to measuring the direct, causal effects of individual chemicals.

(2015, p. 150)

Establishing direct, casual effects is a very difficult, almost impossible thing to do in an uncontrolled environment in which there are many complicated factors that can affect the outcome. Ecological complexity is inherent in diverse ecosystems. There cannot be certainty about exactly how pesticides harm bees in the field. As Hill (1965) argued, "All scientific work is incomplete – whether it be observational or experimental. All scientific work is liable to be upset or modified by advancing knowledge" (p. 300). The actually existing world is dynamic and complex and therefore scientific research about complex ecosystems is always incomplete. However, as critical scientists argue, lack of certainty should not lead to governmental inaction. In fact, not acting may significantly contribute to pollinator defaunation and declining health, causing cascading problems across multiple ecological lifeworlds.

Notes

1 In an article about the negative impacts of pesticides, Goulson gives the example of paraquat, a pesticide made by Syngenta which was banned in the EU in 2007 and continues to be used in the global south. Meta-analysis of this pesticide found that it can cause mortality in humans and can double the risk of Parkinson's disease (Goulson 2020).
2 2,4-D is still used as an herbicide, although glyphosate has replaced its widespread use. Glyphosate is thought to be less harmful than 2,4-D.
3 These different combinations were given code names during the Vietnam War of which Agent Orange was one.
4 Some native bee advocates argue that honey bee extinction is virtually impossible but it should be noted that some domesticated farm animal breeds have become endangered or been extirpated, mostly when they are no longer beneficial to capitalist agriculture.
5 The importance of milkweed to monarch butterflies was central to this de-listing. Milkweed species are the larval hosts for monarchs, which means that the monarch butterfly will only lay her eggs on species of milkweeds. If no milkweed can be found, she may lay her eggs on another plant, but the larvae will not be viable.

References

Abraham, J., Benhotens, G. S., Krampah, I., Tagba, J., Amissah, C., & Abraham, J. D. (2018). Commercially formulated glyphosate can kill non-target pollinator bees under laboratory conditions. *Entomologica Experimentalis et Applictata*, 16 (8), 695–702.

Baron, G. L., Jansen, V. A., Brown, M. J., & Raine, N. E. (2017). Pesticide reduces bumblebee colony initiation and increases probability of population extinction. *Nature Ecology & Evolution*, 1 (9), 1308–1316. https://doi.org/10.1038/s41559-017-0260-1.

Battisti, L., Potrich, M., Sampaio, A. R., Ghisi, N., Costa-Maia, F., Abati, R., Martinez, C., & Sofia, S. H. (2021). Is glyphosate toxic to bees? A meta-analytical review. *Science of the Total Environment*, 767 (1), https://doi.org/10.1016/j.scitotenv.2021.145397.

Benbrook, C. M. (2016). Trends in glyphosate herbicide use in the United States and globally. *Environmental Sciences Europe*, 28 (1), 1–15. https://doi.org/10.1186/s12302-016-0070-0.

Berezow, A. (2018). California's glyphosate judgement: Emotion, bad science and greed win the day. *Outlooks on Pest Management*, 29 (5), 204–205. https://doi.org/10.1564/v29_oct_04.

Borsuah, J. F., Messer, T. L., Snow, D. D., Comfort, S. D., & Mittelstet, A. R. (2020). Literature review: Global neonicotinoid insecticide occurrence in aquatic environments. *Water*, 12 (12), 3388. https://doi.org/10.3390/w12123388.

Brandt, A, Gorenfloe, A., Reinhold, S., Meixner, M., & Buchler, R. (2016). The neonicotinoids thiacloprid, imidacloprid, and clothianidin affect the immunocompetence of honey bees (*Apis mellifera* L.). *Journal of Insect Physiology*, 85, 40–47.

Campbell, K. S., Keller, P. G., Heinzel, L. M., Golovko, S. A., Seeger, D. R., Golovko, M. Y., & Kerby, J. L. (2022). Detection of imidacloprid and metabolites in Northern Leopard frog (*Rana pipiens*) brains. *Science of the Total Environment*, 813, https://doi.org/10.1016/j.scitotenv.2021.152424.

Carson, R. (1962). *Silent Spring*. Boston: Houghton Mifflin.

Colin, T., Meikle, W. G., Wu, X., & Barron, A. B. (2019). Traces of a neonicotinoid induce precocious foraging and reduce foraging performance in honey bees. *Environmental Science & Technology*, 53 (14), 8252–8261, doi:10.1021/acs.est.9b02452.

Conner, C. D. (2020). *The Tragedy of American Science: From Truman to Trump*. Chicago: Haymarket Books.

Cressey, D. (2017). Neonics vs. bees. *Nature*, 551 (Nov.), 156–158. https://doi.org/10.1038/551156a.

David, A., Botias, C., Abdul-Sada, A., Nicholls, E., Rotheray, E.L., Hill, E.M., & Goulson, D. (2016). Widespread contamination of wildflower and bee-collected pollen with complex mixtures of neonicotinoids and fungicides commonly applied to crops. *Environment International*, 88 (3), 169–178.

Dow. (n.d.). Agent Orange. https://corporate.dow.com/en-us/about/legal/issues/agent-orange.html.

Duke, S. O. & Powles, S. B. (2008). Glyphosate: A once-in-a-century herbicide. *Pest Management Science: formerly Pesticide Science*, 64 (4), 319–325. https://doi.org/10.1002/ps.1518.

Environmental Protection Agency (EPA). (2021). Glyphosate. https://www.epa.gov/ingredients-used-pesticide-products/glyphosate.

Fairbrother, A., Purdy, J., Anderson, T., & Fell, R. (2014). Risk of neonicotinoid insecticides to honeybees. *Environmental Toxicology and Chemistry*, 33 (4), 719–731. https://doi.org/10.1002/etc.2527.

Fang, L. (2020). The pesticide industry's playbook for poisoning the earth. *The Intercept*. January 18. https://theintercept.com/2020/01/18/bees-insecticides-pesticides-neonicotinoids-bayer-monsanto-syngenta/.

Fishel, F., Ferrell J., MacDonald G., & Sellers B. (2013) Herbicides: How toxic are they? University of Florida IFAS Extension. http://edis.ifas.ufl.edu/pdffiles/PI/PI17000.pdf.

Florencia, F. M., Carolina, T., Enzo, B., & Leonardo, G. (2017). Effects of the herbicide glyphosate on non-target plant native species from Chaco Forest (Argentina). *Ecotoxicology and Environmental Safety*, 144, 360–368. https://doi.org/10.1016/j.ecoenv.2017.06.049.

Furlan, L., Pozzebon, A., Duso, C., Simon-Delso, N., Sánchez-Bayo, F., Marchand, P. A. ... & Bonmatin, J. M. (2021). An update of the Worldwide Integrated Assessment (WIA) on systemic insecticides. Part 3: Alternatives to systemic insecticides. *Environmental Science and Pollution Research*, 28 (10), 11798–11820.

Gibbons, D., Morrissey, C., & Mineau, P. (2015). A review of the direct and indirect effects of neonicotinoids and fipronil on vertebrate wildlife. *Environmental Science and Pollution Research*, 22, 103–118.

Gill, R. J. & Raine, N. E. (2014). Chronic impairment of bumblebee natural foraging behaviour induced by sublethal pesticide exposure. *Functional Ecology*, 28, 1459–1471.

Goulson, D. (2020). Pesticides, corporate irresponsibility, and the fate of our planet. *One Earth*, 2 (4), 302–305. https://doi.org/10.1016/j.oneear.2020.03.004.

Goulson, D. (2018). Call to restrict neonicotinoids. *Science*, 360 (6392), 973. https://doi.org/10.1126/science.aau0432.

Goulson, D. (2013). Neonicotinoids and bees: What's all the buzz? *Significance*, 10 (3), 6–11. https://doi.org/10.1111/j.1740-9713.2013.00658.x.

Graffigna, S., Marrero, H. J., & Torretta, J. P. (2021). Glyphosate commercial formulation negatively affects the reproductive success of solitary wild bees in a Pampean agroecosystem. *Apidologie*, 52 (1), 272–281. https://doi.org/10.1007/s13592-020-00816-8.

Green, J. M. & Owen, M. D. (2011). Herbicide-resistant crops: Utilities and limitations for herbicide-resistant weed management. *Journal of Agricultural and Food Chemistry*, 59 (11), 5819–5829. https://doi.org/10.1021/jf101286h.

Hallmann C. A., Sorg, M., Jongejans, E., Siepel, H., Hofland, N. ... & de Kroon, H. (2017). More than 75 percent decline over 27 years in total flying insect biomass in protected areas. *PLoS ONE*, 12 (10), e0185809. https://doi.org/10.1371/journal.pone.0185809.

Hamel, M-A. & Dorf, E. (2014). Corn: Canada's third most valuable crop. *Statistics Canada*. http://www.statcan.gc.ca/pub/96-325-x/2014001/article/11913-eng.htm.

Hill, A. B. (1965). The environment and disease: Association or causation? *Proceedings of the Royal Society of Medicine*, 58 (5), 295–300.

Hladik, M. L., Main, A. R., & Goulson, D. (2018). Environmental risks and challenges associated with neonicotinoid insecticides. *Environmental Science & Technology*, 52 (6), 3329–3335. https://doi.org/10.1021/acs.est.7b06388.

Institute of Medicine (US) Committee to Review the Health Effects in Vietnam Veterans of Exposure to Herbicides. (1994). *Veterans and Agent Orange: Health Effects of Herbicides Used in Vietnam*. Washington, DC: National Academies Press. https://www.ncbi.nlm.nih.gov/books/NBK236347/.

IARC. (n.d.). *IARC Monograph on Glyphosate*. World Health Organization. https://www.iarc.who.int/featured-news/media-centre-iarc-news-glyphosate/.

Iverson, A., Hale, C., Richardson, L., Miller, O., & McArt, S. (2019). Synergistic effects of three sterol biosynthesis inhibiting fungicides on the toxicity of a pyrethroid and neonicotinoid insecticide to bumble bees. *Apidologie*, 50, 733–744 (2019). https://doi.org/10.1007/s13592-019-00681-0.

Kaknevicius, A. (2014). Monarch butterflies struggle to survive with loss of milkweed food source. *Canadian Geographic*. https://www.canadiangeographic.ca/article/monarch-butterflies-struggle-survive-loss-milkweed-food-source.

King, J. (2012). US in first effort to clean up Agent Orange in Vietnam. CNN, August 10. https://www.cnn.com/2012/08/10/world/asia/vietnam-us-agent-orange/index.html.

Krupke, C. H., Hunt, G. J., Eitzer, B. D., Andino, G., & Given, K. (2012). Multiple routes of pesticide exposure for honey bees living near agricultural fields. *PLoS ONE*, 7 (1). https://doi.org/10.1371/journal.pone.0029268.

Lu, C., Chang, C. H., Palmer, C., Zhao, M., & Zhang, Q. (2018). Neonicotinoid residues in fruits and vegetables: An integrated dietary exposure assessment approach. *Environmental Science & Technology*, 52 (5), 3175–3184. https://doi.org/10.1021/acs.est.7b05596.

Martin, M. F. (2015). US Agent Orange/Dioxin assistance to Vietnam. Congressional Research Service. https://assets.aspeninstitute.org/wp-content/uploads/2016/06/2015-11-17-MMartin-CRS-Agent-Orange-Report 2015.pdf?_ga=2.44652961.469992199.1645810342-525399080.1645810342.

Mastnak, T., Elyachar, J., & Boellstorff, T. (2014). Botanical decolonization: Rethinking native plants. *Environment and Planning D: Society and Space*, 32, 363–380.

Matsumura, M., Takeuchi, H., Satoh, M., Sanada-Morimura, S., Otuka, A., Watanabe, T., & Van Thanh, D. (2008). Species-specific insecticide resistance to imidacloprid and fipronil in the rice planthoppers *Nilaparvata lugens* and *Sogatella furcifera* in East and South-east Asia. *Pest Management Science: formerly Pesticide Science*, 64 (11), 1115–1121.

Mintz, B. (2021). Neoliberalism and the crisis in higher education: The costs of ideology. *American Journal of Economics and Sociology*, 80 (1), 79–112.

Mogren, C. L. & Lundgren, J. G. (2016). Neonicotinoid-contaminated pollinator strips adjacent to cropland reduce honeybee nutritional status. *Scientific Reports*, 6. https://doi.org/10.1038/srep29608.

Motta, E. V. S. & Moran, N. A. (2020). Impact of glyphosate on the honey bee gut microbiota: Effects of intensity, duration, and timing of exposure. *mSystems*, doi:10.1128/mSystems.00268-20.

OECD. (2018) . *Concentration in Seed Markets: Potential Effects and Policy Responses*. Paris: OECD, https://doi.org/10.1787/9789264308367-en.

Ontario Bee Health Working Group. (2014). Ontario Bee Health Working Group Report. OMAFRA. Accessed July 4, 2017. http://www.omafra.gov.on.ca/english/about/beehealthworkinggroupreport.htm#neon.

Packer, L., Genaro, J. A., & Sheffield, C. S. (2007). The bee genera of Eastern Canada. *Canadian Journal of Arthropod Identification*, 3, 1–32.

Packer, L. (2011). *Keeping the Bees: Why All Bees Are at Risk and What We Can Do to Save Them*. New York: HarperCollins.

Pesticide Management Regulatory Agency. (2016). Imidacloprid: proposed re-evaluation survey. https://www.canada.ca/en/health-canada/services/consumerproduct-safety/pesticides-pest-management/public/consultations/proposed-reevaluationdecisions/2016/imidacloprid/document.html.

Pollinator Network @ Cornell. (n.d.). Neonicotinoids. https://pollinator.cals.cornell.edu/threats-wild-and-managedbees/pesticides/neonicotinoids/.

Ransome, H. M. (2004). *The Sacred Bee in Ancient Times and Folklore*. New York: Mineola.

Richmond, M. E. (2018). Glyphosate: A review of its global use, environmental impact, and potential health effects on humans and other species. *Journal of Environmental Studies and Sciences*, 8, 416–434. https://doi.org/10.1007/s13412-018-0517-2.

Robbins, P. (2007). *Lawn People: How Grasses, Weeds, and Chemicals Make Us Who We Are*. Philadelphia: Temple University Press.

Rundlöf, M., Andersson, G., Bommarco, R., Fries, I., Hederstrom, V., Herbertson, L. ... Smith, H. G. (2015). Seed coating with a neonicotinoid insecticide negatively affects wild bees. *Nature* 521, 77–80. https://doi.org/10.1038/nature14420.

Schafer, J. R., Hallett, S. G., & Johnson, W. G. (2014). Rhizosphere microbial community dynamics in glyphosate-treated susceptible and resistant biotypes of giant ragweed (*Ambrosia trifida*). *Weed Science*, 62 (2), 370–381.

Seeley, T. D. (2019). *The Lives of Bees: The Untold Story of the Honey Bee in the Wild*. Princeton: Princeton University Press.

Seide, V. R., Bernardes, R. C., Pereira, E. J. G., & Lima, M. A. P. (2018). Glyphosate is lethal and Cry toxins alter the development of the stingless bee *Melipona quadrifasciata*. *Environmental Pollution*, 243B, 1854–1860.

Sgolastra, F., Medryzcki, P., Bortolotti, L., Renzi, M. T., Tosi, S., Bogo, G., ... & Bosch, J. (2017). Synergistic mortality between a neonicotinoid insecticide and an ergosterol-biosynthesis-inhibiting fungicide in three bee species. *Pest Management Science*, 73 (6), 1236–1243. https://doi.org/10.1002/ps.4449.

Shaner, D. L., Lindenmeyer, R. B., & Ostlie, M. H. (2012). What have the mechanisms of resistance to glyphosate taught us? *Pest Management Science*, 68 (1), 3–9. https://doi.org/10.1002/ps.2261.

Siviter, H., Richman, S. K., & Muth, F. (2021). Field-realistic neonicotinoid exposure has sub-lethal effects on non-*Apis* bees: A meta-analysis. *Ecology Letters*, 24 (12), 2586–2597.

Suryanarayanan, S. (2015). Pesticides and pollinators: A context-sensitive policy approach. *Current Opinion in Insect Science*, 10, 149–155. https://doi.org/10.1016/j.cois.2015.05.009.

Suryanarayanan, S. & Kleinman, D. L. (2017). *Vanishing Bees: Science, Politics and Honey Bee Health*. New Brunswick: Rutgers.

Szendrei, Z., Grafius, E., Byrne, A., & Ziegler, A. (2012). Resistance to neonicotinoid insecticides in field populations of the Colorado potato beetle (Coleoptera: Chrysomelidae). *Pest Management Science*, 68 (6), 941–946.

Tackenberg, M. C., Giannoni-Guzmán, M. A., Sanchez-Perez, E., Doll, C. A., Agosto-Rivera, J. L., Broadie, K., Moore, D., & McMahon, D. G. (2020) Neonicotinoids disrupt circadian rhythms and sleep in honey bees. *Scientific Reports*, 10, https://doi.org/10.1038/s41598-020-72041-3.

Tarek, H., Hamiduzzaman, M. M., Morfin, N., & Guzman-Novoa, E. (2018). Sub-lethal doses of neonicotinoid and carbamate insecticides reduce the lifespan and alter the expression of immune health and detoxification related genes of honey bees (*Apis mellifera*). *Genetics and Molecular Research*, 17 (2). 10.4238/gmr16039908.

Thompson, H. M., Fryday, S., Harkin, S., & Milner, S. (2014). Potential impacts of synergism in honeybees (Apis mellifera) of exposure to neonicotinoids and sprayed fungicides in crops. *Apidologie*, 45 (5), 545–553. doi:10.1007/s13592-014-0273-6.

Tison, L., Rößner, A., Gerschewski, S., & Menzel, R. (2019). The neonicotinoid clothianidin impairs memory processing in honey bees. *Ecotoxicology and Environmental Safety*, 180, 139–145. https://doi.org/10.1016/j.ecoenv.2019.05.007.

Troiani, I. & Dutson, C. (2021). The neoliberal university as a space to learn/think/work in higher education, *Architecture and Culture*, 9 (1), 5–23, doi:10.1080/20507828.2021.1898836.

Tsvetkov, N., Samson-Robert, O., Sood, K., Patel, H. S., Malena, D. A., Gajiwala, P. H., Maciukiewicz, P., Fournier, V. & Zayed, A. (2017). Chronic exposure to neonicotinoids reduces honey bee health near corn crops. *Science*, 356 (June 30), 1395–1397.

Van Bruggen, A. H., He, M. M., Shin, K., Mai, V., Jeong, K. C., Finckh, M. R., & Morris Jr, J. G. (2018). Environmental and health effects of the herbicide glyphosate. *Science of the Total Environment*, 616, 255–268. https://doi.org/10.1016/j.scitotenv.2017.10.309.

van der Sluijs, J. P. (2020). Insect decline, an emerging global environmental risk. *Opinion in Environmental Sustainability*, 46, 39–42, https://doi.org/10.1016/j.cosust.2020.08.012.

van der Sluijs, J. P., Amaral-Rogers, V., Belzunces, L. P., Bijleveld van Lexmond, M. F. I. J., Bonmatin, J-M., Chagnon, M. ... & Wiemers, M. (2015). Conclusions of the Worldwide Integrated Assessment on the risks of neonicotinoids and fipronil to biodiversity and ecosystem functioning. *Environmental Science and Pollution Research*, 22, 148–154.

Vázquez, D. E., Illina, N., Pagano, E. A., Zavala, J. A., & Farina, W. M. (2018). Glyphosate affects the larval development of honey bees depending on the susceptibility of colonies. *PLoS ONE*, https://doi.org/10.1371/journal.pone.0205074.

Vázquez, D. E., Balbuena, M. S., Chaves, F., Menzel, R., & Farina, W. M. (2020). Sleep in honey bees is affected by the herbicide glyphosate. *Scientific Reports*, 10, 10516 https://doi.org/10.1038/s41598-020-67477-6.

Vergara-Amado, J., Manzi, C., Franco, L. M., Contecina, S. C. C., Marquez, S. J., Solano-Iguaran, J. J., Haro, R. E. & Silvia, A. X. (2020). Effects of residual doses of neonicotinoid (imidacloprid) on metabolic rate of queen honey bees *Apis mellifera* (Hymenoptera: Apidae). *Apidologie*, 51, 1091–1099. https://doi.org/10.1007/s13592-020-00787-w.

Wadiwel, D. (2015). *The War against Animals*. Leiden: Brill.

Weis, T. (2013). *The Ecological Hoofprint: The Global Burden of Industrial Livestock*. London: Zed.

Woodcock, B. A., Bullock, J. M., Shore, R. F., Heard, M. S., Pereira, M. G., Redhead, J., & Pywell, R. F. (2017). Country-specific effects of neonicotinoid pesticides on honey bees and wild bees. *Science*, 356 (June 30), 1393–1395.

5 Bee-washing

Agrochemical corporations and struggles over neonicotinoids

The harm caused by neonicotinoids to pollinators, particularly bees, has galvanized public attention in North America and Europe (Goulson 2018). In this chapter I will examine two struggles against neonicotinoids that had varying degrees of success: the movements to ban neonicotinoids in the European Union (EU) and in the province of Ontario in Canada. I will then interrogate the ways in which food corporations, firmly embedded within the capitalist agricultural system with heavy reliance on agrochemical corporations, have engaged in bee-washing in response to these struggles.

While the ban in Europe and the partial ban in Ontario, Canada may seem like, and to a certain extent, are victories, I argue that the central role played by agrochemical corporations in both struggles diluted and delayed the resulting legislation (Ellis 2019). Agrochemical corporations also launched organized campaigns during this time that attempted to present the industrial agriculture sector as concerned about the flourishing bees with websites such as Bees Matter and pollinator seed giveaways such as Cheerios' #Bringbackthebees. This bee-washing practice attempts to cast agrochemical corporations as part of the solution to the bee crisis in order to weaken critiques of their products and practices and to foster complacency about the prospects of private sector solutions (Suryanarayanan and Kleinman 2017). Ultimately, the struggles of beekeepers, environmentalists, critical scientists, and others to ban or restrict pesticides uncovers the ways in which agrochemicals hold immense power within the global capitalist agricultural system, heavily influencing governmental and international trade policies.

The increasing power of agrochemical corporations

Agrochemical corporations have considerable power and influence within the capitalist agricultural system and over government policy and (in)action. Understanding how agrochemical corporations have come to dominate the global food system is crucial in a discussion about pesticides and pollinator health. In Chapter 4, I explored the connections of the agrochemical industry to the military industrial complex, which after World War II led to a steep increase in biochemical technology that could be used to kill plants and insects in war and within agriculture. This connection highlights that agrochemical corporations are not simply

DOI: 10.4324/9781003142294-5

concerned with agriculture but also continue to be connected to the military industrial complex and pharmaceutical industries. To understand how agrochemical corporations have developed into such powerful and influential global entities, it is important to interrogate the main corporations that dominate this industry.

Over the past five years, the top six agrochemical and seed corporations, sometimes referred to as the 'Big 6' have merged, morphing into four powerful multinational corporations that dominate the agrochemical and seed markets: Bayer-Monsanto, DowDuPont-Corteva, ChemChina-Syngenta, and BASF (OECD 2018). The recent major consolidations include Bayer-CropScience acquiring Monsanto in 2018; ChemChina merging with Syngenta in 2018; Dow and DuPont merging in 2017 (OECD 2018). These mergers represent further integration between corporations that produce agrochemical inputs in the form of pesticides, with corporations that develop genetically engineered (GE) and hybrid seeds. For example, Bayer's CropScience was a leading producer of pesticides when it acquired Monsanto, a leading producer of GE seeds in addition to the herbicide Roundup, in a USD 66-billion-dollar merger (OECD 2018). Similar complimentary mergers occurred with Dow, a producer of pesticides and non-agricultural chemicals, merging with DuPont, a major holder of GE seed patents and ChemChina, a major chemical corporation, merging with Syngenta, a corporation mostly focused on producing GE and hybrid seeds (OECD 2018). Only BASF is focused on one market, primarily being a seed corporation (OECD 2018). This new 'Big 4' holds enormous wealth, capital, power, and influence within the global agricultural system. The Big 4 agrochemical corporations are multinational corporations in terms of their operations and ownership, especially after recent mergers, but their origins are in a very small handful of countries, which also demonstrates the intense concentration of wealth: the United States (DowDuPont-Corteva; the former Monsanto); Germany (BASF; Bayer); Switzerland (Syngenta); and China (ChemChina). The ways in which the agrochemical products developed by a very small group of corporations dominate global agricultural practices and livelihoods; governmental policy; and rural landscapes is a staggering example of the way in which agriculture operates in the Capitalocene.

Some researchers argue that *agrochemical* approaches to food and agriculture and *agroecological*[1] approaches are complementary and a lack of collaboration it is simply due to advocates of both approaches being dogmatic and antagonistic towards one another (Bonny 2017). People with this perspective often argue that there is common ground between the high-tech, high-capital approaches to agriculture often supported by agrochemical and seed corporations, and the agroecological approaches advocated by many small-scale farmers, peasants, and some food science researchers. This perspective fails to consider the role of agrochemical corporations, and the approaches and practices they advocate, in maintaining, intensifying, and expanding capitalist agriculture. The top agrochemical and seed corporations aim, like all corporations under capitalism, to make a profit through continuous economic growth. The histories of the seed and agrochemical sectors demonstrate that profit-making and economic growth drives both industries, at least for the top corporations, with increasing consolidations often occurring when there is a slump in sales of their products. These consolidations stimulate new growth, through increasing research and development and in finding new markets for their products (Phillips 2020; Bonny 2017). The latest set of mergers, for example, has been largely attributed to a desire to combine research and development costs, which is a relatively high expense for agrochemical corporations (OECD 2018). The mergers are also seen as beneficial for corporations investing large amounts of money into the development of precision agriculture and big data technology (OECD 2018). While small seed companies may be agriculturally based and interested in supplying specialty seeds such as diversified vegetable, fruit, flower, and herb seeds that are often organic, open-pollinated, and/or heirloom, to farmers in specific bioregions, the top four companies invest billions of dollars into research and development of new products. It is estimated that to create a new agrochemical product costs approximately USD 286 million (Phillips 2020). After developing new products, agrochemical corporations need to persuade governments to approve them relatively quickly, and to get farmers to purchase them. It is easy to understand why agrochemical corporations spend considerable effort on government lobbying, public relations campaigns, and political manoeuvring. They need to manufacture demand among farmers and the governmental bodies that oversee agriculture to sell the products in which they have invested so much capital.

The merger of agrochemical corporations with seed corporations has a reverberating impact on the global seed market. As Bonny (2017) states, "Because of their chemical origin, these companies have often brought certain economic behaviors into the seed sector, such as the implementation, broadening, and strengthening of intellectual property rights, which are common in the chemical industry, but were previously rather rare in the seed sector." When applied to seeds, intellectual property rights are a contentious issue in which there is no common ground between agrochemical corporations and farmers practicing agroecology and other small-scale forms of agriculture. For most of agrarian history seed saving was something that individual farmers, and collectives of farmers, did as a part of their regular farming activities. The breeding of seeds was also something that was done by farmers at a regional and community level, breeding landraces, varieties of plants that were suited to a particular place as well as to the cultural preferences of the community in terms of taste, size, and aesthetics. Seeds are considered by many advocates of agroecology and small-scale farming to be part of the commons of humanity, with specific seeds being the commons of identifiable groups of people. Corporate ownership of seeds, in which farmers are prohibited from saving seeds and must buy them annually from agrochemical corporations, disrupts this long-standing practice of seed-development and saving.

One of the most important ways in which the Big 4 agrochemical corporations hold power and influence within the food system is in the pesticides they produce. As explored in Chapter 4, these pesticides have serious and long-lasting impacts on bees, and other non-human animals, persisting in soil and waterways. These corporations manufacture demand among farmers for the pesticides they produce, forming powerful lobby groups with other agribusiness sectors. They work to shape international agreements and governmental policy to promote a form of agriculture that is reliant on their pesticides. Far from finding common ground, agroecologists, and small-scale farmers, in alliance with beekeepers and environmentalists, have often formed movements in opposition to pesticides and the corporations who develop, manufacture, and distribute them.

Struggles against neonicotinoids

In 1996, beekeepers in France first raised the alarm about the possible harm that neonicotinoids have on bees, launching a growing movement to restrict the use of this class of pesticides. Beekeepers often have intimate knowledge about the health of their colonies and some began to notice that around the same time that farmers started to use neonicotinoids in large amounts, honey bees started to have increased problems with overwinter mortality. The activism of beekeepers was essential to governments taking the issue seriously, in some cases commissioning research studies and convening advisory groups and public consultations. This activism has led to an alliance of beekeepers, environmentalist, organic farmers, and sympathetic scientists and has put pressure on governments to re-examine the approval and regulation of these pesticides. This activism also helped to stimulate expanded interest among scientists in studying the effects of neonicotinoids on bees of all species, especially since this concern coincided with the phenomenon of Colony Collapse Disorder (CCD).[2] Although there is not consensus (there rarely is among scientists, which is what makes the consensus around climate change remarkable), there is now a large body of evidence indicating that neonicotinoids harm bees, and other non-target animals, something I explore in detail in Chapter 4. Concern about bee health, and debates about what to do about neonicotinoid pesticides, has captured the imagination of the public who are concerned with the plight of pollinators. Recent research about the widespread defaunation of insects, what environmental writer George Monbiot calls an "insectageddon" (2017), adds urgency to the debate (Lister and Garcia 2018; Hallmann et al. 2017). Although there are strong demands, especially among beekeepers and environmentalists, to restrict or ban neonicotinoids, only a few places have instituted such action. The most notable and successful action on neonicotinoids is the European Union. Another very notable action, but ultimately a failure, is the province of Ontario (Ellis 2019). Other than some cities, there have been few other places that have moved in a meaningful way to restrict neonicotinoids, although the state of New Jersey instituted restrictions in 2022 (Rhoads 2022). This section will explore the processes involved in restricting neonicotinoids in the EU and Ontario, including an examination about why these political entities ultimately had very different outcomes. The ultimate failure of legislation to restrict neonicotinoids in Ontario may serve as a cautionary tale for anti-pesticide activists in New Jersey, about realities of corporate control and influence within the agricultural system in North America. The EU ban is important because, although it took years to be permanently implemented, and has been critiqued for not going far enough, it involved a process in which a governmental body accumulated rigorous scientific evidence in the interest of bees, beekeepers, and non-human nature. This process seemed to be largely independent of the influence of agrochemical corporations, although there are some indications that the "emergency exemptions" that are periodically granted to allow regions to use neonicotinoids are driven or supported by these corporations (Dowler and Clarke 2020). In contrast to the process undertaken by the European Union, the partial ban on neonicotinoids in Ontario did not go far enough to address the pollinator crisis, partly due to the role of agrochemical corporations such as Bayer CropScience and Syngenta, manufacturers of neonicotinoids, in the development of the policy, which ultimately led to the legislation ending in failure. Contrasting the ban of neonicotinoids in the EU with the ultimately unsuccessful partial ban in Ontario, may indicate that there is a higher degree of agrochemical influence on governments in North America.

European Union: the precautionary principle at work

Neonicotinoids were first approved by the EU in 2005 (European Commission n.d.), but they had been used by member countries since the early to mid 1990s. In 2013 the EU imposed a two-year moratorium on neonicotinoid use, eventually becoming a permanent ban in 2020. The initial ban was on specific types of neonicotinoids: clothianidin, imidacloprid (the most widely used neonicotinoid until 2018), and thiamethoxam, as well as the non-neonicotinoid systemic pesticide, fipronil (European Commission n.d.). For all types of restricted pesticides, at this time, their use was permitted in greenhouses, and in some cases on field crops that are harvested before going to flower[3] (European Commission n.d.).

After these initial restrictions were put in place, the applicants who were seeking approval for these pesticides from the European Commission (the governing body of the EU), were asked to provide further information about their safety in relation to honey bee health. It is important to note that, initially, the concern about impacts of neonicotinoids and other systemic pesticides was focused on honey bees, not other species of bees or other non-human animals (European Commission n.d.). The restricting of these three neonicotinoids was especially aimed at the use of these pesticides on crops that were designated as "bee-attractive" and included maize,[4] oilseed rape, and sunflowers.

Based on an increasing body of scientific research and strong advocacy from coalitions of beekeepers and environmentalists, the EU put a moratorium on the use of neonicotinoids from 2013–2015. During that time, the European Food Safety Authority (EFSA) undertook an open call for scientific data on the impacts of neonicotinoid pesticides. In doing the open call for scientific data *after* introducing a moratorium, the EU followed a precautionary principle for these systemic pesticides. With this approach, they were willing to accept the responsibility of acting on incomplete science even if it turned out to be wrong (Suryanarayanan 2015). During the open call, the EFSA received 376 contributions from 48 different sources, pushing the deadline to a later date than initially anticipated. Contributions were received from a variety of stakeholders including governmental bodies, non-governmental organizations, producer associations (farmers as well as beekeepers), corporations, universities, research institutions, and a handful of individuals (EFSA 2018). After assessing the data, the EFSA released their assessment on neonicotinoid harm to honey and wild bees, concluding that "Most uses of neonicotinoid pesticides represent a risk to wild bees and honeybees" (EFSA 2018). On 27 April 2018, the EU voted to ban outdoor uses of three main types of neonicotinoids as well as fipronil (European Commission n.d.). After this assessment, the four systemic pesticides of concern were only permitted for use in permanent greenhouses (as opposed to hoop houses which may be moved over or between seasons) (European Commission n.d.).

Agrochemical corporations attempted to manufacture a sense of uncertainty around the banning of pesticides by the EU. The industry commissioned a study in which it was claimed that the pesticide ban would cost the EU economy USD 17 billion in reduced crop yields and would cause 27,000 people working within the agricultural industry in the EU to lose their jobs (Goulson 2020). The question of whether a ban on neonicotinoids affects yields is highly contested. Some research has shown little to no loss of yields (Goulson 2013), while other research (Dewar 2017), shows a loss of oilseed rape in the UK after the EU partial ban on neonicotinoids. Some claim that a ban on neonicotinoids will make it impossible for humans to achieve the 70% growth in agricultural production purported to be needed by 2050 (Walters and Didham 2016). However, this predicted growth is based on a steep increase in a meat-centred diet, which is not necessary for adequate human nutrition and is associated with a variety of serious ecological problems (Weis 2013). The industry also sponsored studies that demonstrated that the pesticides had no negative impact on bees (Goulson 2020). After the decision was made to ban the pesticides of concern in 2018, Bayer took the EU to court to try to overturn the ban, and when this was unsuccessful, appealed the court's decision, which was also unsuccessful for Bayer (Abnett 2021).

It is important to note that while this is the most restrictive use of pesticides in the world, covering several important crop-producing countries, there are problems with this legislation in terms of negative pesticides impact. It is not a complete ban on neonicotinoids, only the three types identified as most harmful to bees. The neonicotinoid acetamiprid, for example, is still allowed as there is evidence that it has a low impact on bees (European Commission n.d.). Although this decision may be aligned with a commitment to the precautionary principle, it does bring into question where the line is for determining the level of acceptable harm. A more concerning limitation is that member countries can apply for "emergency authorization" to use the restricted pesticides (European Commission n.d.). According to Greenpeace UK's online journalism project *Unearthed*, 67 emergency authorizations have been approved, which the authors argue is "rarely justifiable and often repeated" (Dowler and Clarke 2020). To add further complications, Dowler and Clarke (2020) contend that:

> In at least 14 cases, the holder of the "emergency authorisation" was the pesticide manufacturer itself. Bayer, which manufactures imidacloprid and clothianidin, has had six different authorisations approved in its name since the ban, making it one of the EU's three biggest holders of emergency neonic authorisations. There are two sugar beet producer organisations that also have six authorisations apiece. Syngenta, which manufactures thiamethoxam, has had five authorisations approved in that time.

Although there are some loopholes with the EU restrictions of systemic pesticides that agrochemical corporations seem to be able to exploit, at least in some situations, the restriction of these pesticides in the EU allows scientists to gather information about how long they persist in agricultural landscapes after they are largely eradicated from use. In theory, the use of the four systemic pesticides of concern (imidacloprid, clothianidin, thiamethoxam, and fipronil) has been seriously restricted on flowering, "bee-attractive" crops in outdoor settings since 2013. One study found that after the moratorium was implemented, all types of restricted neonicotinoids were detected in oil rapeseed (canola), a crop on which they were not permitted to be used (Wintermantel et al. 2020). Of particular concern was that imidacloprid, which persisted in the soil after the moratorium, was easily taken up by the plant after rainfalls. This is especially concerning because bees do not fly during heavy rainfall, but forage quite intensely (especially honey bees) afterwards, potentially being exposed to higher levels of imidacloprid (Wintermantel et al. 2020). The authors of this study also posit that ground-nesting wild bees may continue to be at risk of exposure due to the persistence of neonicotinoids in the soil (Wintermantel et al. 2020). They ultimately argue that the ban should include all crops that grow outdoors, whether or not they flower, and that further studies should be conducted on the leaching of these pesticides from permanent greenhouses via the water systems (Wintermantel et al. 2020). What this and other studies demonstrate is that the persistent and systemic nature of neonicotinoids and other systemic pesticides cause them to persist in soil and waterways after their use is restricted. Even after these pesticides are restricted, they will likely be present in a variety of plants including crops pollinated by bees for an unknown length of time. Some pro-pesticide advocates use studies like this to argue that restrictions are pointless. Instead, what this, and other studies, demonstrate is that there is an urgent need to ban all pesticides that are shown to have a high probability of negative impact on bees and other non-targeted non-human animals since they may persist for many years, even decades, in soil and waterways.

Ontario: when neo-liberal governance and agrochemical corporations collude

In 2015 the Ontario government imposed a partial ban on neonicotinoids. At the time this was, and remains, the largest level of government in North America to have attempted to restrict the use of neonicotinoids by the agricultural industry. This was made more significant because Ontario is the largest province in Canada in terms of population and the numbers of farms (Ontario Ministry of Agriculture, Food, and Rural Affairs 2017).[5] The restriction on neonicotinoid usage in Ontario officially began in the 2017 growing season but was substantially weakened by the election of a more conservative provincial government in 2018.[6] The agrochemical industry intervened in the debate around neonicotinoid pesticides in Ontario to shape and influence the process, most notably by forming powerful coalitions with large farmers' organizations such as the Grain Farmers of Ontario (GFO), and in the end they were successful in co-producing weak and ineffective provincial guidelines around the use of neonicotinoids by farmers. The Ontario government initially took a similar approach to the EU with their partial ban on 80% of neonicotinoid use in the province, although there was a much higher level of influence and input from agrochemical corporations. While a precautionary principle is more appropriate for the complexity and uncertainty surrounding pesticides and bee health, partial bans and temporary moratoriums have limited effectiveness due to the systemic and persistent nature of neonicotinoids, and so represent a 'win' for the agrochemical industry, indicating the heavy influence this industry has on policymaking.

In response to growing concern about neonicotinoids, the Ontario government established the Ontario Bee Working Group in July 2013 (Ellis 2019) to bring together a "group of experts to support the development and/or implementation of strategies to mitigate the risk to honey bees from exposure to neonicotinoid seed treatments on corn and soybeans" (Ontario Bee Health Working Group 2014). The members of the working group included staff of the Ministry of Agriculture and Rural Affairs Canada and the Ministry of the Environment. It also included an academic from the University of Guelph and representatives from the Ontario Beekeepers Association, the Ontario Federation of Agriculture, and the Grain Farmers of Ontario. Interestingly, a representative each from Syngenta, Bayer CropScience Canada, Crop Life Canada, the Association of Equipment Manufacturers, and the Canadian Seed Trade Association also took part in the working group (Ontario Bee Health Working Group 2014). Collectively, these groups represent various facets of the capitalist agricultural system. Crop Life Canada, an affiliate of Crop Life International, is an especially important organization in lobbying efforts against pesticide bans. Crop Life Canada represents corporations that make up the two main sectors of the agrochemical industry: pesticides and biotech seeds. Their membership when they were engaging in aggressive interventions into Ontario legislation about neonicotinoids was made up of the main corporations who were at that time involved in the industry including Bayer CropScience, Dupont, Syngenta, and Monsanto.[7] There was no representation in the Ontario Bee Health Working Group of small-scale farmers' organizations such as the National Farmers Union (NFU), or of organic farmers' organizations such as the Ecological Farmers Association of Ontario (EFAO) or the Organic Grower's Council (OGC). The Ontario Bee Health Working Group, perhaps unsurprisingly, recommended a *temporary* ban on neonicotinoids for the 2014 growing season (Ontario Bee Health Working Group 2014). The agrochemical industry influence on the working group can be seen with official comments from the working group calling for voluntary approaches instead of what they call "heavy-handed regulated and mandated solutions" (Ontario Bee Health Working Group 2014).

In 2015 the government announced their decision for a partial ban. The partial ban in Ontario began on 1 July 2015, with the restriction on the sale and use of treated seeds, although, it did not take full effect until the 2017 growing season. The goal of the ban was that only 20% of farmed acres in Ontario would be treated with neonicotinoids (Government of Ontario 2015). Due to the systemic and persistent nature of neonicotinoids this was very weak legislation, however, it was stronger than any other jurisdiction's regulation of neonicotinoid pesticides other than the European Union. In order to achieve an 80% reduction of neonicotinoid use in the province, farmers were required to take free training on Integrated Pest Management (IPM) provided by the Ontario government and to justify their usage of neonicotinoid pesticides with soil testing to assess the presence of grubs and larvae of destructive insects (Ontario Ministry of Agriculture, Food, and Rural Affairs 2016). The partial ban on neonicotinoids was fully in place for less than a year, before being threatened by a change in government. This demonstrates the ineffectiveness of a partial ban of pesticide especially when it allows for a significant number of exceptions that agribusinesses and agrochemical corporations can exploit. When the Conservative provincial government was elected in 2018, the partial pesticide ban was so dramatically weakened that it is now essentially voluntary. In 2018, Bill 132 (euphemistically labelled "Better for people, smarter for business act") was introduced to amend the initial pesticide ban and it entails few rules and little monitoring of systemic pesticide use (Legislative Assembly of Ontario 2018), essentially morphing into guidelines about IPM and neonicotinoid use, which is exactly what agrochemical corporations and the agricultural industry organizations wanted.

In the creation of the Ontario neonicotinoid legislation, in the public campaign that ensued, and in media coverage, the main farmers' organization represented was the GFO. The GFO represents 28,000 corn, soybean, and wheat farmers in Ontario who collectively cover 6 million acres of farmland (Grain Farmers of Ontario n.d.). In coverage about neonicotinoids, the GFO leaned into the trope of the struggling family farmer who cannot afford an insect infestation and so must use neonicotinoids until better technology is created to reduce harmful impact on pollinators, waterways, and other aspects of the natural world. This was particularly insidious given that many of their members operate multi-million-dollar agribusinesses. They further argued that the science is too *uncertain* and *incomplete* to risk harming farmers and, by extension, farming communities, parroting the main talking points agrochemical corporations use to manufacture uncertainty about scientific studies that indicate pesticides harm non-human animals.

Using similar tactics as agrochemical corporations in the EU, the GFO repeatedly referenced a study they commissioned with Crop Life Canada from the Conference Board of Canada that claimed that corn and soybean farmers could lose more than CAD 630 million in revenues due to restrictions on neonicotinoids (Grant et al. 2014). The authors of the report claim this would cut the province's revenue by CAD 440 million. This contrasts with other reports commissioned by the GFO where they speak of the positive impact of neonicotinoid reduction, claiming it will "lower production costs and increase economic competitiveness for growers, strengthen relationships with trade and marketing partners, and reduce negative environmental impacts" (Grain Farmers of Ontario 2015). Their main argument was that any reduction in neonicotinoid use should be *voluntary* and tied to technological "innovations" in farm machinery to reduce dust from seed sowing. There is no actual evidence presented that voluntary reductions or machine technology will have a positive impact on pollinators. Nor does the study address the growing concern and scientific evidence for the contamination of waterways by neonicotinoids.

The GFO claimed that the legislation would have no benefit to pollinators and would only rob farmers of an adequate yield. The GFO continually claims that there is little or no evidence to show cumulative harm to pollinators. For example, in their comments on the partial ban, they state they have been willing to work with the Ontario government "despite never seeing the data to support the assertion that there is a direct correlation between bee mortalities and neonicotinoids beyond the acute exposure that farmers are already actively addressing" (Grain Farmers of Ontario 2015). To cast uncertainty and doubt on the neonicotinoid ban, the GFO argued that there are multiple factors negatively affecting honey bees (Grain Farmers of Ontario 2015), a non-controversial statement, agreed upon by most entomologists and beekeepers (Goulson 2013) that should have no bearing on pesticide restrictions.

After the Ontario government announced the decision for a partial ban on neonicotinoids, CBC reported on 12 May 2016, that the GFO launched a campaign to encourage their members to speak out against it on social media (a 'twitter bomb') and through lobbying their MPPs. The GFO, along with the agrochemical corporations, pushed hard to ensure that the neonicotinoid restrictions were weak and largely ineffective from their beginning. Upon examination, these partial bans and temporary moratoriums are not nearly as sweeping as they seem, or as effective as the need to be. The GFO argues strongly that the government should take a position of non-interference in matters of what seeds and pesticides farmers use on their crops. In response to the Ontario government's initial proposal for a partial neonicotinoid ban, they called on the government to "abandon the goal to reduce neonicotinoids by

80% in Ontario and support an agri-industry-led approach that will work for the complexities of both grain farming and beekeeping" (Grain Farmers of Ontario 2015). With the election of the Conservative provincial government in 2018, they essentially got exactly what they wanted in terms of no real restrictions on neonicotinoid use in the province. As advocates of pollinator health have noted, the strong lobbying conducted by Bayer CropScience and other agrochemical corporations has weakened the responses of governments worldwide (Martin 2015).

Bee-washing by agrochemical corporations

The concept of bee-washing, when industries, corporations, or organizations claim to be doing work to help bees when in fact, they are not, has gained some traction over the past few years. The term has widely been used by native bee scientists and advocates in North America to problematize 'save the bee' rhetoric used by beekeepers about honey bees (Westreich 2020). While it is true that honey bees are in no way in danger of going extinct because an entire sector within agriculture and a large group of people are dedicated to keeping their numbers somewhat steady, it has been thoroughly demonstrated by scientists that honey bees are sickly and vulnerable animals. Using the concept of bee-washing in reference to honey bee advocacy seems like a misuse of the term, although it is a fair critique that beekeepers should not imply that honey bees are at risk of extinction and should not conflate honey bees with wild bees in North America where they are not native. However, the term bee-washing can be more accurately applied to the sometimes-sneaky ways in which agrochemical, agribusiness, and food corporations attempt to recast themselves as champions of bees who can offer a real solution to the global pollinator crisis. In this section I will examine bee-washing campaigns that cropped up in North America, at the time in which the public was becoming increasingly concerned about CCD and the widespread use of neonicotinoids. I will examine the Bees Matter front group, and the Bring Back the Bees campaign launched by corporate food giant, General Mills.

Bees Matter?

Leading up to the Ontario government's decision to partially ban neonicotinoids, the GFO formed a public advocacy coalition with several agrochemical corporations, resulting in the creation of front groups and websites such as Bees Matter. With their offers of free organic seeds, these websites confuse people who are genuinely concerned about the pollinator crisis. Bees Matter is a partnership of agrochemical corporations including Bayer-Monsanto, Syngenta, and Dupont, industry groups such as Soy Canada, the Canola Council of Canada, and the GFO. It also lists its 'Buzzing Gardens Partners' as 4H Canada, Communities in Bloom, Pollinator Partnership Canada, and the Canada Honey Council, all non-profit organizations claiming to advocate for pollinator health.

The Canada Honey Council (CHC)'s support of this website is particularly illuminating, as it is the national industry group representing beekeepers. The CHC took a pro-agrochemical stance in debates about neonicotinoids in Canada, something not always shared by its affiliated provincial bodies, most notably the Ontario Beekeepers Association, who supported the Ontario legislation partially banning neonicotinoids (Ellis 2019).

The website claims to be interested in promoting the health of honey bees and does so primarily by encouraging people to grow pollinator-friendly gardens. As of 22 January 2022, it describes itself as, "a partnership of agricultural organizations with a vested interest in pollinator health", and describes its mission as being to, "provide a platform for conversation, dialogue and information sharing regarding *modern agriculture* and the importance of ensuring a healthy environment for honey bees, which play an important role in Canadian food production and agriculture" (emphasis added). This website contributes to a portrayal of the capitalist agriculture industry as trying to do what is best for both people and bees.

As of 22 January 2022, the flashy Bees Matter website claimed that

> In recent years, farmers and scientists have worked more closely with beekeepers to keep their hives healthy. Whether this has meant developing new products to benefit honey bees or *changing the way they use current products* to better protect honey bees, the results have been *innovative and collaborative strategies to mitigate risk*.
>
> (Bees Matter n.d., italics in original)

This statement avoids mentioning pesticides or neonicotinoids, even though it is clearly referring to them in discussing "current products" and "innovative and collaborative strategies to mitigate risk". Furthermore, a romanticised, imaginary relationship between farmers and bees is presented on the website with statements such as, "But farmers aren't just protecting honey bees. They're also providing honey bees with pollen. Canola, for example, is one of the best flowering plants for bees, with a balance of protein and amino acids necessary to support a healthy hive" (Bees Matter n.d.). There is no mention of the potential dangers of pollen from neonicotinoid-treated canola or about the lack of forage (a problem they identify elsewhere) due to monocultures of crops such as canola, soy, and corn. The website goes on to state that, "In many cases, beekeepers and farmers have a mutually beneficial relationship in which the bees, like livestock, are brought to the farm in order to graze on the pollen of the farm" (Bees Matter n.d.). There is also no mention that wildflower forage on farms using neonicotinoid pesticides may do more harm than good especially to wild bees who gather pollen and nectar from native, "weedy" plants (David et al. 2016).

The Bees Matter website acknowledges bees are in trouble but claims it is due to a lack of forage and to parasites that attack them. Nowhere on the slick website are pesticides mentioned. The website also claims, repeatedly, that, "Statistics Canada data shows the number of honey bee hives in Canada is on the rise. They still face a number of health issues, however, and one of their major challenges is finding and collecting food" (Bees Matter n.d.). This statement is particularly problematic, given that honey bee populations in Canada are currently experiencing unsustainably high overwinter mortality rates, so much so that beekeepers' organizations and the province's Ministries of Agriculture, including OMAFRA, are scrambling to protect the struggling industry with grants, partly to compensate beekeepers for unsustainably high overwinter losses of bee colonies (Government of Ontario 2021). The second part of the statement is not backed by science: honey bees in Canada do not face a lack of forage, in fact, some native bee scientists fear that honey bees may outcompete native bees for nectar and pollen (Colla and MacIvor 2016). Furthermore, where honey bees in Canada face nutritional deficiencies (not the same as lack of forage), it is often when they are put to work on monocultured fields in which only one flowering plant is in bloom (Hendriksma and Shafir 2016). Studies also indicate that the combination of nutritional stress and neonicotinoid exposure harms honey bees (Tosi et al. 2017) This last statement on the Bees Matter website can only be understood as intentional misinformation. For people visiting the website to take advantage of the offer of free wildflower seeds it is not immediately evident who runs and funds Bees Matter. This is only one example of an industry-funded organization that seeks to portray industrial agriculture as bee-friendly and to confuse concerned people about the role it plays in harming both wild and honey bees.

#BringBacktheBees

The #BringBacktheBees campaign was launched in North America by General Mills and Burt's Bees during the height of public concern about bee health and decline. General Mills is a US-based multinational food corporation that owns over 100 different food brands (General Mills n.d.). General Mills ranked #21 in *Food Engineering*'s list of top food corporations in the world (Food Engineering 2021) and made a revenue of USD 18.1 billion in 2021 (Investors General Mills n.d.). The campaign was centred on its popular brand of cereal, Honey Nut Cereal, ostensibly because if honey bees disappeared so would honey, an ingredient in the cereal. Materials supporting the campaign featured the mascot of Cheerios, Buzz (a bee), disappearing from Cheerios's packaging (Cheerios Canada n.d.). #BringBacktheBees Canadian website includes annual giveaways of wildflower seed packets to the public, based on a partnership with Vesey's Seeds, a large independent seed company in Canada. This corporate-sponsored campaign takes a different approach than Bees Matter in discussing problems faced by bees. There is a link on the front page of the website to a TED talk by entomologist Marla Spivak (Cheerios Canada n.d.) in which she states that decline in bee health is due to "flowerless landscapes and a dysfunctional food system", and pinpoints both pesticides and monoculture agricultural landscapes as part of the problem (Spivak 2013). Although General Mills does own some organic food brands with an expectation that those sales will increase faster than their conventional brands (Investors General Mills n.d.), the majority of their food brands and products are not organic. This campaign seems less like an intentional disinformation campaign, and more of simple greenwashing campaign. They are willing to discuss problems with the food system but likely anticipate that most people will not make the connection to their actual agricultural practices.

This strategy seems to have mostly succeeded. The rumour-debunking website Snopes addressed criticisms directed at General Mills claiming that they heavily use glyphosate on the grains used to create Cheerios (Emery 2017). In the article, the author claims that while General Mills' products use glyphosate in their production, the herbicide is non-lethal to bees, citing one scientific study (Emery 2017). As examined in Chapter 4, there are conflicting scientific studies about the direct harm that glyphosate causes to bees, with a small but emerging body of evidence showing some harm. Since the #BringBacktheBees campaign focuses heavily on distributing wildflower seeds, it must be noted, but is not in the Snopes article, that glyphosate is used to kill wildflowers deemed as weeds. Confusingly, the author of the Snopes article does not seem to understand that General Mills is a multinational corporation that owns over 100 brands (General Mills n.d.), most of which feature products made up of conventionally grown crops. As neonicotinoids are the most widely used insecticides in the world, and General Mills has made no statement claiming their products do not use them, it is virtually certain many of their products are made from crops whose seeds are embedded with or sprayed with neonicotinoids and other systemic pesticides. The Snopes article demonstrates the misinformation and confusion the public and the media has about pesticide use, harm to bees, and the role of major multinational food corporations. In effect, it demonstrates the success of bee-washing. Although the #BringBacktheBees campaign seems less problematic than the Bees Matter website, both lean into a general lack of education among the public about the influence that agrochemical and food corporations have over governance about pesticides, and the power these corporations hold globally within the capitalist agricultural system.

Learning from success and failure in struggles to ban pesticides

It is important for activists pushing for restrictions on systemic pesticides to note the similarities and differences between the European Commission and the Ontario government's approaches to designing and implementing pesticide legislation. In both situations, agrochemical corporations, agribusiness industry organizations, and their associated lobby groups used similar tactics:

1 They claimed that the science is uncertain and imply systemic pesticides may not harm pollinators. They commissioned their own studies that claimed to demonstrate that systemic pesticides are benign to pollinating insects.[8]
2 They warned that there will be a loss of crop yields and jobs that will negatively affect farmers, the agricultural industry, and even the entire

economy of the jurisdiction affected by the legislation. In order to support this argument, they commissioned studies that forecast dire outcomes for the agricultural industry if there are any compulsory restrictions on systemic pesticides.

3   They take governments to court over the legislation, although this strategy failed for agrochemical corporations in both Ontario and the EU and is likely to fail elsewhere.
4   They attempt to confuse the public about the negative impact of systemic pesticides on pollinators, and on the role that the agricultural industry plays in pollinator health by engaging in bee-washing through campaigns such as Bees Matter and #BringBacktheBees.
5   They exploit any and all exemptions in the legislation that allow for an easing of pesticide restrictions.

For pollinator advocates seeking to push for pesticide restrictions, it is important to refute the claims made by agrochemical corporations and agribusiness industry groups. One important way to do this is to uphold the large body of scientific evidence demonstrating that these pesticides harm pollinators and other insects. It is important for advocates to push for a science-based and precautionary approach to drafting potential legislation. The EU took a mostly science-based approach during their moratorium on four systemic pesticides, calling for empirical evidence of harm, or lack of harm. In contrast the Ontario government formed a consultation group made up of scientists but also featuring several representatives from agrochemical corporations, the agribusiness industry, and agrochemical lobby groups. It is important for advocates of pollinator health to emphasize that science is uncertain and that there is rarely consensus among scientists, however this doesn't mean that governments should not move forward on legislation about ecological issues, especially as a large (and growing) body of evidence supports restricting systemic pesticides. Advocates of pesticide restrictions can address concerns about crop yield and job losses by pointing to research demonstrating that agroecological approaches have higher yield per acre than agrochemical approaches, which tend to have a higher yield per plant (Altieri 2009). Advocates of pesticide restrictions can also point to the actual experience of the EU after the ban on four systemic pesticides in which the agricultural system and economies in the EU did not collapse.

In terms of policymaking, small-scale, organic farmer organizations must be at the table if and when governments consult with industry groups. Although the numbers of these farmers are small in the Global North, they have experience and knowledge about how to farm without the use of systemic pesticides, while also maintaining a yield. The trope of the struggling family farmer, when used by lobby groups and organizations that represent large-scale agribusiness, must be disrupted. The 'get big or get out' attitude that has shaped farming policy in many parts of the world since the mid-20th century has created a reality in which many large farms are highly profitable capitalist enterprises, and the 'farmers' are capitalist owners of these enterprises who oversee a large staff who do the actual work associated with farming in the collective imaginary (Ellis 2019). In order to counter the bee-washing approach pollinator advocacy organizations must have a strong commitment to uncovering corporate misinformation and refuse any attempt to work in collaboration with agrochemical corporations, including a refusal to participate in their campaigns and accept any money or sponsorship from them. Instead, advocates of pesticide restrictions must be part of an interspecies alliance in opposition to agrochemical corporations and, by extension, capitalist agriculture.

In examining the actual legislation created by the Ontario government and the European Commission, advocates should push for full bans on the systemic pesticides that have a large body of evidence demonstrating harm. Partial bans and bans that feature exemptions for the greenhouse industry or crops that are harvested before going to bloom do not go far enough in halting the harm caused by persistent and systemic pesticides. To be effective, legislation restricting pesticides must have as few loopholes as possible and strict standards must be in place if allowing farmers to apply for any exemptions.

Beyond neonicotinoids

Agrochemical corporations hold a prominent place as stakeholders in the development of policy on pesticide use and regulation throughout the world. The industry attempts to intervene in policymaking regarding pesticides in a variety of ways including conducting studies that give results that are favourable to pesticides; taking governmental bodies to court for adopting legislation that restricts pesticides; forming lobbying coalitions with one another and with large farmers' organizations such as the GFO; and devising public campaigns that give incorrect or simplified information. Corporate manipulation of public policymaking over the banning of neonicotinoids is just one example of the power and influence of agrochemical corporations. In response to these manipulations there is need and potential for a powerful movement representing a coalition between small-scale farmers, *bee-centred* beekeepers (Ellis 2021; Moore and Kosut 2013), scientists, and environmentalists. This movement can and should call for the banning of pesticides, and the transformation of global agriculture away from capitalist profit-making and towards an agroecological system in which people grow food using methods and practices that allow for the flourishing of non-human animals, and ecological lifeworlds.

Watson and Stallins (2016) warn that campaigns focused on a ban of neonicotinoids have the potential to fall into a "reductionist regulatory narrative". A neonicotinoid ban *alone* will not 'save' bees or even dramatically improve their health. As studies conducted in the EU have demonstrated, systemic pesticides will likely persist in waterways and soil for many decades (van der Sluijs et al. 2015) and a pesticide ban may not have immediate positive impacts on bees or other non-human natures (Wintermantel et al. 2020). There is also a worry that the banning of neonicotinoids may result in the use of even more harmful pesticides. Davis (2017) points out that, historically, banning pesticides has led to the creation of new classes of pesticides, not a shift towards less pesticide use. There are other types of systemic pesticides on the market that are not neonicotinoids but that likely have similar – or worse – impacts on bees and other non-human natures. Some of these non-neonicotinoid pesticides are already on the market, such as fipronil and flupyradifurone, and some have yet to be made commercially available. In many ways pesticides are a perfect example of the accelerating treadmill of capitalist agriculture. Once farmers start using pesticides to deal with problem insects or plants, they experience contradictions and crises which only intensive and high-tech solutions seem to (temporarily) solve. However, the concern that banning some pesticides will only cause others to be used or developed should not deter the push for pesticide restrictions. Rather, it provides a compelling argument that the neonicotinoid debate should be a catalyst for the building of radical social movements that both disrupt capitalist agriculture and build viable alternatives to the landscapes of scarcity it creates.

These radical social movements can challenge the intervention of agrochemical corporations in debates about neonicotinoids by promoting small-scale farmers, Indigenous farmers and land stewards, and peasants as caretakers of the land who have an interest in the health of pollinators and ecosystems. In many ways, this movement already exists in the form of the international peasants' rights movement as represented by La Via Campesina, which organizes around agroecology, food sovereignty, and social justice, with a strong orientation against the capitalist agricultural system (Martinez-Torres and Rosset 2010). An international agroecological movement can push past the boundaries of national borders through ongoing alignment with La Via Campesina to challenge the global dominance of agrochemical corporations. The harmful effects of neonicotinoids on pollinators and other insects do not stop at national borders and neither should the struggles against them.

The National Farmers' Union in Canada is an affiliate of La Via Campesina, representing small-scale farmers. The NFU-Ontario chapter presents the agroecological perspective very clearly in a submission to the Ontario government about the banning of neonicotinoids:

> We advocate for agricultural practices that are economically, socially, and environmentally sustainable and built on the principles of food sovereignty. By working with and building our own knowledge and skills of agroecology we strive to protect the many organisms, including bees and wild pollinators, which provide economic benefits to our farms and contribute to a more beautiful countryside.
>
> (National Farmers Union 2014)

This is in line with the kinds of changes to agricultural policy promoted by critical entomologists. As Dave Goulson (2013, p. 11), argues:

If we want to ensure healthy populations of honeybees, bumblebees, and other wild pollinating insects upon which we depend for our crop production, and more generally if we wish to support the healthy, diverse ecosystems upon which our future health and well-being depend, then we need to find ways to produce food in a sustainable way which incorporates the needs of biodiversity.

This is especially important at a time when Earth faces an unprecedented defaunation of insect life that could cause widespread ecosystem collapse (Hallmann et al. 2017). It is essential that advocates of pollinator health and biodiversity confront and complicate the claims of agrochemical corporations, which also entails confronting global capitalism. As Suryanarayanan (2015, p. 150) argues, "the contemporary regulatory process that renders the issues of pollinators in relation to pesticides in narrow econometric terms is the outcome of a much broader agenda of neoliberalization … policymaking on pesticides has tended to systematically privilege the interests and values of agribusiness over others". Advocates for pollinator health and biodiversity must go further than partial bans and moratoriums to ensure the mutual flourishing of pollinators alongside people. We know we face an uncertain future of climate chaos and massive threats to biodiversity. In the face of this uncertainty, we can build *interspecies alliances* between bees and people that allow for the creation of landscapes of abundance (Best 2003; Collard et al. 2015). This interspecies alliance can bring together the many people and movements around the world that are confronting capitalist agriculture and nurturing relationships with non-human nature based on care, connection, and mutual flourishing.

Notes

1 Agroecology can be defined as a science, practice, and movement that applies ecological concepts and principles to the design of agricultural systems, while also centring local and regional food sovereignty and Indigenous knowledge systems (Altieri 2009).
2 Colony Collapse Disorder is a phenomenon in which most of the colony disappeared, leaving only a handful of sickly bees. This event did not follow the well-known honey bee behaviours associated with swarming or absconding and the colony was believed to have suddenly died. It was especially widespread in the United States, first noticed in 2006, and peaking in 2007 and while it still occurs is not as serious a problem as high overwinter mortality rates of honey bees. The cause of CCD was never firmly established by scientists and there remains great uncertainty. Suggested causes have, perhaps unsurprisingly, included neonicotinoids, fungicides, viruses, and/or the effects of migratory beekeeping (Watanabe 2008).
3 The logic behind this allowable use is that bees will not be directly harmed because they will not be consuming the nectar or pollen of the plant. However subsequent scientific studies have demonstrated that neonicotinoids make their way into soil and waterways and are taken up by other plants. Due to their persistent and systemic nature, neonicotinoids may be present in the nectar and pollen in non-targeted plants (Botias et al. 2015).
4 Maize is not actually preferred by bees.

5 Ontario is fourth in terms of provinces with largest share of total field crop area for the country, representing 9%. The top province is Saskatchewan, with a whopping 46.8% share of total field crop area in the country. Saskatchewan is the centre of large-scale wheat production in Canada (Statistics Canada 2017).
6 New legislation introduced by the conservative Ontario government has led to the neonicotinoid partial ban being voluntary, essentially a guideline for integrated pest management (IPM), exactly what agrochemical corporations advocated for when the Ontario government first began to research the impact of neonicotinoids on bees and consider legislation to restrict them (Ellis 2019).
7 Due to major mergers, these corporations are now: Bayer-Monsanto; DowDuPont-Corteva; and ChemChina-Syngenta (OECD 2018).
8 Fang (2020) has done an excellent investigative journalist piece on the co-option of scientists by agrochemical corporations.

References

Abnett, K. (2021). EU top court upholds ban on Bayer pesticides linked to harming bees. *Reuters*, May 6. https://www.reuters.com/world/europe/eu-top-court-upholds-eu-ban-bayer-pesticides-linked-harming-bees-2021-2005-06/.

Altieri, M. A. (2009). Agroecology, small farms, and food sovereignty. *Monthly Review*, 61 (3), 102–113.

Bees Matter. (n.d.). https://www.beesmatter.ca, accessed 15 January 2022.

Best, S. (2003). Common natures, shared fates: Toward an interspecies alliance politics. IMPACT Press 42 (January). http://www.impactpress.com/articles/decjan03/interspecies12103.html.

Bonny, S. (2017). Corporate concentration and technological change in the global seed industry. *Sustainability*, 9 (9), 1632. https://doi.org/10.3390/su9091632.

Botías, C., David, A., Horwood, J., Abdul-Sada, A., Nicholls, E., Hill, E., & Goulson, D. (2015). Neonicotinoid residues in wildflowers, a potential route of chronic exposure for bees. *Environmental Science & Technology*, 49 (21), 12731–12740. doi:10.1021/acs.est.5b03459.

Cheerios Canada. (n.d.). Bring back the bees. https://www.cheerios.ca/bringbackthebees/, accessed 15 January 2022.

Colla, S. R. & MacIvor, S. (2016). Questioning public perception, conservation policy, and recovery actions for honeybees in North America. *Conservation Biology*, 31 (55), 1202–1204.

Collard, R., Dempsey, J., & Sundberg, J. (2015). A manifesto for abundant futures. *Annals of the Association of American Geographers*, 105 (2), 322–330.

David, A., Botias, C., Abdul-Sada, A., Nicholls, E., Rotheray, E. L., Hill, E. M., & Goulson, D. (2016). Widespread contamination of wildflower and bee-collected pollen with complex mixtures of neonicotinoids and fungicides commonly applied to crops. *Environment International*, 88 (3), 169–178.

Davis, F. R. (2017). Pesticides and the paradox of the Anthropocene: From natural to synthetic to synthesized nature. *Global Environment*, 10, 114–136.

Dewar, A. M. (2017). The adverse impact of the neonicotinoid seed treatment ban on crop protection in oilseed rape in the United Kingdom. *Pest Management Science*, 73, 1305–1309.

Dowler, S., & Clarke, J. S. (2020). Loophole keeps bee-killing pesticides in widespread use, two years after EU ban. *Unearthed*, July 8. https://unearthed.greenpeace.org/2020/07/08/bees-neonicotinoids-bayer-syngenta-eu-ban-loophole/.

Ellis, R. (2021). Pollinator people: An ethnography of bees, bee advocates and possibilities for multispecies commoning in Toronto and London, ON. [Doctoral dissertation, University of Western Ontario]. Electronic Thesis and Dissertation Repository. 7796. https://ir.lib.uwo.ca/etd/7796.

Ellis, R. (2019). Save the bees? Agrochemical corporations and the debate over neonicotinoids in Ontario. *Capitalism Nature Socialism*, 30 (4), 104–122. https://doi.org/10.1080/10455752.2018.1494748.

Emery, D. (2017). Cheerios gives away 1.5 billion wildflower seeds in 'Save the Bees' promotion. Snopes, March 17. https://www.snopes.com/news/2017/03/17/cheerios-wildflower-seeds-save-bees/.

European Food Safety Authority (EFSA). (2018). Neonicotinoids: Risks to bees confirmed. February 28. https://www.efsa.europa.eu/en/press/news/180228.

European Commission. (n.d.). Neonicotinoids. https://ec.europa.eu/food/plants/pesticides/approval-active-bstances/renewal-approval/neonicotinoids_en.

Fang, L. (2020). The pesticide industry's playbook for poisoning the earth. *The Intercept*. January 18, https://theintercept.com/2020/01/18/bees-insecticides-pesticides-neonicotinoids-bayer-monsanto-syngenta/.

Food Engineering. (2021). 2020 top 100 food & beverage companies. *Food Engineering*. https://www.foodengineeringmag.com/2020-top-100-food-beverage-companies. Accessed January 5, 2022.

General Mills. (n.d.). Brands. https://generalmills.ca/en/Home/Brands/Overview, accessed 20 January 2022.

Goulson, D. (2013). Neonicotinoids and bees: What's all the buzz? *Significance*, 10 (3), 6–11. https://doi.org/10.1111/j.1740-9713.2013.00658.x.

Goulson, D. (2018). Call to restrict neonicotinoids. *Science*, 360 (6392), 973. https://doi.org/10.1126/science.aau0432.

Goulson, D. (2020). Pesticides, corporate irresponsibility, and the fate of our planet. *One Earth*, 2 (4), 302–305.

Government of Ontario. (2015). Neonicotinoid regulations: What you need to know about the new regulations that govern selling neonicotinoid-treated corn and soybean seed. June 9, updated January 30, 2017. https://www.ontario.ca/page/neonicotinoid-regulations.

Government of Ontario. (2021). Governments providing additional supports for Ontario beekeepers. Government of Ontario Newsroom, June 2. https://news.ontario.ca/en/release/1000250/governments-providing-additional-supports-for-ontario-beekeepers.

Grain Farmers of Ontario. (2015). Pollinator health: A proposal for enhancing pollinator health and reducing the use of neonicotinoid pesticides in Ontario. http://gfo.ca/wp-content/uploads/2018/01/Submission-to-EBR-Posting-012-3068.pdf.

Grain Farmers of Ontario. (n.d.). About. https://gfo.ca/about/. Accessed 15 January 2022.

Grant, M., Knowles, J., & Gill, V. (2014). Seeds for success: The value of seed treatments for Ontario growers. The Conference Board of Canada. http://gfo.ca/wpcontent/uploads/2018/01/Seeds-for-Success-the-Value-of-Seed-Treatmentsfor-Ontario-Growers.pdf.

Hallmann C. A., Sorg, M., Jongejans, E., Siepel, H., Hofland, N. … & de Kroon, H. (2017). More than 75 percent decline over 27 years in total flying insect biomass in protected areas. *PLoS ONE* 12 (10), e0185809. https://doi.org/10.1371/journal.pone.0185809.

Hendriksma, H. P. & Shafir, S. (2016). Honey bee foragers balance colony nutritional deficiencies. *Behavioral Ecology and Sociobiology*, 70, 509–517. https://doi.org/10.1007/s00265-016-2067-5.
Investors General Mills. (2021). General Mills Reports Fourth-Quarter and Full-Year Results for Fiscal 2021 and Provides Fiscal 2022 Outlook. *Investors General Mills*. June 30. https://investors.generalmills.com/press-releases/press-release-details/2021/General-Mills-Reports-Fourth-Quarter-and-Full-Year-Results-for-Fiscal-2021-and-Provides-Fiscal-2022-Outlook/default.aspx.
Legislative Assembly of Ontario. (2018). Bill 132, Better for People, Smarter for Business Act, 2019. Accessed January 15, 2020, https://www.ola.org/en/legislative-business/bills/parliament-42/session-1/bill-132#BK6.
Lister, B. C. & Garcia, A. (2018). Climate-driven declines in arthropod abundance restructure a rainforest food web. *PNAS*, 115 (44), https://doi.org/10.1073/pnas.1722477115.
Martin, C. (2015). A re-examination of the pollinator crisis. *Current Biology*, 25, R811–R815.
Martinez-Torres, M. E. & Rosset, P. M. (2010). La Via Campesina: The birth and evolution of a transnational social movement. *The Journal of Peasant Studies*, 37 (1), 149–175.
Monbiot, G. (2017). Insectageddon: Farming is more catastrophic than climate breakdown. *Guardian*, October 20. https://www.theguardian.com/commentisfree/2017/oct/20/insectageddon-farming-catastrophe-climate-breakdown-insect-populations.
Moore, L. J. & Kosut, M. (2013). *Buzz: Urban Beekeeping and the Power of the Bee*. New York: New York University Press.
National Farmers Union. (2014). Importance of bees and bee health. http://www.nfu.ca/story/importance-bees-and-bee-health.
OECD. (2018). *Concentration in Seed Markets: Potential Effects and Policy Responses*, Paris: OECD Publishing, https://doi.org/10.1787/9789264308367-en.
Ontario Bee Health Working Group. (2014). Ontario Health Working Group report. OMAFRA. Accessed 4 July 2017. http://www.omafra.gov.on.ca/english/about/beehealthworkinggroupreport.htm#neon.
Ontario Ministry of Agriculture, Food, and Rural Affairs. (2016). Ontario's Pollinator Health Action Plan. http://www.omafra.gov.on.ca/english/pollinator/action_plan.pdf.
Ontario Ministry of Agriculture, Food, and Rural Affairs. (2017). Number and area of census farms, Canada and the Provinces, 1996, 2001, 2006, 2011 and 2016. http://www.omafra.gov.on.ca/english/stats/census/number.htm.
Phillips, M. W. A. (2020). Agrochemical industry development, trends in R&D and the impact of regulation. *Pest Management Science*, 76 (10), 3348–3356. https://doi.org/10.1002/ps.5728.
Rhoads, L. (2022). New Jersey enacts ground-breaking neonic legislation. NRDC. January 19. https://www.nrdc.org/experts/lucas-rhoads/new-jersey-enacts-groundbreaking-neonic-legislation.
Spivak, M. (2013). Why bees are disappearing. TED. https://www.ted.com/talks/marla_spivak_why_bees_are_disappearing?language=en.
Statistics Canada. (2017). A portrait of 21st-century agricultural operations. *Census2016*, May 17. http://www.statcan.gc.ca/pub/95-640-x/2016001/article/14811-eng.htm.
Suryanarayanan, S. (2015). Pesticides and pollinators: A context-sensitive policy approach. *Current Opinion in Insect Science*, 10, 149–155. https://doi.org/10.1016/j.cois.2015.05.009.

Suryanarayanan, S. and Kleinman, D. L. (2017). *Vanishing Bees: Science, Politics and Honey Bee Health*. New Jersey: Rutgers.

Tosi, S., Nieh, J. C., Sgolastra, F., Cabbri, R. , & Medrzycki, P. (2017). Neonicotinoid pesticides and nutritional stress synergistically reduce survival in honey bees. *Proceedings of the Royal Society B: Biological Sciences*, 284 (169). http://dx.doi.org/10.1098/rspb.2017.1711.

van der Sluijs, J. P., Amaral-Rogers, V., Belzunces, L. P., Bijleveld van Lexmond, M. F. I. J., Bonmatin, J.-M., Chagnon, M. … & Wiemers, M. (2015). Conclusions of the Worldwide Integrated Assessment on the risks of neonicotinoids and fipronil to biodiversity and ecosystem functioning. *Environmental Science and Pollution Research*, 22, 148–154.

Walters, K. F. A. & Didham, R. (2016). Neonicotinoids, bees and opportunity costs for conservation. *Insect Conservation and Diversity*, 9, 375–383.

Watanabe, M. E. (2008). Colony collapse disorder: Many suspects, no smoking gun. *BioScience*, 58 (5), 384–388. https://doi.org/10.1641/b580503.

Watson, K. & Stallins, J. A. (2016). Honey bees and colony collapse disorder: A pluralistic reframing. *Geography Compass* 10 (5), 222–236.

Weis, T. (2013). *The Ecological Hoofprint: The Global Burden of Industrial Livestock*. London: Zed.

Westreich, L. (2020). "Bee-washing" hurts bees and misleads consumers. The Conversation. https://theconversation.com/bee-washing-hurts-bees-and-misleads-consumers-131188.

Wintermantel, D., Odoux, J. F., Decourtye, A., Henry, M., Allier, F., & Bretagnolle, V. (2020). Neonicotinoid-induced mortality risk for bees foraging on oilseed rape nectar persists despite EU moratorium. *Science of the Total Environment*, 704, 135400. https://doi.org/10.1016/j.scitotenv.2019.135400.

6 Which bees shall we save?

Debates over honey bee harm to native bees

In June 2018, as I was conducting my PhD fieldwork in Toronto and London (Canada) on the relationship between urban bees and people, focused on urban beekeeping and pollinator gardening, I noticed a City of Toronto tweet celebrating pollinator week, with an infographic about native bees in the city.[1] I was immediately struck by the fact that while the infographic alludes to multiple threats to native bees, it was specific about just one: "Unregulated European honey bee hives," which it identified as "one of the *largest threats* to native bees because they aggressively outcompete for resources" (emphasis in original).

What struck me about this claim is that the scientific research does *not* indicate that *Apis mellifera* poses one of the biggest threats to wild native bees, but rather that a range of other factors are driving declines including habitat loss and fragmentation, pesticides, pathogens, invasive species (most often referring to plants), and climate change (Goulson et al. 2015). Shortly after I saw this infographic, I attended a monthly meeting of the Urban Toronto Beekeepers Association (UTBA) where a member of the city of Toronto's Pollinator Advisory Group (TPAG) was speaking about the Pollinator Protection Strategy (PPS), which she helped to craft with other bee experts and city staff. Tensions were high at this meeting as beekeepers felt that some of the language in the PPS and on the City of Toronto's website promoting it contained anti-honey bee sentiment. To defuse this tension, the TPAG member explained that the Pollinator Advisory Group had decided to follow the precautionary principle in weighing the potential risks of urban honey bees to wild native bees. As the meeting wore on, the incoming tension turned into expressions of anger and frustration, and I began to realize the extent to which the debate about potential harm honey bees may cause to wild bees was highly emotional, contested, and complicated.

The debate about whether honey bees cause harm to native bees or not was, in fact, the most prominent conflict about urban beekeeping that I encountered during my fieldwork. I begin by examining the evidence of potential harm that honey bees may cause to wild bees, with a focus on urban landscapes which is where the debates about the presence of honey bees have been most contested. I then examine where honey bees belong. Is it only on the monocultured landscapes of the Capitalocene? I argue that hobbyist beekeepers can play an

DOI: 10.4324/9781003142294-6

important role in creating flourishing ecological lifeworlds because they often act as native bee stewards and have the *potential* to raise healthier honey bees. I conclude by arguing that rather than pitting honey bees against wild native bees, the focus of all bee advocates should be to strive to create landscapes of abundance, which involves confronting capitalism.

Are wild native bees harmed by honey bees?

There is a growing body of evidence that demonstrates that honey bees outcompete wild native bees for floral resources. In scientific terms, competition for resources exists between all species who eat the same food sources. Wojcik and colleagues (2018) found that 10 of 19 scientific papers showed some evidence of honey bees outcompeting wild native bees for nectar and pollen. Mallinger and colleagues (2017) also assessed research on competition for floral resources, as well as pathogen transfer, and found that 53% of the studies they included in their review showed negative interactions either in the form of competition or pathogen transfer. It is important to note that most of the studies included in both reviews were conducted in rural landscapes, often in areas that contain some wild native bee habitat (i.e., with unmanaged grasses, shrubs, and trees) bordering areas of monocultured capitalist agriculture. The honey bees in these studies have either been brought to the agricultural fields to provide pollination services or they were migratory bee hives being trucked across landscapes that were resting in between pollination contracts. In both cases, it makes sense that the sudden arrival of hundreds or thousands of honey bee colonies would be disruptive to much smaller populations of wild native bees resident in the area.

Several studies have demonstrated that the type of landscape may play a crucial role in the level of competition for floral resources between honey bees and wild native bees, with increased competition evident in simplified and standardized landscapes of capitalist agriculture that contain a high level of non-native plants (Herbertsson et al. 2016) while more complex, biodiverse landscapes tend to allow for better coexistence between honey bees and wild native bees (Franklin et al. 2018), although some studies indicate the honey bees outcompete with native bees in biodiversity hotspots (Hung et al. 2019). It should be noted that not all studies about competition between honey bees and wild native bees show an *increase* in competition, they simply show that it exists, and it may be that wild native bees have adapted to the competition from honey bees since the arrival of the latter hundreds of years ago, especially where their density is not that great (i.e., where they are not bound up in the relations of industrial agriculture). In fact, it should be noted in this discussion that honey bee colonies decreased in the United States and Europe in the 20th century (Ferrier et al. 2018; Potts et al. 2010), which indicates that if there is an increase in floral competition and viral transfer, it may have to do more with scarcity of landscape or sickly honey bees than the number of colonies. One of the central recommendations given by both Wojcik and colleagues (2018) and Mallinger and colleagues (2017) is that further research is needed on the long-term impacts of honey bees on populations of wild native bees, with respect to both competition and pathogen transfer, and in a variety of other landscapes in addition to the margins of agriculture.

There are a small number of studies about competition and pathogen transfer between honey bees and wild native bees in urban environments. Ropars and colleagues (2019) analyzed whether honey bees compete with wild native bees in Paris, France, and showed that large solitary bees stop foraging when they get within 500 m of a honey bee colony, while bumble bees (who have a larger forging range) stop foraging within 1 km of honey bee colonies. They also demonstrated that small solitary bees and other insects were largely unaffected by the presence of honey bee colonies. Ropars and colleagues (2019) indicate that they were not able to establish correlation, but their results are in line with some of the results of papers done in rural contexts and seem to suggest similar patterns. It is also notable that Ropars and colleagues (2019) found that honey bees have a high preference for managed over wild species of plants while native bees are much more likely than honey bees to visit wild species of plants and exhibit an equal preference for both wild and managed plants. This is in line with other studies that have found that honey bees prefer to forage different flowering plants than many species of native, wild bees including common crops, cultivated ornamental flowers, and 'weeds' that are native to Europe (Urbanowicz et al. 2020). This indicates that while there may be some competition between honey bees and wild native bees in urban environments, the nature of landscape practices within cities can have an important to role to play in the flourishing of all species of bees. Some studies about the relationship between urban honey bees and wild native bees have also shown that competition from honey bees has little to no negative impact on wild native bee populations, with one study from Michigan indicating that other species of non-native bees that are not honey bees were more detrimental to urban native bees than honey bees, perhaps because these non-native wild bees were outcompeting them for nesting sites (Fitch et al. 2019). A study based in Australia found that while non-native honey bees (which Europeans also introduced there) were abundant in an ecologically restored site, the native bees were nevertheless resilient and did not appear to be permanently impacted by the presence of honey bees (Lomav et al. 2010).

However, this should not imply coexistence is benign: clearly there can be an oversaturation of honey bees in specific types of landscapes and this may increase competition, or perhaps more worryingly lead to viral transfer (Casanelles-Abella and Moretti 2022). The authors of the Parisian study estimated that the urban environment in Paris contains 6.5 honey bee colonies per km^2, whereas London, U.K., is estimated to have 10 colonies per km^2 and Brussels has 15 colonies per km^2 (Ropars et al. 2019). One way to assess possible oversaturation of honey bees is to determine if there is a lack of adequate nectar and pollen collection among honey bees outside of dearth periods but this is an inadequate approach given that by the time honey bees are found to be deprived or starving many wild native bees may have already suffered.

Wild, native bees and commercial beekeeping

As indicated in Chapter 2, honey bees have been semi-domesticated for thousands of years in Europe, North Africa, and West Asia and have been present in North American landscapes for hundreds of years. The fact that honey bees and wild native bees have shared landscapes for hundreds or thousands of years suggests that indications of a recent increase in harm caused by honey bees through floral competition and pathogen transfer may be much less about honey bees themselves and more associated with the changing practices associated with beekeeping. The main changes in the scale and practices of honey bee management throughout the world have been driven by the development of large-scale commercial, migratory beekeeping and its integration into increasingly simplified and standardized industrial agriculture landscapes.

As described in Chapter 3, the intensification of agriculture necessitated the creation of a migratory commercial beekeeping industry which mirrors many of the practices utilized within industrial livestock agriculture (Ellis et al. 2020). The level of floral competition that migratory, commercial beekeeping operations bring to wild native bees has also been augmented by intensification on the margins of monocultures. Durant (2019) notes that many large-scale industrial farmers are increasingly removing hedgerows and patches of wildflowers on the edges of their farms to make room for more cash crops. In response, with more acreage devoted to cash crops, migratory beekeepers must find other places to rest their bees between pollination contracts, moving them close to areas of wild bee habitat, including in parks, conservation areas, meadows, or unenhanced pasture. A honey bee scientist at York University in Toronto who I interviewed for my PhD research (Ellis 2021) acknowledges that honey bees do compete with wild native bees at some level,

> I think that there can be competition in places because beekeepers will move hives to areas for specific crop pollination purposes and, for instance, if you're an apple grower and somebody moves in 100 hives during apple bloom, well certainly those 100 hives will be competing with native bees. There is a non-migratory style of beekeeping where the person just keeps the hives on their farm or wherever, that's somewhat less likely to compete because they can't keep more than a certain number of hives because of the amount of food in the neighbourhood.

As noted, along with competing for food, migratory, commercial beekeeping operations risk introducing pests and pathogens to both resident honey bees and wild native bees, as thousands of honey bee colonies get introduced to relatively small areas for short periods of time.

Sometimes native bee advocates argue that even a single honey bee colony is harmful to native bees, flooding the landscape with thousands of additional bees, but this is based on a misunderstanding of the nature of honey bee colonies and the life cycles of bees. In a colony, only a portion of the bees go out to forage in the landscape, while most worker bees remain in the hive carrying out various tasks related to raising brood, caring for the queen, creating honey, and protecting the colony. The foraging bees are adult worker bees older than 21 days, which is about half the natural lifespan of the average worker bee (Abou-Shaara 2014). It is not accurate, therefore, to characterize a single hive as flooding the landscape with 50,000 bees (a number that might be present in a typical honey bee hive in the height of summer) in search of pollen and nectar. However, hundreds of thousands and often many millions of honey bees do flood certain landscapes when commercial beekeeping hives are brought into an area to pollinate blooming monoculture crops.

It is important to recognize that honey bees are not the only managed bees that cause concern for bee scientists and advocates. The use of managed bumble bees in the greenhouse industry to pollinate tomatoes began in 1985 and is a growing industry throughout the world (Evans 2017), that risks spreading bumble bee-specific pests and pathogens (Colla et al. 2006). Bumble bees are efficient pollinators of the small flowers of tomatoes and other plants because of their effective use of buzz pollination (vibrating their body to shake the pollen out of flowers), and managed bumble bees have become crucial to the greenhouse tomato industry (Reade et al. 2015). Although bumble bee production companies do not release public information, Gosterit and Gurel (2018) estimated that worldwide sales of bumble bee colonies for the greenhouse industry is USD$3 million. The main species used in the commercial bumble bee pollination industry is *Bombus terrestris*, sometimes called the buff-tailed bumble bee, a bee native to Europe, coastal Africa, and West and Central Asia (Reade et al. 2015). The North American species *Bombus impatiens*, or the common eastern bumble bee, is also used commercially (Reade et al. 2015). A commercially produced bumble bee colony consists of a cardboard box containing 75 to 100 bees and pollen for their sustenance (Reade et al. 2015). As Reade and colleagues (2015) argue, these colonies are a "ready-made shelf product that is easily suitable for transport and marketing". Managed bumble bees face some of the same problems with increased pathogens that are familiar to honey bee colonies and domesticated animals more generally, due to being kept in closer proximity to one another than they would be in the wild, which allows for more rapid pathogen transfer. These bees occasionally escape the greenhouses in which they are contained and, as a result, *Bombus terrestris* can be found in regions of the world to which it is non-native including Japan, Israel, Tasmania, Chile, and Israel (Gosterit and Gurel 2018). Even though *Bombus impatiens* is the main commercial bumble bee species used in North America, there is concern that escapee commercial bumble bees may transfer pathogens to wild bumble bees (Murray et al. 2013; Otterstatter and Thomson 2008) and, in some cases, out compete for forage (Gosterit and Gurel 2018).

Urban beekeepers who I interviewed for my PhD research (Ellis 2021) expressed concern that the bumble bee industry poses a more serious problem than is presently acknowledged. According to one urban beekeeper, "if you really want to look for a villain in the native bee issue honey bees aren't it," because they "are very well regulated" whereas "bumblebees are not. So, there is a bumble bee industry in Ontario that has pretty much zero oversight." Another urban beekeeper noted that:

> There has been some good research about how bumble bees escaped from these greenhouses and basically decimated the local bumble bee population, because they were screened for honeybee diseases, but not bumblebee diseases. And that had a major impact. That's probably why we've … seen some bees disappear. I think only two or three companies in the world that are rearing these bumblebees en masse in the largest scale imaginable for a bumblebee, and they're being shipped worldwide and that's an issue [for genetic diversity and risks of pathogen transfer]. That is completely horrible, and no one's talking about that. I think honey bees can be an easy target because they're out there and there is some bad beekeeping going on.
>
> (Ellis 2021)

There are also a few other bee species that are commercially managed on a smaller scale in North America and Europe, leafcutter bees (*Megachile rotundata*) and blue orchard bees (*Osmia lignaria*), which are used primarily by the orchard industry as they are very efficient at pollinating the blossoms of fruit-bearing trees. These are also commonly available for anyone to purchase at nurseries for their own backyards or small farms. Unlike managed bumble bees, these bees are not contained, but are put into human-created nests in orchards or backyards, where they may or may not stay. While honey bees are the most populous and impactful non-native bee species in North America, there are also several other bee species that were unintentionally introduced from Europe or Asia, and it is possible that they too could increase competition for floral resources and nesting sites.

What does it mean for a species to be invasive?

Another layer of this debate in North America centres on whether honey bees, as a non-native species, are invasive when they fly outside of landscapes of capitalist agriculture. On the surface the definition of an invasive species might be simple and straightforward, focusing on whether a given species is presently established outside of their natural range and causing clear harm to a native plant or animal species. But it gets far more complicated depending on the animal or plant in question, which becomes quickly apparent when we consider how some non-native species get considered naturalized, and in the case of domesticated animals, are often seen to belong in a landscape. Almost all domesticated animals in Canada and the United States, for example, are non-native species, apart from turkeys (Larson et al. 2014) and dogs. Indigenous societies in pre-invasion North America did not have any other large, domesticated animal for labour or food (Perri et al. 2021). The matter of invasiveness is also complicated by the fact that many species of plants and animals have moved dynamically across landscapes, often with humans, over long periods of time, accelerating in recent centuries and now with climate change. A series of very complex questions arise. For instance, how do we determine harm when an animal plays important roles in human-created landscapes, systems, and lives? What if the benefits to humans (e.g., livestock) comes at the expense of wild animals (e.g., through habitat loss)? How do we determine if the non-native animal (or plant) is creating the harm or if the harm is caused by the socio-economic systems in which they are embedded?

As discussed in Chapter 2, many plants and animals were brought to the Americas by European colonialists, both intentionally and unintentionally, and the impacts have been largely destructive to ecological lifeworlds in the Americas as well as having many devastating effects on Indigenous societies. Although these plants and animals often had initial devastating impacts on ecological lifeworlds in the Americas, they have adapted, some over hundreds of years. The focus on invasive species within ecology and ecological restoration is often on individual species and specific ecosystems without contextualizing the historical and socioeconomic systems in which these species were moved – colonialism and capitalism.

Another problem with the concept of invasiveness is that it is often deployed in confused ways that uphold capitalist industries. For example, the Government of Canada (n.d.) defines an alien species as "species that have become established in areas outside their natural range," and indicates that

> generally, alien species do not pose a significant risk, and many are even beneficial. However, when alien species are capable of causing significant harm to our environment, *the economy* or to society, they are referred to as "invasive alien species". (emphasis added)

In this definition, a non-native species of plant or animal can be targeted as invasive if they cause no ecological harm but do interfere with crop cultivation or livestock farming. Within the field of ecology, there is no consensus on what exactly an invasive species is, how to determine invasiveness, and what to do with invasive species; in fact, there are heated debates about these issues within the sub-field of invasion biology that have been ongoing for at least two decades (Cassini 2020; Crowley et al. 2017).

In defining alien species, governments rarely attempt to place them in a wider historic context, and do not recognize that the extent of environmental impacts is often contingent on the socioeconomic systems in which they are embedded (e.g., cattle occupy a tremendous amount of Canadian land). The damage wrought by non-native species to the ecological lifeworlds of the Americas is, therefore, not necessarily inherent in various species but relates to their role in colonial and capitalist transformations. In other words, while some introduced species are harmful to ecological lifeworlds, negative impacts cannot

114 *Which bees shall we save?*

be separated from their socio-ecological relations within colonialism and capitalism. This relates directly to my contention that honey bees are not inherently ecologically destructive, but rather that their negative impacts are principally connected to their place in capitalist agriculture.

Do honey bees only belong in landscapes of capitalist–industrial agriculture?

The concerns about floral competition and pathogen transfer between honey bees and wild native bees has led to some heated debates about where honey bees belong. When I asked a prominent pollination biologist at the University of Toronto if and where honey bees belong in North America, he insisted that they do have a necessary function in conventional agriculture, but nowhere else. When I asked about the role of honey bees in small-scale agriculture, he indicated his belief that it is possible to maintain polycultural and organic agricultural landscapes without managed honey bees. Conservation biologists Colla and MacIvor (2016) argue that "there are important yet often ignored reasons why increasing their numbers outside intensive agricultural systems should be avoided. Honeybees have large colonies and have become invasive in all regions outside of their Old-World origin" (pp. 1202–1203).

In making this argument, Colla and MacIvor seem to be proposing that agro-industrial monocultures should be sacrifice zones in which we accept that most species of bees cannot thrive, which includes a view of honey bees as something close to a sacrifice animal. When viewing this argument through the lens of a political ecology that is critical of capitalist agriculture, there are a few problems. First, as outlined in the previous section the honey bees contained in large-scale migratory beekeeping operations tend to be very unhealthy, and are frequently moved over large distances in response to a problem posed by industrial capitalist agriculture. If one of the main concerns about the impacts of honey bees on wild native bees is pathogen transfer, then this system is the root of the problem, because the populations are so much greater and because sickly honey bees do not simply stay on monocultured fields or resting areas on their margins. Unlike other livestock animals, honey bees leave human created enclosures and ranges to find their own forage, which is clearly influenced by humans (reflected in the fact that pollination services can be bought and sold) but also reaches beyond human control at some level, with bees frequently moving as many as 5 km in the landscape, and up to 12 km if they are unable to find good sources of nectar and pollen, which can happen in heavily monocultured landscapes. Even if honey bees were only kept on monocultured orchards and fields, they would continue to swarm and sometimes go feral because swarming behaviour cannot be completely prevented by beekeepers. Although honey bees only swarm within a couple of kilometres of their origin hives, bee colonies kept in heavily populated areas of the world such as midwestern United States, Southern Ontario, and most of Europe, will quickly become established outside of industrial agriculture landscapes.

Another concern with the notion that honey bees should be relegated to sacrifice zones of chemical intensive monocultures is that the negative impacts of capitalist agriculture are not spatially bounded as some might like to imagine, but rather have serious impacts on nearby human settlements and ecological lifeworlds. In many countries around the world rural landscapes are increasingly dominated by monocultures of grain-oilseed crops such as corn, soy, and canola, with pockets of intensive fruit and vegetable production and concentrated animal feeding operations (CAFOS) scattered throughout. If more rural landscapes are converted to monocultures that require mechanization and high inputs of pesticides and artificial fertilizers, it will further reduce wild native bee habitat and necessitate more sickly honey bees are brought into these spaces as what Watson and Stallins call "rescue pollinators" (2016, p. 229). As an urban beekeeper said to me during an interview,

> focusing on honey bees versus native bees is entirely asking the wrong question ... you gotta ask, "why are we at the point where we need our cities to be pollinator sanctuaries in the first place?" It all comes down to the insanity of our agricultural practices.
>
> (Ellis 2021)

Which animals need saving?

Wild native bee advocates who are critical of hobbyist and small-scale beekeeping rightly point out that honey bees are not wild animals and should not be understood as subjects of conservation efforts. Some native bee advocates argue that people who misconstrue the problems facing honey bees in terms of biodiversity conservation are in fact engaging in 'bee-washing', in the sense that they are justifying expanding honey bee colonies at the expense of attention to wild native bees (Westreich 2020). While it is mistaken to consider the flourishing of domesticated and semi-domesticated animals as a conservation issue, it is important to recognize that agriculture has momentous environmental impacts and ethical implications, and that domesticated animals are still part of ecological lifeworlds. Weis' (2018) description of the way in which capitalist agriculture turns some animals into ghosts while others are made into things, is instructive here. Domesticated animals that are used in agriculture are vulnerable to polluted environments, toxic chemical exposure, and physical harms (Weis 2013), and the impact of pollutants and toxins on domesticated animals can give humans important early signals of wider public health risks and ecological problems. For instance, an attentive farmer will notice his cows are suddenly sick after eating poisoned food, and a mindful beekeeper will notice her colony's health is deteriorating after a field of corn is sprayed (Maderson and Wynne-Jones 2016).

Considering the strong evidence that capitalist agriculture is central to the problems facing populations of both honey bees and wild native bees, it is important to consider why some wild native bee advocates are putting so much focus on the presence of beekeeping in cities. To return to the example that I began this chapter with, why does the city of Toronto identify honey bees as one of the biggest threats to wild native bees during Pollinator Week and not even mention any of the larger threats? There has been limited empirical research on pathogen transfer and competition between urban honey bees and native bees, with only a few studies focusing on the relations between honey bees and wild native bees within urban environments. In contrast, there are many studies indicating that there are multiple and intersecting risks to wild bees (Goulson et al. 2015), including pesticides (Siviter et al. 2021; Woodcock et al. 2017), loss of habitat (Kline and Joshi 2020), and, increasingly, climate change (Soroye et al. 2020; Miller-Struttman et al. 2015; Faleiro et al. 2018; Kerr et al. 2015).

In my interviews with scientists who research bees, pollination, and ecology, they all acknowledged the fact that wild native bees are adversely affected by pesticides and habitat loss at some level, although one scientist downplayed the impact of pesticides and one claimed it is not as big a problem for North American native bees as European native bees (even though most of the same pesticides were widely used on both continents before the ban in the EU). These scientists also recognize that the loss of habitat and forage from urbanization and capitalist agriculture are major causes of population declines among wild native bees, and that there is growing evidence that climate change is negatively impacting wild native bees (Soroye et al. 2020; Miller-Struttman et al. 2015; Faleiro et al. 2018; Kerr et al. 2015). Considering these problems, I struggled to understand the focus on urban honey bees as a threat to wild native bees, and came to suspect that it may stem from a perception among some scientists that the negative impacts of both capitalist agriculture and climate change are 'wicked issues' that are too big for any viable, immediate interventions and therefore not worth focusing on, unlike the presence of honey bees in cities. Clearly, it will be much easier to eradicate the practice of hobbyist beekeeping through restrictive bylaws in cities like Toronto, Paris, or New York City than it will be to stop the global production and use of neonicotinoids or transform the global agricultural system.

In the debate about honey bee competition with wild native bees that I encountered in Toronto, some scientists have taken clear political stances and engaged in lobbying action against urban hobbyists and small-scale beekeepers. While I generally applaud the willingness of scientists to engage in political activism, in this instance I believe that there has been a misguided focus on the relatively small threat posed by honey bees, where there is limited empirical evidence. This is all the more jarring because it entails downplaying the much larger threats associated with capitalist agriculture and pesticides where there is ample evidence of harm, which in turn means, whether consciously or unconsciously, choosing not to confront agrochemical corporations (Fang 2020).

The idea that landscapes can contain large sacrifice zones of industrial capitalist agriculture without negatively impacting other ecological lifeworlds is simply not tenable, which is clearly reflected in evidence about things like honey bee foraging patterns and the persistence of neonicotinoid pesticides. Furthermore, efforts to increase sustainable food production from small-scale polycultures will require more pollination by animals, not less, and with the growing evidence that some wild native bees are already suffering from climate change (which is poised to get much worse), it seems even more important that people engage in efforts to manage healthier colonies of honey bees than prevail in most rural environments. I strongly agree with an urban beekeeper in my research who argued:

> Pitting one bee against another is taking away from the important issues, the way more important issues that are affecting native bees are pesticides, lack of habitat, climate change. You know, these are issues that are much bigger than having competition. And to pit bees against each other is, it's not really worth it. I think it's harmful for moving forward in terms of trying to get things changed.
>
> (Ellis 2021)

Even if it were somehow possible to confine honey bees to landscapes of capitalist agriculture, it would not be desirable to humans, honey bees, wild bees, or the global agricultural system for several reasons.

One, confining honey bees to capitalist landscapes in which they have been shown to encounter a variety of stressors may cause a plummeting of their populations that cannot be prevented even by the most vigilant beekeepers. The combination of poor nutrition, pesticide exposure, and possibly virulent viruses is widely agreed upon to be the cause of Colony Collapse Disorder (CCD) (Watanabe, 2008). Although CCD seems to not be as serious an issue for beekeepers currently, CCD or a similar phenomenon could rise again especially if honey bees are almost universally kept in poor conditions. In an article about debates over managed honey bees in Europe (which is part of *Apis mellifera*'s native range), Alaux and colleagues (2019) argue, "rather than creating opposition between managed honey bees and wild pollinators, and creating conflicts between stakeholders, we need to find ways to reconcile wild pollinator conservation with responsible and sustainable beekeeping practices in natural and/or protected areas of the honey bee native range". While they are discussing regions in which honey bees are within their native range, it seems equally important to support the development of sustainable, small-scale beekeeping practices in parts of the world where they are endemic and crucial to the agricultural system. Feeding 7 billion or more people a diverse diet made up of an ample amount of fruit and vegetables is likely impossible without the pollination work of honey bees. As has been demonstrated in previous chapters, some species of wild bees simply cannot thrive in the landscapes of scarcity created by monocultured agriculture with high inputs of pesticides and high levels of mechanization. Honey bees have been a feature of agricultural systems in much of the world throughout the 20th century, a time in which the human population, and need for food, has increased from 1.65 billion in 1900 (Roser et al. 2013) to more than 7.8 billion in 2021 (United Nations Population Fund n.d.). Although there is currently more food grown in the world than consumed (undernourishment is a symptom of inequality and poverty, not lack of food), it is uncertain how much food can be produced if an essential component of the agricultural system (honey bees) is removed.

Two, humans and honey bees have a long and entangled relationship, as described in Chapter 1. Not only do individual beekeepers often feel a strong sense of connection to honey bees, honey bees, and beekeeping, are culturally important in various regions of the world. This connects to a larger discussion about the cultural, spiritual, and emotional connections humans have cultivated over millennia towards domesticated farmed animals. For critical animal theorists concerned with the health and wellbeing of farmed animals, there is considerable debate and discussion about whether the solution to the misery and suffering of farmed animals is to eradicate domesticated species of farmed animals by letting them die out (Francione 2021) or to retain a relationship between humans and farmed animals, particularly older heritage breeds of animals, while eradicating the violence and exploitation of animal agricultures (Weis and Ellis 2020; Donaldson and Kymlicka 2010).

Three, and perhaps the biggest reason why honey bees should not be confined to the landscapes of capitalist agriculture is that this form of agriculture is extremely harmful and should itself be eradicated. As explored in previous chapters, the simplification and standardization of monocultured agricultural landscapes creates and requires landscapes of scarcity in which neither wild nor domesticated animals thrive. A domesticated or semi-domesticated animal being *numerous* in population should not be confused with that animal *thriving*. One has only to look at the short, brutal lives of chickens, whose populations have risen from 14.3 billion in 2000 to 33 billion in 2020 (Shahbandeh 2022), and who are typically bred to grow quickly; confined to small, cramped cages; prone to serious disease; and mutilated to prevent fighting (Weis 2018). Landscapes of scarcity have also been created through a high level of exploitation of human workers and the poisoning of soil, waterways, and ecological lifeworlds. Lastly, the agricultural system of the Capitalocene contributes to, and is threatened by climate chaos, which is likely to have devastating impacts on many species of non-human animals, including wild bees.

Climate change and the role of honey bees

Climate change presents a serious risk to bees of all species, particularly wild bees and this may make the presence of healthy and resilient honey bees even more important to agricultural systems, even small-scale, organic, and/or polycultural farms that reject the harmful practices of capitalist agriculture. In the often antagonistic debates between beekeepers and native bee advocates, climate change, and the effects it will have on insect pollinators is the proverbial elephant in the room. The 6th IPCC report indicates the extent to which the climate crisis is expected to accelerate in the next few decades,

> Global surface temperature will continue to increase until at least the mid-century *under all emissions scenarios considered*. Global warming of 1.5°C and 2°C will be *exceeded* during the 21st century unless deep reductions in carbon dioxide (CO_2) and other greenhouse gas emissions occur in the coming decades.
>
> (IPCC 2021, emphasis added)

A growing body of evidence indicates that many species of native bees are at risk from the increasing temperatures associated with climate change (Soroye et al. 2020; Pyke et al. 2016; Giannini et al. 2020; Gonzalez et al. 2021). In an analysis of 216 wild bee species in the Carajas National Forest in Brazil, scientists' projections indicate that 95% of bee species surveyed will experience decline caused by climate change (Giannini et al. 2020). The authors of this study posit that many species of crop-pollinating wild bees will be included in this decline, although they do not know what effect this will have on agricultural systems in the region (Giannini et al. 2020). In another study on several species of stingless bees in Columbia, scientists' modelling indicated that seven out of nine species would "experience a significant reduction in climatically suitable areas", and that this will have "significant economic and social consequences, particularly for species involved in crop pollination" (Gonzalez et al. 2021). The loss of stingless bees will be particularly disruptive for local and Indigenous people in the region, as they are managed by humans and are the subjects of beekeeping livelihoods, producing a rich and valuable honey, as well as other products of the hive, and are used to pollinate agriculture landscapes in the regions in which they live (Gonzalez et al. 2021). Stingless bees, wherever they are managed by humans, are also important culturally and socially. Their loss would reverberate across ecological lifeworlds and among the people who are in relationship with them. Similarly, in a recent study on bumble bees in North America and Europe, the authors found that recent climate changes have driven declines in bumble bees, especially in Europe, and warn that the effects of climate change, combined with other pressures such as agricultural intensification and pesticide use, may increase the extirpation of bumble bees (Soroye et al. 2020).

The proper response to predicted defaunation and extirpation of wild bees due to climate change is not to accept the loss, as there are clear actions that can be taken to promote the health of wild bees including banning systemic pesticides, engaging in ecological restoration, protecting forests from clearcutting, and engaging in ecological farming and urban landscaping. However, I do think that because honey bees already play a role as 'rescue bees' in agricultural landscapes that cannot be adequately pollinated by wild bees, this will expand as some species of wild bees continue to decline due, in part, to climate change. This is vastly better response than grim searches for high-tech solutions to animal pollinator defaunation and crises such as so-called robobees. The development of high-tech alternatives to animal pollinators involves the investment of large amounts of capital and STEM research and funding that would be better used to figure out how to transition away from agrochemical agriculture; or to create viable renewable energy sources so that humans can, as the IPCC recommends, burn dramatically fewer fossil fuels (IPCC 2021).

The focus, for all species of wild and/or native bees, should be to preserve their habitats and forage; and drastically reduce the amount of pesticides in the landscape. However, the threat that climate change poses is different than other threats faced by bees. Although there are powerful agrochemical corporations who will fight pesticides bans, pesticides can be banned and, over time, perhaps decades or centuries, the systemic pesticides in soil and waterways will dissipate. Habitats that have been destroyed can be restored to a degree, although like the dissipating of systemic pesticides, this will take place over decades or centuries depending on the type of ecosystem. However, changes to the climate that have already occurred due to historic greenhouse gas emission cannot be altered, nor can the climate chaos that will occur based on current levels of greenhouse gas (GHG) emissions. Even though humans can and should dramatically decrease the amount of GHG emissions released into the atmosphere, the amount of emissions already released will cause rising temperatures and chaotic weather events that are largely out of control of humans. Part of a mitigation strategy for agriculture should include raising healthy honey bees that can be used as rescue pollinators if native and wild bee populations decline in crop-producing regions of the world. Defaunation, it should be noted, is not the same as species extinction and of course there are species of bees such as 'wide habitat generalists', who gather nectar and pollen from a wide variety of plants and adapt easily to differing bioregions who are expected to experience little, if any, decline (Giannini et al. 2020). Honey bees should not be viewed as a replacement for wild or native bees. Instead, they should be part of agroecological systems that also include native and wild bee species. Honey bees should not be numerous yet sickly; instead, they should be healthy and thriving, and play a complementary role in an agroecological strategy to feed people with as little negative impact on ecological lifeworlds as possible. Healthy honey bees are an important aspect of agroecological systems in a future that is uncertain due to climate chaos.

Bee-centred beekeeping and healthy honey bees

If sickly honey bees have the potential to spread pathogens to wild native bees, it follows that efforts to raise healthier honey bees have the potential to improve wild native bee health. Hobbyist and small-scale beekeepers do not follow most of the harmful practices of commercial beekeeping outlined earlier, although they may not do enough to manage pathogens and pests, which are now endemic to all honey bees. Many small-scale and hobbyist beekeepers practise bee-centred beekeeping, which I define as an entangled and embodied form of beekeeping in which the physiological needs of the bees are consciously put ahead of the needs of the beekeeper. This is not to suggest that hobbyist beekeeping is unproblematic for wild native bees. Some hobbyist beekeepers are reluctant to treat their bees for mites or to monitor for other pathogens, which increases the potential for sickly bees and in turn potential pathogen transfer to wild native bees.

Some small-scale beekeepers are finding that cities are healthier places to raise honey bees. A research participant (Ellis 2021) who worked for rural commercial beekeeping operations before co-founding an urban beekeeping operation explained to me why he now focuses entirely on urban beekeeping:

> the move was 100% dictated by pesticide usage. So cosmetic pesticide bans in municipalities meant that it [the urban environment] was the only safe place to keep bees anymore. I was so discouraged and angry about pesticide damage that I was seeing that I just quit beekeeping for two years. ... I didn't want to get more bees just to watch them die again.

While some native bee advocates point to their concern about the competitive threat from honey bees for floral resources, as indicated earlier, studies have shown that honey bees and wild native bees tend to prefer different things, with honey bees more inclined towards non-native plants and the plants associated with human agriculture (Urbanowicz et al. 2020). This is something that a number of my beekeeper participants explicitly noticed, which this beekeeper summarizes well:

> everything in my personal experience out in the field suggests that when one pollinator does well, they all do well. And also ... we have so many different species of pollinators because they are all occupying different niches. And so, I pay attention to what's happening when I'm out in the bee yard, what's blooming, what bees are on and almost all the time, I will see plants directly beside my beehives without a single honeybee on them that are covered in different species of native bees.

Small-scale beekeepers have the potential to foster healthier honey bees because they do not generally move their bees, they do not maintain overcrowded apiaries or use miticides excessively, and they generally only supply artificial feed when they believe their bees are starving. The benefits for bee health are amplified when coupled with practices associated with mindful and organic beekeeping. One example of this relates to propolis, the sticky glue that honey bees make from the resin of trees. While several studies have shown that propolis has medicinal value for honey bees (Simone-Finstrom et al. 2017; Simone-Finstrom and Spivak 2012), it is a common practice in commercial beekeeping enterprises to scrape propolis off hives because it makes removing frames a quicker process.

It is also useful to examine how the scaling up of capitalist industries that involve non-human animals can increase the suffering of the animal. Like any form of work under capitalism, the various efforts and interventions associated with beekeeping can become regimented, and workers can be alienated from the products of their own labour. Further, when animals are directly involved in a capitalist industry, their bodies – and the products their bodies produce – become commodities and part of the mechanization and regimentation of the process, further increasing alienation of the human worker to the non-human animal. The relationship between humans and 'livestock' animals is always present at some level, but capitalist imperatives incline it towards exploitation and alienation and away from connection and care. Hobbyist and small-scale beekeeping, on the contrary, are often centred upon connection and care, and their unregimented nature allows beekeepers to engage in practices that are mindful and bee-centred (Ellis 2021; Moore and Kosut 2013).

My research of small-scale and hobbyist beekeepers indicates that an interest in honey bees can be a crucial stepping stone for people to develop and deepen their concerns for other bee species and insects more broadly (Ellis 2021). Because of this urban, hobbyist, and small-scale beekeepers may be some of the most important stewards for wild native bees. Many beekeepers tend to be highly visible in their neighbourhoods and communities. This visibility can relate to simple things like chatting with neighbours over their fence about their honey bees. It is also common for small-scale beekeepers to sell or gift their honey to neighbours or sell it at craft fairs and farmers markets, which are also great spaces for engaging in conversations with people about pollinator-friendly practices.

In many ways honey bees are the charismatic micro-fauna of the insect world, along with monarch butterflies, a suggestion that was echoed throughout many interviews with my research participants. As an urban beekeeper involved in a Toronto-based beekeeping collective states,

> I feel like honey bees are … the charismatic bee that everyone knows. I would love if people had a greater understanding, even myself, about how important native bees are too. And how we can help them, but I feel like exposure to and education about honey bees is important.
>
> (Ellis 2021)

A beekeeper who does a significant amount of community outreach also described the powerful education role honey bees can have:

> Honey bees can be a great [basis for] advocacy. They're like the panda of the insect world. People love them. People like honey and we can use that to bring up these other issues. No one is really looking after the native bees. They're suffering from the same issues the honey bees are suffering from. As beekeepers, we are in the industry and we're able to actually put some weight behind these issues, and make it part of our daily conversation, which we do. I think it's important if we sell bees, we should talk about what's harming the bees and not sugar-coat it.
>
> (Ellis 2021)

Hobbyist and small-scale beekeepers who are active and visible members of their communities may play an important role in promoting pollinator-friendly practices and building an interspecies alliance that can help all species of bees to flourish.

Against scarcity: creating landscapes of abundance

A philosophical and political aspect of the debates around beekeeping in relation to wild native bees that is often overlooked on both sides is a tacit acceptance of a starting point that needs to be contested; that is, both sides often accept the inevitability of the manufactured scarcity of the Capitalocene. Scarcity has been naturalized within capitalist societies to an extent that makes it seem as though there is limited space and resources for humans, let alone sufficient space for other species like bees. However, as I stressed in Chapter 2, the nature of scarcity is constructed within capitalism and the landscapes of scarcity that exist have been manufactured by colonialism and capitalism (Mehta et al. 2019).

An anti-capitalist critique of scarcity, according to Mehta and colleagues (2019, p. 228), illuminates how scarcity serves to sustain "elite and capitalist power" by justifying "resource acquisitions and enclosures, large-scale policy reforms in the name of 'austerity' and intensification of extraction whilst politically side-stepping more thorny politics of (re)distribution, mis-appropriation, dispossession and social justice". Further, the use of scarcity in justifying capitalist enclosure and austerity "has thus become an instrumentalized and totalising hegemonic and largely unquestioned discourse, with the application of particular forms of scientific knowledge, technology, governance, market mechanisms and innovation evoked as the appropriate solutions" (Mehta et al. 2019, p. 224). An anti-capitalist and anti-colonial critique of the politics and geography of scarcity needs to be coupled with an anti-capitalist, anti-colonial aspiration for abundance. For Collard and colleagues (2015, p. 323), the pursuit of abundance means striving towards "futures with more diverse and autonomous forms of life and ways of living together". Calls to create abundance, in this conception, can be important in political and organizing work, especially around food systems. There is, after all, far more than enough food produced in the world to feed the human population, and yet widespread hunger and food insecurity persists due to capitalist mechanisms of supply and demand (Patel 2009).

As Robbins (2007) argues and every gardener and farmer knows, ecological lifeworlds are constantly moving towards dynamic succession. Capitalist landscapes of scarcity are often very resource intensive and hard to maintain. Some ecologists seem to accept landscapes of scarcity as inevitable and following this, actively participate in creating more scarcity by focusing on removing further elements from landscapes, including people, non-native plants, or non-native animals such as honey bees. For some entomologists and pollination biologists, cities are conceived as important sites for ecological restoration precisely because rural areas are accepted to be monocultured sacrifice zones. However, this conception of ecological restoration is still limited, as cities are not treated as potential landscapes of abundance but instead as spaces where there cannot possibly be enough flowers to sustain both wild native bees and managed honey bees.

I believe that an alternative framework for multispecies flourishing is necessary, and this must involve rejecting the politics of scarcity and the ways in which it is deployed to justify capitalist enclosures, land grabs, and eradications. It should involve a new conception of abundance that focuses not on capital, money, and resources, but on the creation of ecological lifeworlds in which multiple species can flourish in the context of the ruins caused by colonialism and capitalism (Collard et al. 2015). As Collard and colleagues (2015, p. 329) state, "orienting toward abundant futures requires walking with multiple forms of resistance to colonial and capitalist logics and practices of extraction and assimilation". Part of this work must include confronting capitalist agriculture rather than accepting it as inevitable. Although there continues to be uncertainty about the impact of honey bee colonies on wild native bees, biologically simplified landscapes filled with mostly non-native crops do not tend to provide sufficient food supplies capable of supporting a diversity of bee species, and are therefore likely to foster competition rather than co-existence.

Given their role in pollinating many important food crops, heathy populations of honey bees are essential to feeding the human population in an uncertain future of climate breakdown. While large populations of sickly honey bees are presently managed in capitalist agricultural landscapes, there are many reasons to believe this is not sustainable for either honey bees or wild native bees. Because pathogen transfer can occur from honey bees, and other managed bees, to wild native bees, it is imperative for the health of wild native bees that honey bees are healthy. Although honey bees must be carefully managed, the potential that they can thrive in a variety of landscapes alongside wild native bees gives an indication of how multispecies flourishing can be pursued in capitalist ruins, if their mindful care is accompanied by efforts to create and expand landscapes of abundance.

Note

1 Pollinator week occurs every year in North America during the last week of June. It began in 2007 when the US Senate designated that particular week as "National Pollinator Week" (Pollinator Partnership) and is currently celebrated across Canada and the US, typically through events organized by various non-profit environmental organizations that focus on native pollinator health, often in collaboration with municipal governments.

References

Abou-Shaara, H. F. (2014). The foraging behaviour of honey bees, *Apis mellifera*: A review. *Veterinarni Medicina*, 59, 1–10.

Alaux, C., Conte, Y. L., & Decourtye, A. (2019). Pitting wild bees against managed honey bees in their native range, a losing strategy for the conservation of honey bee biodiversity. *Frontiers in Ecology and Evolution*. March 13. | https://doi.org/10.3389/fevo.2019.00060.

Casanelles-Abella, J. & Moretti, M. (2022). Challenging the sustainability of urban beekeeping using evidence from Swiss cities. *Urban Sustaiability* 2 (3). https://doi.org/10.1038/s42949-021-00046-6.

Cassini, M. H. (2020). A review of the critics of invasion biology. *Biological Reviews*, 95 (5), 1467–1478.

Colla, S. R., Otterstatter, M. C., Gegear, R. J., & Thomson, J. D. (2006). Plight of the bumble bee: Pathogen spillover from commercial to wild populations. *Biological Conservation*, 129 (4), 461–467. https://doi.org/10.1016/j.biocon.2005.11.013.

Colla, S. R. & MacIvor S. (2016). Questioning public perception, conservation policy, and recovery actions for honeybees in North America. *Conservation Biology*, 31 (55), 1202–1204.

Collard, R., Dempsey, J., & Sundberg, J. (2015). A Manifesto for Abundant Futures. *Annals of The Association of American Geographers*, 105 (2), 322–330.

Crowley, S. L., Hinchliffe, S., & McDonald, R. A. (2017). Conflict in invasive species management. *Frontiers in Ecology and the Environment*, 15 (3), 133–141.

Donaldson, S. & Kymlicka, W. (2010). *Zoopolis: A Political Theory of Animal Rights*. Oxford: Oxford University Press.

Durant, J. (2019). Where have all the flowers gone? Honey bee declines and exclusions from floral resources. *Journal of Rural Studies*, 65 (1), 161–171. doi:0.1016/j.jrurstud.2018.10.007.

Ellis, R. (2021). Pollinator people: An ethnography of bees, bee advocates and possibilities for multispecies commoning in Toronto and London, ON. [Doctoral dissertation, University of Western Ontario]. Electronic Thesis and Dissertation Repository. 7796. https://ir.lib.uwo.ca/etd/7796.

Ellis, R., Weis, T., Suryanarayanan, S., & Beilin, K. (2020). From a free gift of nature to a precarious commodity: Bees, pollination services, and industrial agriculture. *Journal of Agrarian Change*, 20 (3), 437–459, https://doi.org/10.1111/joac.12360.

Evans, E. (2017). From humble bee to greenhouse pollination workhorse: Can we mitigate risks for bumble bees? *Bee World*, 94 (2), 34–41.

Faleiro, F. V., Nemesio, A., & Loyolo, R. (2018). Climate change likely to reduce orchid bee abundance even in climatic suitable sites. *Global Change Biology*, 24 (6), 2272–2283, https://doi.org/10.1111/gcb.14112.

Fang, L. (2020). The pesticide industry's playbook for poisoning the earth. *The Intercept*. January 18, https://theintercept.com/2020/01/18/bees-insecticides-pesticides-neonicotinoids-bayer-monsanto-syngenta/.

Ferrier, P. M., Rucker, R. R., Thurman, W. N., & Burgett, M. (2018). *Economic Effects and Responses to Changes in Honey Bee Health*, ERR-246, U.S. Department of Agriculture, Economic Research Service, March.

Fitch, G., Wilson, C. J., Glaum, P., Vaidya, C., Simao, M., & Jamieson, M. A. (2019). Does urbanization favour exotic bee species? Implications for the conservation of native bees in cities. *Biology Letters*, 15 (12).

Francione, G. L. (2021). *Why Veganism Matters: The Moral Value of Animals*. New York: Columbia University Press.

Franklin, E., Carroll, T., Rickard, K., Blake, D., & Diaz, A. (2018). Bumble bee forager abundance on lowland heaths is predicated by specific floral availability rather than the presence of honey bee foragers: Evidence for forage resource partitioning. *Journal of Pollination Ecology*, 24 (19), 172–179.

Giannini, T. C., Costa, W. F., Borges, R. C., Miranda, L., da Costa, C. P. W., Saraiva, A. M., & Imperatriz Fonseca, V. L. (2020). Climate change in the Eastern Amazon: Crop-pollinator and occurrence-restricted bees are potentially more affected. *Regional Environmental Change*, 20 (1), 1–12. https://doi.org/10.1007/s10113-020-01611-y.

Gonzalez, V. H., Cobos, M. E., Jaramillo, J., & Ospina, R. (2021). Climate change will reduce the potential distribution ranges of Colombia's most valuable pollinators. *Perspectives in Ecology and Conservation*, 19 (2), 195–206. https://doi.org/10.1016/j.pecon.2021.02.010.

Gosterit, A. & Gurel, F. (2018). The role of commercially produced bumblebees in good agricultural practices. *Scientific Papers. Series D. Animal Science*, 5, 61–63. http://animalsciencejournal.usamv.ro/pdf/2018/issue_1/Art34.pdf.

Goulson, D., Nicholls, E., Botias, C., & Rotheray, E. L. (2015). Bee declines driven by combined stress from parasites, pesticides, and lack of flowers. *Science*, 347 (6229). doi:10.1126/science.1255957.

Government of Canada. (n.d.). Invasive alien species strategy. Accessed October 10, 2019. https://www.canada.ca/en/environment-climate-change/services/biodiversity/invasive-alien-species-strategy.html.

Herbertsson, L., Lindstrom, S. A. M., Rundlof, M., Bommarco, R., & Smith, H. G. (2016). Competition between managed honeybees and wild bumblebees depends on landscape context. *Basic and Applied Ecology*, 17 (7), 609–616.

Hill, A. B. (1965). The environment and disease: Association or causation? *Proceedings of the Royal Society of Medicine*, 58 (5), 295–300.

Hung, K.-L. J., Kingston, J. M., Lee, A., Holway, D. A., & Kohn, J. R. (2019). Non-native honey bees disproportionately dominate the most abundant floral resources in a biodiversity hotspot. *Proceeding of the Royal Society B*, 286 (1897). http://doi.org/10.1098/rspb.2018.2901.

IPCC. (2021). Summary for policymakers. In Masson-Delmotte, V., Zhai, P., Pirani, A., Connors, S. L., Péan, C., Berger, S. … & Zhou, B. (eds.), *Climate Change 2021: The Physical Science Basis. Contribution of Working Group I to the Sixth Assessment Report of the Intergovernmental Panel on Climate Change*. Cambridge and New York: Cambridge University Press, pp. 3–32, doi:10.1017/9781009157896.001.

Kerr, J. Y., Pindar, A., Galpern, P., Packer, L., Potts, S. G., Roberts, S. M. ... & Pantoja, A. (2015). Climate change impacts on bumblebees converge across continents. *Science*, 649 (6244), 177–180. doi:10.1126/science.aaa7031.

Kline O. & Joshi N.K. (2020) Mitigating the effects of habitat loss on solitary bees in agricultural ecosystems. *Agriculture*, 10 (4), 115. https://doi.org/10.3390/agriculture10040115.

Larson, G., Piperno, D. R., Allaby, R. G., Purugganan, M. D., Andersson, L., Arroyo-Kalin, M. ... & Fuller, D. Q. (2014). Present and future of domestication studies. *Proceedings of the National Academy of Sciences*, 111 (17), 6139–6146; doi:10.1073/pnas.1323964111.

Lomav, B., Keith, D. A., & Hochuli, D. F. (2010). Pollination and plant reproductive success in restored urban landscapes dominated by a pervasive exotic pollinator. *Landscape and Urban Planning*, 96 (4), 232–239. https://doi.org/10.1016/j.landurbplan.2010.03.009.

Maderson, S. & Wynne-Jones, S. (2016). Beekeepers' knowledges and participation in pollinator conservation policy. *Journal of Rural Studies*, 45, 88–98.

Mallinger, R. E., Gaines-Day, H. R., & Gratton, C. (2017). Do managed bees have negative effects on wild bees? A systematic review of the literature. *PLoS ONE*, 12 (12). https://doi.org/10.1371/journal.pone.0189268.

Mehta, L., Huff, A., & Allouche, J. (2019). The new politics and geographies of scarcity. *Geoforum*, 101, 222–230. https://doi.org/10.1016/j.geoforum.2018.10.027.

Miller-Struttman, N. E., Geib, J. C., Franklin, J. D., Kevan, P. G., Holdo, R. M., Ebert-May, D. ... & Galen, C. (2015). Functional mismatch in a bumble bee pollination mutualism under climate change. *Science*, 349 (6255), 1541–1544. doi:10.1126/science.aab0868.

Moore, L. J. & Kosut, M. (2013). *Buzz: Urban Beekeeping and the Power of the Bee*. New York: New York University Press.

Murray, T. E., Coffey, M. F., Kehoe, E., & Horgan, F. G. (2013). Pathogen prevalence in commercially reared bumble bees and evidence of spillover in conspecific populations. *Biological Conservation*, 159, 269–276. https://doi.org/10.1016/j.biocon.2012.10.021.

Otterstatter, M. C. & Thomson, J. D. (2008). Does pathogen spillover from commercially reared bumble bees threaten wild pollinators? *PloS ONE*, 3 (7), e2771. https://doi.org/10.1371/journal.pone.0002771.

Patel, R. (2009). *Stuffed and Starved: Market, Power, and the Hidden Battle for the World's Food System*. New York: HarperCollins.

Perri, A. R., Feuerborn, T. R., Frantz, L. A. F., Larson, G., Malhi, R. S., Meltzer, D. J., & Witt, K. E. (2021). Dog domestication and the dual dispersal of people and dogs into the Americas. *Proceedings of the National Academy of Sciences*, 118 (6), e2010083118; doi:10.1073/pnas.2010083118.

Potts, S. G., Biesmeijer, J. C., Kremen, C., Neumann, P., Schwiger, O., & Kunin, W. E. (2010). Global pollinator declines: Trends, impacts and drivers. *Trends in Ecology and Evolution*, 25 (6), 345–353. https://doi.org/10.1016/j.tree.2010.

Pyke, G. H., Thomson, J. D., Inouye, D. W., & Miller, T. J. (2016). Effects of climate change on phenologies and distributions of bumble bees and the plants they visit. *Ecosphere*, 7 (3), e01267. https://doi.org/10.1002/ecs2.1267.

Reade, C., Thorp, R., Goka, K., Wasbauer, M., & McKenna, M. (2015). Invisible compromises: Global business, local ecosystems, and the commercial bumble bee trade. *Organization & Environment*, 28 (4), 436–457. https://doi.org/10.1177/1086026615595085.

Robbins, P. (2007). *Lawn People: How Grasses, Weeds, and Chemicals Make Us Who We Are*. Philadelphia: Temple University Press.

Ropars, L., Dajoz, I., Fontaine, C., Muratet, A., & Geslin, B. (2019). Wild pollinator activity negatively related to honey bee colony densities in urban context. *PLoS ONE*, 14 (9). https://doi.org/10.1371/journal.pone.0222316.

Roser, M., Ritchie, H., & Ortiz-Ospina, E. (2013). World population growth. https://ourworldindata.org/world-population-growth.

Seeley, T. D. (2019). *The Lives of Bees: The Untold Story of the Honey Bee in the Wild*. Princeton: Princeton University Press.

Shahbandeh, M. (2022). Number of chickens worldwide from 1990 to 2020. *Statista*, https://www.statista.com/statistics/263962/number-of-chickens-worldwide-since-1990/.

Simone-Finstrom, M. D. & Spivak, M. (2012). Increased resin collection after parasite challenge: A case of self-medication in honey bees? *PLoS ONE*, 7 (3). https://doi.org/10.1371/journal.pone.0034601.

Simone-Finstrom, M., Borba, R. S., Wilson, M., & Spivak, M. (2017). Propolis counteracts some threats to honey bee health. *Insects*, 8 (2), 46. http://doi.org/10.3390/insects8020046.

Siviter, H., Richman, S. K., & Muth, F. (2021). Field-realistic neonicotinoid exposure has sub-lethal effects on non-Apis bees: A meta-analysis. *Ecology Letters*, 24 (12), 2586–2597.

Soroye, P., Newbold, T., & Kerr, J. (2020). Climate change contributes to widespread declines among bumble bees across continents. *Science*, 367 (678), 685–688.

United Nations Population Fund. (n.d.). World population dashboard. https://www.unfpa.org/data/world-population-dashboard.

Urbanowicz, C., Muniz, P. A., & McArt, S. A. (2020). Honey bees and wild pollinators differ in their preference for and use of introduced floral resources. *Ecology and Evolution*, 10 (13), 6741–6751. https://doi.org/10.1002/ece3.6417.

Watanabe, M. E. (2008). Colony collapse disorder: Many suspects, no smoking gun. *BioScience*, 58 (5), 384–388. https://doi.org/10.1641/b580503.

Watson, K., & Stallins, J. A. (2016). Honey bees and colony collapse disorder: A pluralistic reframing. *Geography Compass*, 10 (5), 222–236.

Weis, T. (2018). Ghosts and things: Agriculture and animal life. *Global Environmental Politics*, 18 (2), 134–142.

Weis, T. (2013). *The Ecological Hoofprint: The Global Burden of Industrial Livestock*. London: Zed.

Weis, T. & Ellis, R. (2020). Animal functionality and interspecies relations in regenerative agriculture: Considering necessity and the possibilities of non-violence. In Duncan, J., Carolan, M., & Wiskerkerke, J. S. C. (eds.), *Routledge Handbook of Sustainable and Regenerative Food Systems*. Abingdon: Routledge, pp. 141–153.

Westreich, L. (2020). 'Bee-washing' hurts bees and misleads consumers. *The Conversation*. https://theconversation.com/bee-washing-hurts-bees-and-misleads-consumers-131188.

Wojcik, V. A., Morandin, L. A., Davies Adams, L., & Rourke, K. E. (2018). Floral resource competition between honey bees and wild bees: Is there clear evidence and can we guide management and conservation? *Environmental Entomology*, 47(4), 822–833. doi:10.1093/ee/nvy077.

Woodcock, B. A., Bullock, J. M., Shore, R. F., Heard, M. S., Pereira, M. G., Redhead, J., & Pywell, R. F. (2017). Country-specific effects of neonicotinoid pesticides on honey bees and wild bees. *Science*, 356 (June 30), 1393–1395.

7 Pollinator people

Hopeful possibilities for multispecies flourishing in cities

One of the hopeful possibilities for the flourishing of bees of all species and the creation of landscapes of abundance are the practices of 'pollinator people'. Pollinator people are people who construct some of their identity based on their relationship with pollinators, engaging in practices and behaviours that are aimed to create pollinator-friendly spaces (Ellis 2021). This term contrasts with what geographer Paul Robbins (2007) calls 'lawn people', people who construct their identity, in part, around the maintenance of lawns. In Robbins' definition of lawn people, they become so deeply committed to the practice of creating a pristine lawn that they uncritically consume the products and ideologies of agrochemical corporations and are, in a sense, put to work by invasive grasses to keep them in a state of immaturity. Lawn people, Robbins argues, develop a concept of what it means to be a good neighbour and even a good citizen based on lawn-care practices and dismiss concerns that their practices may harm their or others' health or cause environmental destruction, even in the face of empirical evidence to the contrary. During my PhD research into the relationship between people and bees in the cities of Toronto and London (Canada), I discovered that pollinator people construct an identity around what they perceive as pollinator-friendly practices, often explicitly in opposition to agrochemical corporations and industrial agriculture and, in a sense, can be seen to be put to work by bees, native plants, and weeds to create landscapes of abundance. In this chapter I will discuss the practices of pollinator people, explored during my research with pollinator gardeners and urban, hobbyist beekeepers.

The North American lawn

The idea that cities are 'concrete jungles', thoroughly human-dominated spaces devoid of biodiversity, is being eroded by a growing recognition that some animal species manage to flourish in cities. For the past two decades, there has been increasing attention paid to the complexity of multispecies cities from a range of disciplinary perspectives (Philo and Wilbert 2000; Buller 2014; Jerolmack 2008; Moore and Kosut 2013). As explored in previous chapters, rural landscapes across North America, and many parts of the world, have become

DOI: 10.4324/9781003142294-7

increasingly hostile to both honey and wild bees with the loss of forage (Durant 2019; Roger et al. 2017), reduced habitat (Kim et al. 2006), standardized and biologically simplified monocultures (Tsvetkov et al. 2017; Ellis et al. 2020), and the high use of pesticides (Dance et al. 2017; Brandt et al. 2016; David et al. 2016; Goulson et al. 2015; Gill and Raine 2014). An increasing body of scientific evidence indicates that cities are partial refuges for honey bees and many species of native wild bees (Hall et al. 2017; Frankie et al. 2009), which has contributed to increasing advocacy and awareness about urban bees. Studies have indicated that urban bees of all species flourish in urban spaces that have a diversity of forage and habitat materials including home gardens, community gardens, and vacant lots[1] (Sivakoff et al. 2018; Garbuzov et al. 2015; Frankie et al. 2009; Matteson et al. 2008). While bee species flourish in a wide variety of green, urban spaces, few thrive in lawns, one of the most common urban and suburban landscapes in North America.

To understand the possibilities for bee flourishing in cities it is necessary to interrogate the ubiquitous North American lawn and to draw connections between the lawn and capitalist agriculture. Most North American lawns are made up of non-native grasses kept in a state of immaturity, and constantly tended by humans so they do not bloom, go to seed, or die back (Robbins, 2007). The most common grass in North American lawns is Kentucky bluegrass (*Poa pratensis*), which is not actually native to the US state of Kentucky, but rather is an herbaceous perennial species of grass native to Europe and North Asia. Unlike native grasses, especially those allowed to go to seed and form deep roots, Kentucky bluegrass has little value for biodiversity in North America. Robbins (2007) argues that lawncare practices aimed at keeping grasses lush, green, and short have huge benefits for *Poa pratensis*, as humans propagate it and allow it to colonialize urban and suburban landscapes while the plant expends little energy. Keeping it in a state of immaturity requires a vastly higher level of input than if it was allowed to express its seasonal lifecycle as a perennial grass. Robbins (2007, pp. 38–39) argues that the idealized aesthetic of the lush, green, weed-free lawn is incredibly hard to maintain for five basic reasons: polyculture is inevitable; grasses naturally go dull or brown; insects are the most abundant creatures on earth; lawn grasses inevitably go to seed; and organic materials decay.

In general, for lawns to have the lushness and uniformity that many homeowners and landscapers strive for, they need some level of external fertilization, watering, and herbicides.[2] Robbins (2007, p. 42) argues that the grasses in the typical North American lawns have agency that shapes the way in which people interact with them, requiring huge amounts of the time, energy, and money to maintain, to an extent that "lawn people have remarkably little 'choice' in the matter of labor and inputs, except insofar as they might choose not to have a lawn". He further suggests that

> if we consider these actions are repeated from household to household, block to block, across the densely yarded regions of suburban areas, we can

begin to imagine the rhythm of whole neighbourhoods, indeed whole cities, synchronized with the habits of grass.

(Robbins 2007, p. 43).

Some of the practices required to maintain the widely idealized lawn are harmful to both humans and non-human nature, something known by many of the people who engage in these lawncare practices. Robbins (2007) argues that the maintenance of 'attractive' lawns is deeply connected to conceptions of what it means to be not only a good neighbour but also a good citizen, especially the front lawn – which can be seen as pseudo-public space despite technically being a mostly private space. Researchers have found that people have very strong and sometimes contradictory feelings about their yards and lawns (Harris et al. 2012), and it is important to briefly consider how lawns became so ubiquitous in urban and suburban North American landscapes and how a particular conception of a nice lawn came to be seen as something that is, for many people, an important part of being a good neighbour.

The North American lawn cannot be understood outside of the violent history of settler-colonialism and capitalist agriculture. The expansion of lawns is an integral part of the enclosure of the commons, which is not simply an historical event integral to early capitalism but an ongoing process through which capitalism finds news markets, commodities, and frontiers (Federici 2004). Lawns became popular in 18th-century Europe when the homes of the wealthy were largely surrounded by pastoral landscapes (Harris et al. 2012), which had been created through the clearance of forests and the eradication of most non-human natures and humans. Lawns, ornamental gardens, and private hunting reserves – largely unproductive landscapes in terms of food and other materials needed for human survival – became important signifiers of extreme wealth (Jenkins 1994; Bormann et al. 2001).

The clearing of complex ecological lifeworlds to create simplified and standardized landscapes is a key aspect of colonial capitalism, and this was mostly associated with the expansion of agriculture and resource extraction until the 20th century. Prior to the mid-20th century, the expansion of lawns was largely dominated by the wealthy, though some lawns had been established in public parks, the policing of which helped to enforce bourgeois sensibilities (Bruck, 2013). It is safe to assume that the modern lawn was not something that most North Americans before the mid-20th century would either have aspired to or had the means to establish. For rural inhabitants, land was primarily thought of in productive terms, such as for cultivation, pasture, orchard, or woodlot. For most working people in North American cities prior to World War II, housing was dense and property was limited. Thus, the ability to have a lawn was overwhelmingly associated with large concentrations of wealth, and this did not begin to change until cities began to spread out dramatically following the rise of the automobile and suburban property became more broadly distributed. But it was not only the expansion of property among middle- and working-class households that began to make lawns both desirable and viable, it was also due to the rise of mass-produced pesticides, fertilizers, and gas-powered machinery which is where the lawn becomes intertwined with both the military industrial complex and capitalist agriculture (Robbins, 2007).

The post–World War II housing boom found some working people able to purchase modest homes in newly developing suburbia,[3] accessed through expanding public transportation and networks of highways (Jackson 1985). To draw young families to these suburban developments, they were marked as places to escape the dirtiness, pollution, and intensity of large city cores (Harris et al. 2012). One of the main draws was that people would have a little bit of land, along with their single-family home, a space to grow a garden or, more commonly, have a lawn. The lawn, in a sense, became democratized, but only for homeowners (Robbins, 2007). Lawns, cars, and the nuclear family became some of the most essential, defining elements of the ideal suburban life, continuing to dominate the way in which cities are currently planned (Alexander & Gleeson 2019; Hurley 2019).

The pesticides and artificial fertilizers first created for the military industrial complex made it possible for lawns to become the dominant landscape in suburban neighbourhoods across North America. The widespread application of pesticides and artificial fertilizers enabled a sharp increase in yield of crops (Robbins 2007) that allowed for an abundance of cheap food to flood the North American market. In the 1950s and 60s it was not as necessary for working people to cultivate a vegetable garden or keep chickens, a common practice to supplement diets especially during wartime and recessions when fruits and vegetables were rationed or otherwise scarce (Lawson 2005). Secondly, lawns would not have been accessible for working people owning modest suburban homes if they were not able to maintain them using cheap inputs in the form of mass-produced pesticides and artificial fertilizers (Robbins 2007).

Currently lawns are ubiquitous especially in suburban areas of large cities and 'green' areas of moderate to small cities and towns, typically in higher-income countries of the Global North. The country in which lawns seem to be most important culturally is the United States, although the American lawn has spilled over into Canada and other countries of the world. It is, therefore, not hyperbole to assert that lawns are the industrial monocultures of North American cities. Both capitalist agricultural landscapes and lawns require the standardization and simplification of landscapes to an extreme degree. Both capitalist agriculture and lawns put people in a war-like antagonistic relationships with insects, 'weeds', and other non-human natures, deploying similar weapons of pesticides, artificial fertilizers, and mechanization, owned and marketed by the same agrochemical corporations but on different scales. Both capitalist agriculture and lawns deploy these weapons to protect a small number of desired plants, such as corn and soy in rural areas and a mix of non-native grasses in urban and suburban areas. Both these landscapes are harmful to wild native bees. In the United States, 50% of urban and suburban areas are lawns, constituting the dominant form of land cover in urban areas (Lerman and Milam 2016) similar to the way in which monocultures dominate agricultural landscapes.

The pesticides many people use to maintain lawns directly harm wild native bees. Insecticides harm all or most insects that encounter them (Woodcock et al. 2017) and herbicides kill plants that may be important sources of nectar and pollen (Florencia et al. 2017), and may also cause harm to insects (Battisti et al. 2021; Abraham et al. 2018; Seide et al. 2018). Mechanization and fertilizers also negatively affect wild native bees, particularly ground nesters, as these processes can destroy their nests or make the soil uninhabitable (Packer 2011). Even the seemingly benign act of raking up autumn leaves can harm pollinators, especially overwintering butterflies, and moths, but also bumble bee queens who hibernate in leaf litter or just below ground under leaf litter as it provides added protection from the elements (David Suzuki Foundation, n.d.). A lush, green, and weed-free lawn is the opposite of what most species of bees need to thrive. Bees of all species need a diversity of flowers, with specialist bees needing the presence of certain types of native flowers, and wild native bees needing suitable materials and places to nest, which can include bare ground, pithy stems, or rotting wood depending on the species (Packer et al. 2007).

Rise of urban pollinator people

There is growing popular awareness and concern about the plight of pollinators, especially bees, which has sparked increasing interest in many North American and European cities in pollinator gardening and hobbyist beekeeping. Urban beekeepers and pollinator gardeners are two groups of people, often overlapping, who provide a glimpse of what it might be like to create backyards, neighbourhoods, landscapes, and lives in which humans flourish alongside bees. As I discovered in my PhD fieldwork (Ellis 2021), these pollinator people often construct part of their identity around the pollinator-friendly practices in which they engage, and promote counter-hegemonic ideas about how to interact with non-human nature and landscapes. The following sections discuss my qualitative research project, a multi-sited ethnography in London (Canada) and Toronto, about the entangled and embodied relationship between people and urban bees, including both wild and managed species. The fieldwork for this research included a variety of ethnographic methods: participant observation, semi-structured interviews, and 'walking while talking' backyard tours, and this variety allowed me to arrive at a comprehensive understanding of the urban bee advocacy landscape in London and Toronto. I participated in 500 hours of participant observation at urban farms, urban gardens, collectively managed apiaries, and pollinator conferences and events. My participant observation activities with beekeepers were conducted with two beekeeping collectives, the Toronto Beekeepers Collective (TBC) and the London Urban Beekeepers Collective (LUBC). I interviewed a total of 61 participants, most in one-to-one conversations, although a minority (11 in total) wanted to be interviewed with the people with whom they kept bees or gardened. Most of the interviews were just over one hour in length, with the shortest being 34 minutes and the longest being almost two hours. The sections of this chapter on pollinator people will largely draw from these qualitative interviews, which necessitates a change in tone from previous chapters. Pseudonyms have been used for research participants, except for people who wanted their real names used.

Urban beekeeping and bee-centred beekeeping

In my research (Ellis 2021) with urban hobbyist and small-scale beekeepers, I discovered that most of these beekeepers consider themselves to be involved in meaningful relationships with honey bees. For those urban beekeepers, beekeeping is pursued because honey bees are viewed as fascinating, interesting, and 'delightful' animals, and because they enjoy the conviviality of the human communities associated with urban beekeeping. Whether some products of the hive are collected or not, urban hobbyist beekeepers generally view their honey bees as companion species who possess a considerable degree of agency: that is, they are seen as rightful co-creators of both backyard and common spaces. My participants consistently expressed that what mattered most to them about beekeeping was its emotional, sensuous, and/or relational aspects. They saw themselves as being in an entangled and transformative relationship with bees. Over the course of my research, I came to see this aspect of beekeeping as something that allows beekeepers to express parts of themselves that are generally discouraged under capitalism and helps them overcome at least part of the alienation to non-human nature that is so common in everyday urban life in North America.

This chapter explores the central findings from my participant observation with the TBC and the LUBC together with an analysis of the qualitative interviews conducted with 14 members of the TBC and LUBC and 12 individual beekeepers (Ellis 2021). The type of beekeeping that is practised by most of my research participants lies outside the realms of wage labour and entrepreneurial commodity production. The time and effort invested in the practices of beekeeping can be considered part of a hobbyist beekeeper's social reproductive labour, in that they are engaged in an activity that (for most but not all) produces useful products for their household, brings joy and delight into their lives, and involves immersion in (and ongoing building of) convivial communities. For my research, I categorize beekeeping into three basic groups: hobbyist beekeepers (those with 25 or fewer hives who derive little to no income from beekeeping), small-scale beekeepers (those with 200 or fewer hives, and who derive some of their livelihood from beekeeping), and large-scale commercial beekeepers (those who manage operations with more than 200 hives).[4] Using this definition, most urban beekeeping in cities fall into the hobbyist category, with some small-scale operations. In this research project, 75% of the individual beekeepers (operating outside of the collectives) I interviewed are hobbyists.

Urban landscapes inherently limit the scale and restrict the mobility of beekeeping, and help to foster some distinct and common practices and it is important to stress the significant and sometimes contentious differences between urban beekeepers and large-scale commercial beekeepers (Andrews 2019). Urban beekeepers generally do not move their bee hives in the season unless there is a problem, such as a complaint from a neighbour or an inadequate hive location. They do not fulfil pollination contracts in cities and do not identify pollination 'services' as the core reason why they keep bees, although some frame neighbourhood-based pollination as a benefit of urban beekeeping. Most of my beekeeper participants practice organic beekeeping methods with varying levels of intervention, preferring to avoid miticides and prophylactic antibiotics if possible, and not routinely feeding sugar syrup or pollen patties, but do not dismiss these practices entirely and are willing to turn to them under certain circumstances. Most opt for an integrated pest management (IPM) approach, which essentially entails starting with cultural practices and using the least invasive methods as much as possible.

One of my central discoveries in this research is that beekeeping is an activity that demands all of one's senses and invokes a wide range of emotions. In many ways, hobbyist and small-scale beekeeping embodies Marx's argument that sensuous, concrete human activity with non-human natures is an essential part of what it is to be human (2004). The relational and sensual aspects of beekeeping are part of what makes these beekeepers become enchanted with honey bees, to the extent that they become pollinator people. For urban beekeepers, much of their time is spent closely observing the bees. Outside of the hive, beekeepers watch bees as they carry in pollen, noticing its different colours. During these observations, beekeepers often become accustomed to the colour of pollen produced by different plants and trees and notice the seasonal fluctuations in pollen-gathering activity among honey bees. Upon opening a bee hive, beekeepers carefully examine the bees on a frame hoping to find the queen and signs that indicate she is laying well. It takes time to be able to assess this, and beekeepers become skilled in spotting the tiny rice-shaped eggs located at the bottom of brood cells. When checking hives, beekeepers also look carefully for other things: signs of illness such as deformed wing virus and chalkbrood; mites on the bodies of adult bees; and the larvae of wax moths. Observant beekeepers also spend time watching and learning from the movement of the bees. Jenn, a Toronto beekeeper who managed a hive in friend's backyard, noted how she was captivated by the movement of bees:

> It was really cool … getting used to their little bee highways, the paths they took to go foraging. Cause it was like an invisible thing, but you get so used to it that you find yourself ducking and it was just like, I don't know, it really changed the way I felt about space in general. You just feel, like, it was really nice to get the opportunity to see how it's used by non-human creatures.

The sense of smell is activated with the rich scent of the beeswax and the intense, sweet smell of honey. Experienced beekeepers also become attuned to seasonal changes in the smell of the honey in the hive, as well as smells associated with sick hives. The taste of honey is a big part of the sensuous experience of beekeeping. Beekeepers often taste honey when a piece of the honey comb breaks during a hive check. Dan, co-founder of an urban beekeeping business in Hamilton, Ontario, and a paid mentor in the TBC, explained how he has developed a tongue for honey and can identify the types of flower nectar from which a particular batch of honey has been created. Touch is another important sense used regularly in beekeeping, although beekeepers differ in how much they utilize this sense because it requires using bare hands. Beekeepers in the TBC were not allowed to wear gloves during hive checks because without gloves they will be less clumsy, move slower, and be more mindful of the bees.

Another important sense that beekeepers develop over time is listening to the sounds of the colonies, as it is important to be able to hear and understand differences in the pitch of the buzz of the bees and notice when it changes. A higher pitch often indicates that the bees are agitated while a more frenzied pitch, combined with lots of bees circling a colony, can mean that they are about to swarm, which is an incredible sight to witness. Fran, a beekeeper and teacher in the Urban Sustainable Beekeeping Certificate program at Humber College in Toronto, describes the power of careful listening very well:

> As you get to understand them a little bit better, you can sense when you walk into the yard from the sound of them, you know, are they in a good mood? Are they a little testy today? And things of that sort. That helps in how you approach and sometimes you say, "okay, let's back off a little bit, give them a few minutes here". The more you understand them, the easier it is in a sense to work with them.

Over time beekeepers develop control over their own emotions. Many seasoned beekeepers believe that bees can sense fear and anger emanating from humans, and that the best way to ensure calm bees during a hive check is for the beekeeper to stay calm themselves. This is one reason why some beekeepers choose to wear beekeeping suits, as suits do not protect from all stings but can provide nervous beekeepers with a feeling of security that makes them feel and act confident and calm when checking a bee hive.

At the same time as it is important to be calm in the presence of bees, bees can also have a calming effect on the humans who care for them. Several research participants spoke about the calming quality of working with bees due to the intentional practice of mindful behaviour. Jenn explained how she finds beekeeping "meditative, it was a very relaxing exercise, very calming. Every time I went, I felt great and then you just notice small things more." Her friend and beekeeping partner Xavier described how keeping bees encouraged him to move slower and more mindfully, noting that "I am normally a pretty erratic mover and I wasn't forcing myself, but it was training me to move slower because the bees react to how you move and how you're feeling." Several beekeepers also reported that they find the sounds, smells, and presence of honey bees to be calming. Roberta, a founding member of the TBC, reflected on how this might seem contradictory to some: "It has always sort of struck me as amazingly soothing in a funny sort of way, because you think it's going to be scary. And then suddenly, when you're there, it's like you're in the middle of a ceremony. It's kind of, there's a hush. And it's lovely."

Research participants often spoke of the sensuous aspects of beekeeping. Fran noted how she was an artist and that beekeeping "actually fills or meets some of those needs. When I open up the hive, and I see, I smell, it's a very sensory experience." In a similar vein, Linda, a recently retired teacher and member of the TBC, insists that "it doesn't matter how many times I go in. It's such a sensory experience, the smell, the sight of the bees but that sound is so calming that it just brings my blood pressure right down." Claire, a hobbyist beekeeper in London, Ontario and member of the LUBC, highlighted the sensuous aspects of beekeeping in her explanation of why she enjoys it, explaining that "I like the hum; I like the smell. I like everything about it. I like watching them forage, I like them coming in with their little pollen sacks. I like watching them like on the side buzzing away. I just, I adore them."

In short, beekeeping is an activity that offers people the ability to concretely engage with non-human nature, engaging all their senses and intimately attuning people to the weather and seasons in new ways, including through fluctuations in nectar flow and the changing pollen availability of flowering plants. Part of the intensity of the experience relates to risk, as a wrong move when working in the hive can lead to the pain of the sting. The necessity of mindful engagement with honey bees can be transformative for the beekeeper. As Maureen, who hosts Xavier and Jenn's hive in her backyard, puts it, the decision to get involved with beekeeping is "a moment where your whole life can, like, I'm not trying to be too dramatic when I say this, but it is an invitation to a change right?"

My beekeeper participants reported that part of what made beekeeping meaningful to them was that it allowed them to engage with the non-human world in curious, creative, and joyful ways. For example, when asked how he feels when he sees a bee, Xavier noted that "I generally get pretty curious and want to like go up and touch it and like see it." When asked what honey bees brought to her life, Sylvia, a backyard hobbyist beekeeper in London, put it in clear terms: "Delight, it's just delightful to have them."

These ideas also came through strongly during my participant observation. During the bee checks done by the TBC and LUBC, I regularly sensed a collective feeling of awe and that people were genuinely excited to spend time with the bees, with feelings of both enjoyment and amazement often expressed, especially about certain activities. For instance, spotting the queen during collective hive checks was commonly regarded as a playful activity, and when she was found there was invariably a sense of excitement with people who may have been doing other tasks coming over take a look. In both LUBC and TBC hive checks, sneaking a taste of honey is another shared joyful activity, in which people often marvel about the delicious taste. Many of my beekeeper participants described "curiosity" as one of the most rewarding aspects of beekeeping. Emma, a member of the TBC, described this sense while recalling the dynamic of a smaller than usual TBC hive check:

> One day, there were only three of us that ended showing up to a hive check, and that was really good. I could be a little more curious and a had a bit more time to play ... and that was really nice.

Hobbyist and small-scale beekeeping allowed my research participants to engage in playful work, a term Ferguson (2017, p. 119) uses to describe labour that "approximates the sort of unalienated self-objectification that Marxists identify with self-actualization and freedom. It engages all the senses and brings imagination and concrete interactions with the environment together to produce a material and social world that satisfies human desires and need." Several participants described with pride various creative ways they had dealt with beekeeping problems, sometimes partly for the fun of it. Jeff, a small-scale beekeeper in London, Ontario, explained this creativity while discussing how he began beekeeping right after being laid off from his factory job:

> This was such a refreshing breeze, on a hot muggy day. I was 53. I missed my [full] pension by 18 months [by taking a buyout package], but it was like parole, I actually got out of jail 18 months early. And straight into the bee thing and I see so much interesting stuff. It's got a little woodworking component to it, something I never did a lot of, but I can be innovative.

After retiring he used his pension to scale up his beekeeping. As this quote indicates, being forced to retire early not only gave him a chance to focus on beekeeping but also to play around with new modifications to the hive. Linda, who had recently retired at the time of our interview and was transitioning to provide elder-care for her father, spoke in depth about how beekeeping with the TBC transformed her post-teaching life, reflecting that at the same time as she is "making their lives so much better" the bees "are helping me through a fairly lonely period in my life." Linda reported attending all but one of the hive checks in her first season of beekeeping with the TBC in 2017, as well as attending most of the community outreach events. She also described feeling a special connection to Black Creek Community Farm,[5] where we conducted the interview, which is near her home:

> I don't have an outdoors ... in all my teaching career I've taught in bunkers. Schools now are like bunkers. I taught in a very modern school that

had no windows. and I've lived in a high rise ever since I moved out of the house. So, all my grown-up life. I've never had that experience ... I always thought I would love to live in the country, in a small little farm and just have, you know, nothing hard, bees and ducks and so on. That's not going to happen ... this is my way of kind of seeing, you know, kind of realizing that dream. I can't have my own farm. So, I have this [gestures to the gardens of BCCF].

As these stories from Jeff and Linda make clear, beekeeping enabled them to engage in invigorating forms of playful work, and brought them a different (and in some ways greater) sort of intellectual and sensual reward than they found in their waged labour.

The relationship between many of my beekeeper participants with their honey bees is based on care and connection which led many of them to practise bee-centred beekeeping. For example, some beekeepers are very intentional about not killing any bees during hive checks. For instance, Claire described feeling both excited and scared the first time she checked her bee hives,

> because I didn't want to hurt them and I'm always thinking about you know, when you're sliding down the frames if anyone, any bee, got caught in there. I'd hate to hurt them. I knew that they had a great place to be and there was lots of nice spring flowers coming enough for them and they had a good water source and they had a windbreak and they were in the best place.

Linda also gives a sense of the emotional connection despite the numbers of individual animals, in describing her first time checking the TBC's bee hives, noting how she was suddenly handed a frame full of bees:

> I think I wasn't frightened. I just thought this is really powerful stuff. This is amazing. You're holding like 1000, maybe more, bees in your hand. And frames kept flying out. So, it was a full on, you know, sock in the face kind of experience. And I loved it.

The unregimented nature of hobbyist and small-scale allows beekeepers to move at a slower pace when conducting hive checks and to be more mindful within the hive. Moore and Kosut argue that people who work with bees (researchers and beekeepers) should strive towards "intra-species mindfulness" which entails "an attempt at getting at, and with, another species in order to move outside of our human selves" and involves "acquiring new modes of embodied attention and awareness" (2014, p. 520) through an engagement of all human senses. Along with specific practices, the slower pace is an important aspect of bee-centered beekeeping. In practice this requires beekeepers to minimize harming and agitating the colony as a whole, including individual bees when conducting hive checks and to ensure the bees can exercise as much agency as possible within the constraints of necessary animal husbandry.

In the case of hobbyist beekeeping, the formation of relationships with bees based on sensuous and playful human activity may allow beekeepers to become enchanted with the non-human world and to share that enchantment with others. My beekeeper participants regularly described feelings of awe and delight when encountering wild native bees, just as they do when interacting with their honey bees. Because of this attention and affection, beekeepers often relate to their land in ways that incline them towards pollinator gardening and makes them good stewards of wild native bees and insects of all kinds.

Swarming and honey bee agency

There are various ways that bees force beekeepers to confront and consider the realities of bee autonomy and agency, and I believe the ways in which bee-centred beekeepers integrate bee democracy into their practices can help to create new forms of co-existence with honey bees and other stinging insects. One of the principal expressions of bee agency and autonomy happens through or in relation to swarming in which half the colony, anywhere from 10,000 to 30,000 bees, leave the hive with the old queen, while the rest of the colony stays in the hive and nurtures new, developing queens. Although there is a common belief among people, even among some beekeepers, that queen bees are 'in charge' of the colony, this is not accurate, and the term 'queen' is a misnomer, implying power over subjects that is not the case in a honey bee colony. In fact, no individual bee is in charge of the colony and it is a collective colony decision when to start preparing to swarm based on the conditions of the hive including over-crowding and, more importantly, as a way to manage pests and pathogens in the hive. Swarms fly up to a few hundred feet from the hive, and form a cluster, usually in a tree, with the queen at the centre. Scout bees are then sent out to look for potential sites to set up a nest, and when scouts find a good nest site they return to the swarm and through dances, give the other bees information about their chosen site. Bees 'vote' for the location that has the best conditions by mimicking the dance of the scout bee they support. Once the decision is made, the swarm leaves en masse to the new location (provided they are not caught by a beekeeper first) (Seeley 2011).

Swarming demonstrates that bees have their own agency, and the complexity of swarming behaviour in spaces shared with humans shows some of the ways in which honey bee agency can collide with human activities, in ways that are both awe-inspiring and frustrating. Multispecies commoning does not always invoke feelings of magical enchantment, and there will inevitably be some friction between species that have autonomy and the people seeking to manage them, as well as between different groups of people. Swarming is one of the most powerful forms of bee autonomy because, as Seeley (2011) argues, the decision to swarm and the subsequent decision about where to make a new nest, happens through complex decision-making within the colony. As all beekeepers know (or eventually will learn), bees do not necessarily change their decision to swarm when humans intervene to stop them, and hives sometimes swarm even when beekeepers do various things to try to inhibit the swarming such as split the hive or destroy queen cells. To an extent, bee-centred beekeepers learn to live with swarming behaviour, accepting that it may occur and learning how to negotiate this behaviour while maintaining positive relationships with other people living nearby or using the space in which the bees are located.

In addition to dramatic episodes of swarming, bees also sometimes express their agency to beekeepers during hive checks in more modest ways, such as demonstrating their agitation by increasing the pitch of their buzz, incessantly following beekeepers, and stinging people when they do not want certain actions taking place within their hives. Sometimes beekeepers must take these actions anyway, even when it is clear the bees are expressing some opposition, especially if it involves treating or checking for mites or other pests, but sometimes the best response is simply to close the hive and leave the bees alone for the day. Bees can also affect beekeepers' behaviour in other more subtle ways. For instance, if beekeepers stand in the way of flight paths or in front of the hive, guard bees will intentionally and repeatedly fly into them to get them to move. A mindful beekeeper must learn to move out of the way. Beekeepers learn to recognize, respond to, and respect bee agency and autonomy. In collectively managed apiaries or apiaries located in or near public spaces, this can also involve discussion with other people about learning to live with and among stinging insects, reverberating beyond honey bees to wild bees and even to the often despised but absolutely essential bee cousin – wasps.

The long and entangled relationship humans have with honey bees can be based on care and connection rather than exploitation. In building meaningful and transformative relationships with honey bees in which their agency is recognized and respected, bee-centred beekeepers often also become advocates for insect stewardship beyond honey bees. With honey bees as the catalyst, this can create an opening to new ways of living, co-creating, and empathizing with insects. In the Capitalocene, marked by climate chaos and a 6th mass extinction, this might be the most important aspect of small-scale and hobbyist beekeeping.

Pollinator gardeners and landscapes of abundance

Although much of the media attention and environmental advocacy about bees has focused on honey bees, pollinator gardeners tend to focus their efforts on creating landscapes of abundance in which wild bees flourish. Efforts to promote the flourishing of wild native bees in urban settings often centre around campaigns to change lawn care practices and, in North America, to encourage people to plant native plant species in their gardens. Conscious efforts to cultivate pollinator-friendly gardens can bring people into meaningful co-creative relationships with bees and other non-human natures. Pollinator people can be powerful members of an interspecies alliance against capitalist agriculture and urban/suburban lawncare regimes. This section is principally based on participant observation and qualitative interviews I conducted with 20 people who describe themselves as pollinator gardeners (13 in London, 7 in Toronto), 9 of whom are also honey beekeepers or have a strong interest in honey bees in addition to their deep concern for wild native bees (Ellis 2021). These interviews took two basic forms: sitting down for interviews in a home, garden, or coffee shop, and 'walking while talking' interviews (13) in which the gardener gave me a tour of their front and backyards and, in one case, neighbourhood (Pitt 2015).

Pollinator people who focus on gardening practices foster a relationship not only with bees, and other insects, but with the plants they nurture in their spaces. Some social scientists acknowledge that plants have agency and a certain degree of autonomy (Brice 2014; Ryan 2012; Pitt 2015). 'Planty agency' can be seen when plants grow where they want and shape human behaviour in ways that encourage the further flourishing of their species along with complimentary plants and animals (Brice 2014). Robbins (2007) discusses the planty agency of non-native grasses, which have successfully colonized a large amount of the North American landscape, partly through their own physiological activity and partly through humans, who are dedicated to their propagation. In order to create spaces in which wild native bees flourish, humans must nurture specific plants based on scientific evidence about their habitats and key food sources. While this can vary to some degree for different wild bee species, in general it requires planting a variety of perennial plants, with an emphasis on ones that are native to the bioregion (Pardee and Philpott 2014; Morandin and Kremen 2012). In this way, pollinator gardening can be understood as native plants acting to partly shape human-managed biodiverse landscapes, in a similar way to how Robbins characterizes non-native grasses acting to foster human-managed lawn landscapes – though with a drastically different outcome.

Pollinator gardening is a deeply sensuous activity and is distinct from vegetable gardening. While vegetable gardening is also sensuous, embodied, and meaningful for gardeners, there is a focus on obtaining a human-oriented outcome. If a plant does not produce a crop as expected in a vegetable garden, the gardener is likely to consider it unsuccessful and may not grow it again, or may attempt to grow it only under changed conditions. In contrast, pollinator gardening typically does not produce anything other than nectar and pollen for pollinators, with the main purpose of providing food and habitat for bees and butterflies. Although pollinator gardeners can obviously cherish the aesthetics of the garden and experience delight and beauty in observing pollinators, in general human needs can be seen to be secondary. Throughout the course of my research, my pollinator gardener participants consistently described how pursuing this activity brought them pleasure. Mariam, a pollinator gardener in London, summarized this well, explaining that "the pleasure of being in a garden is part of it [her motivation], and seeing things grow, and to see the bees and the butterflies. I get great pleasure from that." She also gave an illuminating description of the changes that she has noticed since planting native plants in her boulevard:

> Last summer, there was a buzz in the boulevard section that is all native. It was fabulous. The sound was just beautiful. The bees were there and there was a lot of different butterflies in the garden also. So, I think that they are starting to know that there are possibilities here.

Roger, a honey bee researcher at York University in Toronto who has an extensive native plant backyard in central Toronto, also gave a good sense of the key motivations behind pollinator gardening, which for him is at once oriented towards non-human nature while providing enjoyment as well as a basis for education. When I asked Roger what motivates him to maintain his garden, he explained:

> One is for my personal pleasure where I simply try to enjoy flowers and the variety of bees that come to them and that's one of the reasons why my continued battle with the racoons is important to me because there's a plant, pickerelweed in the pond, which attracts a very rare kind of native bee but the racoons like to munch it. So that's for my pleasure and then as a community engagement activity I teach people to do pollinator gardens and help get them installed.

When I asked my pollinator gardener participants what this activity brings to their lives, the answers had very strong echoes to the sorts of answers given by my urban beekeeper participants, including regular use of terms like 'delight', 'joy', and 'awe'. Andris, a gardener in London who has founded several community garden initiatives, described his motivation in clear terms, simply stating that "I love it, and in fact, when I walk through my garden and I see the various plants buzzing with bees, I feel overjoyed."

Similar to urban and hobbyist beekeepers, pollinator gardeners contrasted the playful work they do in their gardens with their paid work. Carol, an enthusiastic gardener, clearly distinguished the sense of enjoyment she gets from the work done in her garden and the work done at her paid job. She described working long hours during weekdays, including long commutes on public transit, and how she cherished her time in the garden, both because of the direct enjoyment it brings and because of how this helps her relax from her weekly working rhythm:

> I would spend almost all my spare time in my garden if I can, but I don't because I work in the West End. I'm not usually in the garden during the week, I might go through and pick off a few things, pull a few weeds and

that kind of thing. But I don't do anything really extensive. On the weekends I'll probably spend, If I'm lucky, I spend six hours in my garden ... It's almost like meditation without sitting doing nothing sort of thing. Like, you can be busy and accomplish something. But you're not really thinking about a lot except for like, clearing some weeds or that kind of thing. So, it's a meditative sort of thing. Its relaxing. I started it when my kids were little cause, I'd be like, "Oh, I need to go out and garden". It's a way for me to unwind.

While my pollinator gardener participants identified a range of motivations, the primary reason overarching them all is a concern about the declining health and population of pollinators, with a focus on bees and butterflies. Lily, a prolific pollinator gardener in London, conveys this general motivation succinctly, as well as reflecting on how this benefits her at an emotional level:

I read the news. I saw that pollinators were in trouble and I love the look of hummingbirds and butterflies. So, it was partly aesthetic. I partly wanted beauty around me, and birds and bees are a part of that and the more I got into it the more interested I got at helping all pollinators and not just the poster children.

The work that pollinator gardeners pursue in their gardens is mostly aimed at creating conditions for pollinators to flourish. In order to create these conditions, pollinator gardeners engage in sensuous human activity that is spatially bound – meaning that it is deeply rooted in their specific bioregion – and this in turn leads to a strong attachment to place. Working a garden for a long period of time can lead to an intimate knowledge about the conditions of the soil, such as whether it is dry or moist, lacking in organic matter, sandy, or heavy with clay. While this intimate relationship to the soil is common to all types of gardening (at least for serious gardeners), pollinator gardeners can face particular challenges, especially at the outset, as most species of native and perennial plants thrive once established but will take off only under the right initial conditions. For example, woodland plants need moist, nutrient-rich soil and partial shade and simply will not thrive in full sun with sandy soil, while meadow plants need sun and well-draining soil.

My pollinator gardener participants consistently expressed taking great pride in their ability to attract an abundance of individual pollinators and a wide diversity of species to their gardens, as well as spending considerable time observing them. Some of my participants described how they enjoyed learning to identify specific species of bees and butterflies. Serena, a member of TBC and enthusiastic pollinator gardener in Toronto, shares her gardening tasks with her three young daughters, including the raising of mason bees and praying mantises, and she explained how it is part of a process of continual learning:

Certainly, when I started gardening, I don't think I really made the connection [between specific plants and insects] and since having bees I like allowing the mint to [flower]. [For instance] last year we just decided we were going to just let it [the mint] take over and let the whole thing flower. And then it was like this haven and I feel like that was really nice to watch all the bees come and the variety you see when walking around the city.

My pollinator gardener participants consistently indicated a willingness to accept the agency of wild native bees in choosing the habitats they want, and often adapt their lives to some degree to protect or avoid disturbing nesting bees. If pollinator gardeners know that ground dwelling native bees are nesting in their garden, rather than feeling threatened, they tend to feel a responsibility to protect these areas and encourage bees to continue living there. This is illustrated in a story that Carol told me about first discovering the sweat bee nests in her garden: "we have the sweat bees, we have quite a few little colonies. At first, I didn't know what they were, they're kind of creepy, this little green head. Like, 'Hey, I'm not sure what you are but …' and [now] they've lived there for years." During our interview, she showed me the nesting holes and described how it has affected her garden work, noting that "I try to remember not to cover their holes when I'm working in this area," and that whereas she first found them creepy now finds them "kinda cute, their little green heads. Because sometimes they'll just sit there in the hole and like just look and you think 'what the heck?!'"

Pollinator gardeners are not only forming new and embodied relationships with insects, but their deep focus on pollinators is propelling them to be stewards of wild spaces, however small, of multispecies flourishing. A key part of this is helping to regenerate ecological lifeworlds by encouraging native plant species to flourish alongside the non-native plants – 'weedy' and cultivated – that thrive in urban landscapes. Advocacy for native plant gardening that is explicitly political, rooted in both a critique of colonialism and capitalist agriculture, has transformative potential. Lorraine Johnson, a native gardening author and expert, illustrates the form this might take, with her advocacy against property standard by-laws, which she characterizes as attempts to enforce colonial control over landscapes. She articulates this powerfully in a *Toronto Star* op-ed responding to a native plant gardener being ordered by the City of Toronto to cut down her native, front-yard garden:

> A meadow might look "messy" and disordered, but whose health and safety does its diversity threaten? The only threat it offers is to an aesthetic of control — the "normal" look of yards and gardens that treat all insects as pests and all abundance as an affront. Are we really still comfortable defending an aesthetic that is rooted in colonial ideas of control? Landscapes that weed out difference and subvert indigenous plants?
>
> (Johnson 2020)

Another potentially political aspect of native plant gardening is that it can lead people to establish forms of commoning based on sharing seeds and plants and collective gardening in public spaces (Lang 2014). Native plant enthusiasts often gather to exchange seeds, plants, knowledge, and skills, most of which is done through seed and plant swaps and without any monetary exchange. Roberta is active in the Toronto Seed Library, and she indicated to me that her main priority in maintaining her community garden plot is to grow native plants whose seeds go into the library. Andris and Roger have set up pollinator gardens in public spaces, with Andris also establishing two community food forests that contain some native trees and shrubs. Mariam reported removing the fence between her yard and her neighbours yard in order to share garden space, as well as installing a pathway in her garden that starts on the public boulevard and goes into her backyard so that neighbourhood children can meander among the bees and butterflies. Sara, a native gardener and butterfly enthusiast in London, described participating in native plant 'rescue missions' with her neighbours under cover of darkness as bulldozers tore down an old hospital and threatened the surrounding vegetation.

Of course, the sharing of seeds, plants, knowledges, and skills happens among all types of gardeners, and is not unique to pollinator and native plant gardening; indeed, this is an aspect of gardening that gives it such great community-building and commoning potential. However, gardening with native plants seems to generate an even bigger compulsion for pollinator people to engage in acts of commoning. A big part of this stems from the fact that native plants are mostly perennial, which means that they reproduce quickly once established in appropriate conditions. It is common for gardeners to have to cut back rootstock to keep plants under control and for the plant to produce an abundance of seeds, which means that in thriving gardens, there is abundant plant material available for sharing every year. If this work stays within the boundary of one's private property or the lines of an individual community garden plot, it can have ecological benefits for pollinators and social benefits for gardeners. However, pollinator gardening can become more broadly transformative when it pushes beyond those boundary lines, spilling out into pseudo-public spaces, like boulevards, and public spaces, like parks, where it can begin to unsettle the landscape. It is notable that none of my research participants described their gardening practices in terms of the property value of their home, and instead posited their gardening as being in direct opposition to ecological destruction. For many of these pollinator people, they viewed their gardening as a political act of resistance, however small, and while this did not directly lead them towards more radical critiques of colonization and private property it was often infused with a critique of the destruction of non-human nature by capitalist industries that can potentially be mobilized.

During my research, I found that many of my participants shared a sense of pollinator gardens as enchanted spaces, as they often described very familiar perceptions and experiences. Although seemingly very different activities, there are important similarities between pollinator gardening and hobbyist beekeeping, as both bring people into relationships with insects and both are sensuous practices that require considerable time, energy, and skill, but are not tied directly to livelihood or subsistence for most people (though they can contribute to meeting some basic needs). They are also activities that nurture a diversity of life, that can replicate itself largely outside of the reaches of capitalism. So, while capitalist imperatives might shape the nature of the landscapes they inhabit, honey bees still swarm and perennial plants still go to seed and multiply through runners and roots. They are non-human natures that cannot be fully commoditized, because while they can be encouraged (and discouraged) they can never be fully controlled by humans.

In sum, pollinator gardeners strive to co-create spaces with wild native bees in ways that allow for bee autonomy and agency by carefully observing the interactions of pollinators with plants, removing plants that are not well-liked by pollinators, and keeping or establishing plants that they observe a lot of pollinators visiting. This means accepting the locations of bee nests, gardening around bee nests so as not disturb the bees, engaging in practices that create habitat sites, and providing nesting materials. For some people this entailed changing long-held practices, such as the mulching of garden beds or the raking of dead leaves. At a broader philosophical or spiritual level, pollinator gardeners tend to conceive of themselves as being in a mutually beneficial relationship with bees, butterflies, and other pollinators, in which they derive considerable benefits, not only through their activities as pollinators but as co-creating enchanting and delightful spaces in which the gardeners also clearly benefit, finding joy, a sense of calm, and purpose.

Pollinator people and bee flourishing

Pollinator people have an important role to play in promoting bee flourishing in cities, which is crucial because many species of bees, including managed honey bees, are vulnerable animals in the landscapes of capitalist agriculture. In their engagement in the playful work of hobbyist beekeeping and pollinator gardening, pollinator people form an embodied and transformative relationship with bees, and often other non-human natures. In my research, I found that this relationship led to pollinator people being highly critical of the capitalist agricultural system, including of the practices of commercial beekeeping and the monocultured and pesticide-laden landscapes. Pollinator people can be important members of an interspecies alliance to confront capitalist agriculture because they are often dedicated to and draw part of their identify from the creation of landscapes of abundance in which non-human nature flourishes. Marxist-feminist Silvia Federici (2019) argues that to break out of capitalist-induced alienation with non-human natures, people must become re-enchanted with the world, and I believe that insects have an important part to play in this, though even dedicated animal liberation advocates often find insects difficult animals with which to emotionally connect. The encounters that urban pollinator people have with both honey bees and wild native bees may be an important way in which humans can become enchanted with and delighted by insects.

Notes

1 It is important to note that while many species of wild bees flourish in cities, some do not. In Ontario, for example, some species of bees fail to flourish in both agricultural landscapes and urban or suburban landscapes, the most notable being the rusty-patched bumble bee. The rusty-patched bumble bee was estimated to be the most common species of bumble bee in Ontario in the mid-1900s but is now likely extirpated in the province as it has not been seen since 2009 at Pinery Provincial Park (Government of Ontario n.d.).
2 Insecticide use on lawns is not as common as there are few adult insects that eat the grass. However, there are larvae of insects, grubs, who live in the soil and these are killed in various ways the main reason being to prevent urban wild animals such as skunks from digging them up, thereby messing up the uniformity of the lawn.
3 It is important to note here how white supremacy in Canada and the United States restricted home ownership for many racialized people to certain neighbourhoods and, in many cases, restricted it altogether. For example, see Woods (2012) and Harris and Forrester (2003).
4 I do this with the recognition that there can be no absolute definition between hobbyist and small-scale beekeepers: the divide is simply too fuzzy in some instances, with governmental definitions varying depending on the criteria they set for grants or information gathering. Yet while there is a difference that is worth indicating between hobbyist and small-scale beekeepers, at the same they tend to share many common practices that sharply distinguish them from large-scale commercial operations, and therefore I interviewed both types of beekeepers.
5 Black Creek Community Farm is a not-for-profit urban farm in Toronto that is committed to organic farming, racial justice, and ecological sustainability. It hosts one of the TBC's apiaries.

References

Abraham, J., Benhotens, G. S., Krampah, I., Tagba, J., Amissah, C., & Abraham, J. D. (2018). Commercially formulated glyphosate can kill non-target pollinator bees under laboratory conditions. *Entomologica Experimentalis et Applictata*, 16 (8), 695–702.

Alexander, S. & Gleeson, B. (2019). *Degrowth in the Suburbs: A Radical Urban Imaginary*. London: Palgrave Macmillan.

Andrews, E. (2019). To save the bees or not to save the bees: Honey bee health in the Anthropocene. *Agriculture and Human Values*, 36, 891–902, https://doi.org/10.1007/s10460-019-09946-x.

Battisti, L., Potrich, M., Sampaio, A. R., Ghisi, N., Costa-Maia, F., Abati, R., Martinez, C., & Sofia, S. H. (2021). Is glyphosate toxic to bees? A meta-analytical review. *Science of the Total Environment*, 767 (145397), https://doi.org/10.1016/j.scitotenv.2021.145397.

Bormann, F. H., Balmori, D., & Geballe, G. T. (2001). *Redesigning the American Lawn: A Search for Environmental Harmony*. New Haven: Yale University Press.

Brandt, A., Gorenfloe, A., Reinhold, S., Meixner, M., & Buchler, R. (2016). The neonicotinoids thiacloprid, imidacloprid, and clothianidin affect the immunocompetence of honey bees (*Apis mellifera* L.). *Journal of Insect Physiology*, 85, 40–47.

Brice, J. (2014). Attending to grape vines: Perceptual practices, planty agencies and multiple temporalities in Australian viticulture. *Social and Cultural Geography*, 15 (8), 942–965.

Bruck, J. (2013). Landscapes of desire: Parks, colonialism and identity in Victorian and Edwardian Ireland. *International Journal of Historical Archaeology*, 17 (1), 196–223.

Buller, H. (2014). Animal geographies I. *Progress in Human Geography*, 38 (2), 308–318.

Dance, C., Botias, C., & Goulson, D. (2017). The combined effects of a monotonous diet and exposure to thiamethoxam on the performance of bumblebee micro-colonies. *Ecotoxicology and Environmental Safety*, 139, 194–201.

David, A., Botias, C., Abdul-Sada, A., Nicholls, E., Rotheray, E. L., Hill, E. M., & Goulson, D. (2016). Widespread contamination of wildflower and bee-collected pollen with complex mixtures of neonicotinoids and fungicides commonly applied to crops. *Environment International*, 88 (3), 169–178.

David Suzuki Foundation. Why you should leave the leaves. Accessed September 29, 2020, https://davidsuzuki.org/queen-of-green/how-to-leave-the-leaves/.

Durant, J. (2019). Where have all the flowers gone? Honey bee declines and exclusions from floral resources. *Journal of Rural Studies*, 65 (1), 0.1016/j.jrurstud.2018.10.007.

Ellis, R. (2021). Pollinator people: An ethnography of bees, bee advocates and possibilities for multispecies commoning in Toronto and London, ON. [Doctoral dissertation, University of Western Ontario]. *Electronic Thesis and Dissertation Repository*. 7796. https://ir.lib.uwo.ca/etd/7796.

Ellis, R. (2022). Social reproduction, playful work, and bee-centred beekeeping. Agriculture and Human Values. https://doi.org/10.1007/s10460-022-10319-0

Ellis, R., Weis, T., Suryanarayanan, S., & Beilin, K. (2020). From a free gift of nature to a precarious commodity: Bees, pollination services, and industrial agriculture. *Journal of Agrarian Change*, 20 (3), 437–459, https://doi.org/10.1111/joac.12360.

Federici, S. (2019). *Re-enchanting the World: Feminism and the Politics of the Commons*. Oakland: PM Press.

Federici, S. (2004). *Caliban and the Witch: Women, the Body, and Primitive Accumulation*. Brooklyn: Autonomedia.

Ferguson, S. (2017). Children, childhood and capitalism: A social reproduction perspective. In Bhattacharya, T. (ed.), *Social Reproduction Theory: Re-mapping Class, Re-centering Oppression*. London: Pluto Press, pp. 112–130.

Florencia, F. M., Carolina, T., Enzo, B., & Leonardo, G. (2017). Effects of the herbicide glyphosate on non-target plant native species from Chaco Forest (Argentina). *Ecotoxicology and Environmental Safety*, 144, 360–368. https://doi.org/10.1016/j.ecoenv.2017.06.049.

Frankie, G. W., Thorp R. W., Hernandez, J., Rizzardi, M., Ertter, B., Pawelek, J.C. … & Wojcik, V. C. (2009). Native bees are a rich natural resource in urban California gardens. *California Agriculture*, 63 (3), 113–120.

Garbuzov, M., Schurch, R., & Ratnieks, F. (2015). Eating locally: Dance decoding demonstrates that urban honey bees in Brighton, UK, forage mainly in the surrounding urban area. *Urban Ecosystems*, 18 (2), 411–418.

Gill, R. J. & Raine, N. E. (2014). Chronic impairment of bumblebee natural foraging behaviour induced by sublethal pesticide exposure. *Functional Ecology*, 28, 1459–1471.

Goulson, D., Nicholls, E., Botias, C., & Rotheray, E. L. (2015). Bee declines driven by combined stress from parasites, pesticides, and lack of flowers. *Science*, 347 (6229). 10.1126/science.1255957.

Government of Ontario. *Rusty-patched bumble bee*. Accessed October 15, 2020. https://www.ontario.ca/page/rusty-patched-bumble-bee.

Hall, D. M., Camilo, G. R., Tonietto, R. K., Ollerton, J., Ahrne, K., Arduser, M. … & Threlfall, C. G. (2017). The city as a refuge for insect pollinators. *Conservation Biology*, 31(1), 24–29. https://doi.org/10.1111/cobi.12840.

Harris, R. & Forrester, D. (2003). The suburban origins of redlining: A Canadian case study, 1935–54. *Urban Studies*, 40 (19), 2661–2686, https://doi.org/10.1080/0042098032000146830.

Harris, E. M., Martin, D. G., Polsky, C., Denhardt, L., & Nehring, A. (2012). Beyond "lawn people": The role of emotions in suburban yard management practices. *The Professional Geographer*, 65 (2), 345–361.

Hurley, A. K. (2019). *Radical Suburbs: Experimental Living on the Fringes of the American City*. Cleveland: Belt Publishing.

Jackson, K. T. (1985). *Crabgrass Frontier: The Suburbanization of the United States*. New York: Oxford University Press.

Jenkins, V. (1994). *The Lawn: A History of an American Obsession*. New York: Penguin Random House.

Jerolmack, C. (2008). How pigeons became rats: The cultural-spatial logic of problem animals. *Social Problems*, 55 (2), 72–79.

Johnson, L. (2020). Battle over front-yard meadow thick with irony. *The Toronto Star*, 1 September 2020, https://www.thestar.com/opinion/contributors/2020/09/01/battle-over-front-yard-meadow-thick-with-irony.html.

Kim, J., Williams, N., & Kremen, C. (2006). Effects of cultivation and proximity to natural habitat on ground-nesting native bees in California sunflower fields. *Journal of the Kansas Entomological Society*, 79 (4), 309–320.

Lang, U. (2014). The common life of yards. *Urban Geography*, 35 (6), 852–869.

Lawson, L. J. (2005). *City Bountiful: A Century of Community Gardening in America*. Berkeley: University of California Press.

Lerman, S. B. & Milam, J. (2016). Bee fauna and floral abundance within lawn-dominated suburban yards in Springfield, MA. *Annals of the Entomological Society of America*, 109 (5), 713–723. https://doi.org/10.1093/aesa/saw043.

Marx, K. (2004). Theses on Feuerbach. In K. Marx & F. Engels, *The German Ideology*. New York: International Publishers (first printed 1947).

Matteson, K. C., Ascher, J. S., & Langellotto, G. A. (2008). Bee richness and abundance in New York City urban gardens. *Annals of the Entomological Society of America*, 101 (1), 140–150. https://doi.org/10.1603/0013-8746(2008)101[140:BRAAIN]2.0.CO;2.

Moore, L. J. and Kosut M. (2014). Among the colony: Ethnographic fieldwork, urban bees and intra-species mindfulness. *Ethnography*, 15 (4), 516–539.

Moore, L. J. & Kosut, M. (2013). *Buzz: Urban Beekeeping and the Power of the Bee*. New York: New York University Press.

Morandin, L. A. & Kremen, C. (2012). Bee preference for native versus exotic plants in restored agricultural hedgerows. *Restoration Ecology*, 21 (1), 26–32. https://doi.org/10.1111/j.1526-100X.2012.00876.x.

Packer, L. (2011). *Keeping the Bees: Why All Bees Are at Risk and What We Can Do to Save Them*. New York: HarperCollins.

Packer, L., Genaro, J. A., & Sheffield, C. S. (2007). The bee genera of Eastern Canada. *Canadian Journal of Arthropod Identification*, 3, 1–32.

Pardee, G. L. & Philpott., S. M. (2014). Native plants are the bee's knees: Local and landscape predictors of bee richness and abundance in backyard gardens. *Urban Ecosystems*, 17, 641–659. https://doi.org/10.1007/s11252-014-0349-0.

Philo, C. & Wilbert, C. (2000). *Animal Spaces, Beastly Places*. London: Routledge.

Pitt, H. (2015). On showing and being shown plants: A guide to methods for more-than-human geography, *Area*, 47, 48–55.

Robbins, P. (2007). *Lawn People: How Grasses, Weeds, and Chemicals Make Us Who We Are*. Philadelphia: Temple University Press.

Roger, N., Michez, D., Wattiez, R., Sheridan, C., & Vanderplanck, M. (2017). Diet effects on bumblebee health. *Journal of Insect Physiology*, 96 (Jan.), 128–133.

Ryan, J. C. (2012). Passive flora? Reconsidering nature's agency through human-plant studies (HPS). *Societies*, 2 (3), 101–121.

Seeley, T. D. (2011). *Honeybee Democracy*. Princeton: Princeton University Press.

Seide, V. R., Bernardes, R. C., Pereira, E. J. G., & Lima, M. A. P. (2018). Glyphosate is lethal and Cry toxins alter the development of the stingless bee *Melipona quadrifasciata*. *Environmental Pollution*, 243B, 1854–1860.

Sivakoff, F. S., Prajzner, S., Gardiner, M. M. (2018). Unique bee communities within vacant lots and urban farms result from variation in surrounding urbanization intensity. *Sustainability*, 10 (6), 1926. doi:10.3390/su10061926.

Tsvetkov, N., Samson-Robert, O., Sood, K., Patel, H. S., Malena, D. A., Gajiwala, P. H., Maciukiewicz, P. ... & Zayed, A. (2017). Chronic exposure to neonicotinoids reduces honey bee health near corn crops. *Science*, 356 (June 30), 1395–1397.

Woodcock, B. A., Bullock, J. M., Shore, R. F., Heard, M. S., Pereira, M. G., Redhead, J., & Pywell, R. F. (2017). Country-specific effects of neonicotinoid pesticides on honey bees and wild bees. *Science*, 356 (June 30), 1393–1395.

Woods II, L. L. (2012). The Federal Home Loan Bank board, redlining, and the national proliferation of racial lending discrimination, 1921–1950. *Journal of Urban History*, 38 (6). https://doi.org/10.1177/0096144211435126.

8 Building movements to confront capitalist agriculture

As I have demonstrated throughout this book, the harms caused to bees of all species, and other non-human natures, within capitalist agriculture is astounding. Capitalist agriculture requires the standardization and simplification of landscapes that results in habitats being destroyed; soil, waterways, plants, and living beings poisoned; and farmed animals and people being enrolled in labour regimes that distort relationships and cause irreparable harm. Agrochemical corporations, and other industries invested in the global capitalist agricultural system, hold enormous power over the policymaking of governments and international decision-making bodies. When this is assessed within the context of increasing climate chaos and a 6th mass extinction of life on Earth, the future seems more than uncertain, it seems grim and frightening.

However, building on Chapter 7 about the creation of urban-based pollinator people, this concluding chapter offers hopeful possibilities for an interspecies alliance that not only confronts capitalist agriculture but presents tangible alternatives to the current food system. In cities, organic urban farms and pollinator gardens are replacing vacant lots and lawns to create bee forage and habitat. In rural areas, agroecological and organic farming practices are being taken up by small-scale farmers and peasants, who are organizing into international, movement-based networks such as La Via Campesina (Von Redecker and Herzig 2020; Martinez-Torres and Rosset 2010). Widespread concern about the health of bees in North America and Europe has led to a sharp increase in hobbyist and small-scale beekeeping, along with an interest amongst beekeepers in organic and bee-centred practices. While these practices are sometimes problematic, they present a *possibility* for healthier honey bees that are not embedded in capitalist agriculture. Instead of scaling *up*, these forms of gardening, agriculture, and apiculture can scale *out* to involve and feed billions of people while also creating landscapes of abundance in which non-human animals thrive. In alliance with one another, along with environmentalists and native bee advocates, these movements can help lay the foundation for a post-capitalist agricultural system that allows for the flourishing of people and bees of all species through the creation of landscapes of abundance.

DOI: 10.4324/9781003142294-8

Alliances in struggles against capitalist agriculture

In order to build a movement that has the capacity to disrupt and confront capitalist agriculture and transform it into new, post-capitalist ways of feeding people, while also allowing for the flourishing of non-human nature, it is imperative to build interspecies alliances that connect and build solidarity between movements. This interspecies alliance must bridge the rural and the urban, uniting diverse groups of people including farmers, environmentalists, farm workers, Indigenous land stewards, bee-centred beekeepers, animal advocates, urban 'pollinator people', and aligned scientists. The building of a powerful interspecies alliance requires the willingness to break down false binaries that separate people from acting in solidarity with one another including the urban versus rural and farmer versus environmentalist binaries. In their place movements can form alliances that promote the interests of urban and rural people as aligned against agrochemical corporations, and can cast small-scale farmers, Indigenous land stewards, and organic gardeners as environmental stewards at the forefront of struggles against capitalist agriculture. In sparring with those in power who oppose these movements such as agrochemical corporations (Montenegro de Wit 2021), this coalition can acknowledge the uncertainty inherent in complex ecosystems and can insist that within and because of that uncertainty, other forms of agriculture must be nurtured.

Movements for multispecies flourishing and commoning therefore need to build alliances with people who are struggling against capitalist agriculture in both urban and rural areas. In terms of bees, the biggest threats to the health of both honey *and* wild bees is capitalist agriculture and climate change, and the former is a major contributor to the latter. This means that there is potentially fertile ground for alliance-building between native bee advocates, conservation scientists, beekeepers, environmentalists, gardeners, and small-scale organic farmers, and there is an urgent need for these groups to come together to confront the power and influence of capitalist agriculture. This movement should also attempt to build bridges with both rural and urban Indigenous communities who are struggling for land rights, as well as with farmworkers who are struggling for decent wages, working conditions, and citizenship rights.

This movement must include people who advocate for the flourishing of wild animals, alongside people concerned with the wellbeing and health of domesticated animals. All bees, and other insect pollinators, are harmed by capitalist agriculture. As I have argued throughout this book, pervasive monocultures and heavy pesticide use contribute significantly to the defaunation of multiple species of bees and the embeddedness of commercial beekeeping within industrial agriculture makes most honey bees in rural areas sick and vulnerable (Ellis et al. 2020). Capitalist agriculture should be understood to harm both wild animals (by effectively occupying a large amount of land through feed crops and through wide-ranging pollution loads) and the farmed animals who face miserable lives within intensive livestock operations (Weis

2018). Confronting and disrupting the misery capitalist agriculture causes to animals, both domesticated and wild, can create the conditions in which new ways of living with and among all species of animals can be imagined and explored.

There is much potential for alliance-building, yet it is important to recognize that it will take considerable effort, especially since some of these groups might presently see themselves in conflict with one another. To overcome these conflicts, it is essential to create hopeful narratives about how intersecting problems can be overcome, and how unequal and ecologically destructive landscapes can simultaneously become sites of abundance, multispecies flourishing, ecological regeneration, and social justice.

Can bees join the struggle?

On 4 January 2022, beekeepers in Santiago, Chile held a protest outside government buildings to highlight the plight of bees and beekeepers, especially those suffering due to a drought in the Colina commune north of Santiago (Reuters 2022). The beekeepers had an unusual accomplice in their action: they brought 60 bee hives, each containing approximately 10,000 bees. As one beekeeper, Jose Iturra, told reporters, "Bees are dying, there would be no life if the bees die. That's what we wanted to highlight with this demonstration" (Reuters 2022). The protest ended with four beekeepers arrested and seven police officers stung. These bees are not like the famous protest dogs of Chile and Greece, who chose to join activists in struggles against police, but bees do express agency and autonomy in ways that disrupt their status as an ownable commodity and help to shape other, better worlds.

In animal rights scholarship and activism, there has been attention given to the idea that animals, particularly domesticated farmed animals, resist their exploitation by humans (Colling 2020). Extending beyond animal rights theory, some Indigenous ways of knowing posit non-human nature, including animals and plants, as being in relationships of reciprocity that can push against the brutality and death-making of colonialism and capitalism (Simpson 2017; Kimmerer 2013). Leanne Betasamosake Simpson describes how Nishnaabeg relationships with other people and non-human nature is based on nation-to-nation internationalism grounded within "consent, reciprocity, respect and empathy" (2017, p. 61). Inspired by conceptions of interspecies resistance and solidarity, I believe bees can play an important role in the building of interspecies alliances in opposition to capitalist agriculture. Honey bees resist their status as commodities, and all species of bees work within ecological lifeworlds to create landscapes of abundance, something that mindful beekeepers, farmers, and gardeners can see as part of the co-creation of post-capitalist ways to grow food in both rural and urban spaces (Ellis et al. 2020).

Learning to live among honey bees in ways that respect their autonomy and agency, as many bee-centred beekeepers try to do, may allow people to think through how to live with a range of other animals, especially ones that are difficult to know as individuals, as well as helping us learn to navigate some of the difficulties and disruptions to our lives that autonomy and agency of non-human animals necessarily entail. Although honey bees are highly managed by beekeepers, there are certain aspects of honey bee lifecycle and behaviour that makes them an impossible animal to fully domesticate, including the fact that they travel relatively far distances for forage and swarm as a form of colony reproduction, which is an act of democratic decision-making *within* honey bee colonies (Seeley 2011). When swarming is understood in its entirety, it can be seen an act of collective agency for honey bees. For commercial beekeepers, swarming removes their source of income if they fail to capture the swarm and for this reason, it can be seen to complicate the status of honey bee colonies as a commodity. Swarming is a key behaviour in relation to their status as partially domesticated animals and at the same time it is a reason why they can never be fully owned by humans. Another aspect of honey bee behaviour that makes them instructive animals to co-create space with is that while they forage, they are not under the control of their beekeeper or any other human. Indeed, the benefits provided by honey bees to humans, and the very reasons why humans sought to domesticate them, *requires* that bees forage freely and there is no feasible way to stop this behaviour. Yet while the foraging behaviour of honey bees can be seen to be beneficial, it is not controllable by humans. As Nimmo (2015) says the beehive is "an apparatus that stages and mediates co-constitutive interaction between bodies...the outcome of which is always at least partly open-ended, contingent, and negotiated" (p. 189).

Commercial beekeeping is therefore a contradictory activity under capitalism because honey bees, while technically owned by their beekeeper, are never fully ownable. They may be purchased and sold, as well as themselves producing commodities, but they also disrupt human attempts to commoditize their bodies and their work and there is no real way to overcome this barrier to their complete domestication and deeper commodification. Bees must be free to come and go as they please in order to pollinate flowers and gather nectar for honey. What does liberation entail for an animal species that is partly domesticated and deeply embedded in capitalist agriculture and yet allowed to exercise considerable agency and regularly capable of going feral? And more importantly, how can bee agency and autonomy be respected and integrated into post-capitalism forms of agriculture?

The preferences of bees (and other insects) can be included in deliberations about the commoning of land and can help humans understand how to respect the agency and autonomy of all animals we live with and among. In the Capitalocene, the harm caused to bees of all species forces farmers and beekeepers onto the treadmill of capitalist agriculture with its accelerating contradictions and crises. In a post-capitalist agricultural system, farmers and beekeepers will have to collectively get off that treadmill. Landscapes in which bees thrive, will have to be consciously created, especially in areas of the world where oceans of monocultures dominate. In a sense, bees of all species will collectively show mindful humans the types of landscapes in which they want to live.

Although they have diverse needs based on species and region, evidence demonstrates that bees thrive in ecological lifeworlds that are polycultures of plants, guaranteeing almost continuous bloom during the growing season (Mallinger et al. 2017). They thrive in spaces that have low or no pesticides (Goulson 2020); minimal soil disruption; and contain at least some species of plants that are native to the bioregion (Pardee and Philpott 2014). The types of agricultural and other landscapes that bees of all species need to flourish can be the foundations of post-capitalist landscapes of abundance.

Abundance in the ruins of capitalism

As I have argued throughout this book, the capitalist agricultural system creates landscapes of scarcity in which pollinators, especially bees, cannot flourish. An important way to fight the destruction wrought by capitalist agriculture is to understand and communicate how it actually manufactures scarcity. But it is not enough to confront landscapes of scarcity, it is equally important to develop and support practices, strategies, and philosophies that create landscapes of abundance. Collard and colleagues (2015, p. 327) point to the need to "ally ourselves with … strategies to produce abundance" while at the same time directly confronting the ruins and violence caused by colonialism and capitalism, noting that "to recall this violence is neither nostalgic nor anachronistic but central to understanding that any intervention today is unavoidably linked to processes of imperial ruination". They call for the pursuit of a sort of abundance that includes an intention to act pluriversally instead of universally, which entails supporting "already existing worlding practices that enact worlds different from those produced by European imperialism and settler colonialism". It also includes supporting Indigenous sovereignty struggles as well as a resurgence of Indigenous political thought and alternative forms of governance.

Further, the vision of abundance Collard and colleagues (2015, p. 328) set out also calls for the recognition of animal autonomy, explaining that they take autonomy to "mean the fullest expression of animal life, including capacity for movement, for social and familial association, and for work and play," while stressing that they "are not advocating a return to conservation's old misanthropy but an orientation in which wildness is understood relationally, not as the absence of humans but as interrelations within which animals have autonomy". The conception of abundance set out by Collard and colleagues (2015) serves as a guide for my intervention into debates about creating an agricultural system beyond capitalism, in which people, bees, and other non-human natures can flourish. Landscapes of abundance that promote multispecies flourishing can be nurtured, even in the ruins of capitalist landscapes and acting as experiments and models for moving beyond it. If we take seriously the need to act pluriversally by being open to multiple forms of other-worlding that are and will take place, we cannot know the paths that will become available in post-capitalist worlds before we begin to walk. The not knowing about the future is the gift and scourge of uncertainty. However, other worlding is happening in various ways even within capitalism that can be instructive in imagining the possibilities of post-capitalist agricultural systems.

Agroecology and landscapes of abundance

Although there are hopeful possibilities emerging for bee flourishing in cities, as outlined in Chapter 7, the disruption of the capitalist agricultural system requires transformative changes in the ways in which rural landscapes are shaped, used, and exploited. As described in Chapter 5, there is considerable bee-washing promoted by agrochemical corporations in alliance with farming organizations, claiming that with a few tweaks to farming practices, such as the planting of flowering strips adjacent to monocultured fields, and applying pesticides via seed coatings instead of spraying, agriculture as it is currently practiced can be bee-friendly. However, as social reproduction theorists argue, capitalist value-making is, at its heart, a system of death-making (Ferguson 2021). Flowering strips near fields saturated with pesticides are toxic to pollinators (David et al. 2016). Pesticide-coated seeds still enable pesticides to make their way into soil and waterways (Rundlöf et al. 2015). The only solution to the global pollinator crisis is to confront the death-making of the Capitalocene and replace it with an agricultural system with the central aim of life-making which must be post-capitalist. A life-making agricultural system is one that promotes multispecies flourishing through the creation of landscapes of abundance. Although the trajectory within the global agricultural system has been towards bigger farms growing one or two crops with a high level of inputs, including pesticides, there are farmers throughout the world who nurture and defend abundance.

Agroecology: in/against/and beyond capitalist agriculture

Agroecology is a science, practice, and movement that applies ecological concepts and principles to the design of agricultural systems, while also centring local and regional food sovereignty and Indigenous knowledge systems (Altieri 2009). Agroecology is an open and dynamic concept that encompasses wide and varied practices appropriate to the bioregion in which it is practiced. The concept of food sovereignty is central to agroecology causing it to be pluralistic as opposed to universalistic, allowing for 'many worlds' in terms of types of farms and food systems. Agroecology as a concept emerged from the movements of smallholder farmers and peasants in Latin America and has been adopted globally by international peasants and smallholder farmers movements, largely but not entirely under the banner of La Via Campesina. There are 182 organizations in 81 countries affiliated to La Via Campesina, especially concentrated in Central and South America, sub-Saharan Africa, and South Asia. Although this movement is strongest and most transformative in the Global South, there are farmers' organizations in the Global North that advocate agroecology among their members and see themselves in solidarity with agroecological struggles in the Global South. These organization include the National Farmers' Union in Canada; The Landworkers' Alliance in the UK, and the National Family Farm Coalition in the United States (La Via Campesina 2018). Although the advocacy of affiliated organizations in the Global North have mainly centred on family farms, there has been a push to incorporate other types of smallholder farming such as cooperative and non-profit farms and, in Canada, to include Indigenous food systems (National Farmers Union n.d.). Agroecology has developed into an important political movement with many leading advocates including La Via Campesino moving beyond an anti-corporate orientation to an approach that is staunchly in opposition to global capitalism (La Via Campesina n.d.). In this regard, some agroecology activists and practitioners question private land ownership, advocate for land reform, and develop collective and cooperative forms of farm organization (Selwyn 2021). La Via Campesina and many of its member organizations also advocate for the rights of farm workers, including supporting unionization of the rural workforce, and work to advance agrarian feminism which acknowledges the labour, experiences, and knowledges of women farmers.

Although agroecology is a diverse and dynamic movement, grounded in science and the everyday lived experiences of farmers, there are some common features that make it highly compatible with multispecies flourishing and incompatible with capitalist agriculture. One of the central tenets of agroecology is that human agriculture and food-procuring systems can and should be part of flourishing ecological lifeworlds. Agroecology practitioners, "promote beneficial biological interactions and synergies among the components of the agroecosystem so that these may allow for the regeneration of soil fertility and maintain productivity and crop protection" (Altieri and Toledo 2011). Agroecological approaches involve creating polycultural mosaics in which a variety of cultivars are grown, many of which are landraces, developed over time in specific bioregions, making them especially useful for native and wild bees (Altieri 2009).

Agroecology practitioners eschew pesticides and artificial fertilizers placing a high emphasis on the use of on-site or locally available natural fertilizers such as compost or manure (Altieri and Toledo 2011). Insect control varies but often involves increasing the presence of natural predators such as wasps in the landscape physically covering crops with netting or cloth, and manually removing problem insects. Studies have shown that bee abundance and richness is higher in diversified, organic landscapes (Kennedy et al. 2013) with studies of agroecological systems in Chile (Henríquez-Piskulich et al. 2021) and traditional, diversified, Indigenous systems in Mexico (Landaverde-González et al. 2017) and Bolivia (Catacora-Varagas et al. 2017) showing higher levels of bee diversity and richness. The type of diversified, polycultural farming practised by agroecologists enhances local diversity of non-human animals and plants while also having higher yields when calculated per land area rather than per plant (Altieri 2009; Gliessman et al. 1998).

Can agroecology and small-scale farming feed the world?

One of the main criticisms of agroecology and small-scale farming and, by extension, post-capitalist agriculture is that it cannot possibly feed the world, especially in the midst of a climate crisis that will cause additional, uncontrollable stresses for farmers and agroecosystems. In response, agroecologist practitioners and activists argue that agroecology can be more resilient to the crises brought about by climate change and can mitigate some of the effects of climate change through the planting of more resilient polycultures and the integration of perennial plants including trees and shrubs into agroecological landscapes (Altieri 2009). Although many agroecologists advocate integrating livestock into farming systems, it is clear that industrial livestock agriculture, which is responsible for a high amount of GHG emissions, would not exist under post-capitalist agroecology as it is a wildly unsustainable way to get food to people (Weis and Ellis 2020; Weis 2013). Further, they argue that agroecology nurtures and promotes biodiversity, helping to slow the loss and defaunation of species (Altieri et al. 2017; Wanger et al. 2020). Lastly, in the aftermath of the COVID-19 pandemic, which brought about serious concerns about food supply, and unmasked some of the most exploitative aspects of the global food system, especially around the rights of workers, agroecology activists argue that capitalist agriculture has shown itself to be vulnerable to and ineffective in the face of crises (Montenegro de Wit 2021).

In fact, it is entirely possible to transform the global agricultural system so the world's human population is fed, largely though small-scale, organic agriculture in which regional food needs are met first, and only after these needs have been met, select foods are exported. This transformation would not be simple but not because it is difficult to grow enough food for people without the use of pesticides and other inputs. In fact, at least one third of the world's food is grown on tiny farms of less than 2 hectares (FAO 2021), although this is a highly disputed figure with NGOs who work with peasant and smallholder farmers arguing that the previous statistic used by the FAO, that 70% of the world's food is grown by small farmers and peasants, is more accurate (GRAIN 2022). Critics of the revised FAO statistic argue that the studies on which it is derived confuse production of food as commodities with the consumption of food (ETC. Group 2022), harkening to Marx's important distinction between the use value of an item and the exchange value of an item (Marx 2018). A significant amount of food produced in the world is consumed directly by people, valued for its direct use as food, and does not enter into capitalist commodity production, which is where food and other items are bestowed with exchange value. It should be noted that much of the production of food that is directly for consumption is done by women within the realm of social reproduction, and to ignore this labour renders gendered, social reproduction work, crucial to human existence, as invisible. In the most populous areas of the world, up to 80% of food consumed is grown by small-scale farmers and peasants (ETC. Group 2022), and much of that food is grown, raised, and produced either in the household or informal sector. Critics of the revised FAO statistic also argue that the definition of a small farmer, the amount of land on which a farm is deemed to be small-scale, can significantly change the statistic (ETC. Group 2022). There is no one measure for what constitutes a small-scale farm because sizes of farms fluctuate depending on geographical region and crop. For example, due to the nature of the plants, a small-scale grain operation will be much larger than a small-scale vegetable operation. Regardless, even if the amount of food grown by small-scale farmers is only one third of all food produced, given the extreme hostility to small-scale farming by governments, agrochemical corporations, and some billionaire-backed philanthropic organizations, it is an astounding number that indicates in a post-capitalist world many billions more people can be fed. Imagine how many people could be fed by small-scale farmers in a world in which they are supported by governmental policies, funding, and action (including land reform), and in which farm work is well-paid, safe, and highly valued.

The difficulties in creating such a world lie in reversing the entrenched land use, labour, and meatification patterns that have occurred throughout the world in the 20th and 21st century without returning to systems of extreme exploitation of human labour. In regions of the world such as the United States and Canada in which most of the population lives in cities and huge swaths of rural areas have been turned into high-input monocultures, it would take a monumental societal-wide transformation to move towards a mosaic of polycultural small-scale farms. For such a transformation to occur, intensive livestock agriculture would have to be dismantled and meat would, once again, be on the periphery of most people's diets, except for people living in the far north. This transformation would entail that human and non-human labour in agriculture increases exponentially, meaning in some parts of the world an extensive re-population and revitalization of rural areas. To figure out how to make agricultural labour fair and just, providing good livelihoods and working conditions for all human workers; and excellent quality of life to animal labourers will be one of the biggest challenges of this transformation. This transformation will not be simple or easy but neither will the future for capitalist agriculture. It certainly will be almost impossible for the global capitalist agricultural systems to recover from a crash in the population of the world's pollinators or the chaos caused by climate change. As Naomi Klein (2014) reminds us, the realities of climate chaos ensure that the future will be radical regardless, and, knowing this, we can choose to create worlds of collective flourishing and abundance.

Agroecology and small-scale, organic farming cannot be easily *scaled up* because at the centre of the concept is the idea that agriculture must be integrated into local and regional ecological lifeworlds in beneficial ways that allow for the flourishing of people alongside non-human nature. Instead, these agricultural systems must *scale out*. Capitalist imperatives have forced a trajectory in which small farms and farmers are replaced with large agribusinesses that are fully integrated into global capitalist agriculture. The push to farmers and peasants has been, and continues to be, 'get big (or at least adopt agrochemical practices) or get out'. In contrast a post-capitalist food system will involve a multiplying of diverse small farms and, with it, a multiplying of farmers. But a post-capitalist agroecological system must go further than a multiplication of small, diversified, polycultural farms towards the commoning of urban and rural land; widespread land reform to correct class, racial, and colonialist injustices; the organizing of workers and collectivizing of work throughout the entire food system; and the decommodifying of food (Selwyn 2021). It may be hard to imagine these transformative, radical changes, however the urgency of climate change, biodiversity loss, and widespread suffering among people makes it a necessity. As Montenegro de Wit argues (2021, p. 119), drawing from the lesson of abolition,

> The systematic cheapening of nature, labor, care, and lives that renders food so cheap can be delegitimized just as slavery (the original cheap lives institution) was. What appears radical now, in terms of practicing biodiversity-based farming, establishing worker-owned farming and food cooperatives, and enacting agency and power in agrifood governance can evolve into common sense. How? Abolition history shows that this evolution, while possible, is not "natural"; new normals were not re-established without sustained counter-hegemonic organizing – and people willing to take risks.

Radical changes to the global food system will not be brought about by governments, although they can be pushed, to an extent, to make changes. In order to radically transform the way in which humans grow, procure, and raise food, there must be an interspecies alliance that unifies intersecting food and agriculture-based movements on the principles of diversity, solidarity, and collective flourishing.

Multispecies commons as landscapes of abundance

In order to create a future of collective flourishing, there must be a focus on the commoning of urban and rural spaces. The commons refer to commonly owned and governed land, resources, and knowledges. The origin of the word is in European legal conceptions of land use, especially in regard to the early capitalist processes of the enclosure of the commons. However, in many human societies some land and resources, especially those crucial for survival, were, and a few still are, held in common. The commons in any given society are governed by complex rules and guidelines including sets of obligations, rights, and responsibilities, to ensure fairness and decrease destruction of the land or resources being held in common (Ostrom 1990). In response to the ecological destruction and human injustice brought about by the continuous wealth accumulation and resource extraction of capitalism, there is an urgent need for the defence, expansion, and creation of commons. Commoning is "the production of the commons ... the creation of social relations and spaces built on solidarity, the communal sharing of wealth, and cooperative work and decision-making" (Federici 2019, p. 183). This commoning of space must be conceived of as multispecies, in order to bring about the transformative change that is necessary to confront and recover from the harms of capitalist agriculture. Multispecies commons can include urban farms, community gardens, pollinator gardens in public or pseudo-public spaces, community farms, community and agricultural land trusts, collective apiaries, common pastureland, and co-operatively shared farms.

It is useful to think about the co-creation of collective spaces through the perspective of bee flourishing for several reasons. If spaces that enable bees to flourish can also integrate the needs and wants of people who live around them, through democratic decision-making processes, it can help to foster social change and food justice. Pollinator gardens and spaces of ecological regeneration can become spaces in which people experience a sense of belonging, and have some of their basic needs met. The colonial myth of wilderness, that has long promoted the idea that wild areas must be set apart from people's everyday lives, can be challenged, while democratic decision-making processes can ensure fair and just access to land that does not harm non-human natures and that seeks to wrong the injustices of colonialism.

Spaces of human flourishing in which food is grown, from rural agroecological farms to urban community garden plots, can incorporate multispecies flourishing into their design in ways that benefit not only honey bees but native bees, wasps, and other insects and small pollinators. The flourishing of insects and pollinators is essential for the healthy functioning of every terrestrial ecological lifeworld, and spaces that contain insect habitats also contain habitats for other animals. For example, many species of insects and birds need dead standing perennials both for the habitat created by their stems and through the food source that seed heads provide. Likewise, rotting logs and old trees provide habitat for a wide range of animals including insects, birds, mammals, reptiles, and amphibians. They also serve as important sites for the propagation of mushrooms which are essential to healthy soil. The variety of forage needed by bees of all species is also crucial to other animals, especially native plants which have a symbiotic relationship to many native species of insects, spiders, and birds. The crops that humans plant also provide food to other animals, including insects, birds, and mammals, sometimes to the chagrin of gardeners. The presence of food-growing spaces where humans are committed to actively fostering food supplies and habitat for wildlife can shift the relationship humans have to non-human natures more generally. Co-creating landscapes with insect pollinators that sting can help people to learn to live with 'despised others' such as wasps, who regularly show up in bee-friendly landscapes, and with whom humans must learn to co-exist. The creation of landscapes where humans flourish alongside other animals entails considering their behaviours, food needs, and habitat demands in planning.

Creating spaces where both humans and bees flourish can challenge a pervasive myth about scarcity, which is that it is principally caused by absolute limits, that there are just too few resources to go around. As I argued throughout this book, landscapes of capitalist agriculture are very productive in a narrow way, designed to maximize capital and wealth for a few, while constituting a landscape of scarcity for most other species (and many other humans). If suddenly abandoned by people, such biologically simplified landscapes of scarcity would quickly be transformed through succession into more diverse ecological lifeworlds. The idea that scarcity is a natural or inevitable state must be problematized, and shown to be a defeatist premise for thinking about contemporary environmental problems, especially when we are in the midst of a biodiversity crisis and climate breakdown. Instead, it is important to show how specific industries and corporations are actively working to manufacture landscapes of scarcity, through practices including biological simplification, widespread pesticide use, and mechanization.

A central argument of this book is that post-capitalist landscapes of abundance can be created to foster both human and bee flourishing through diverse assemblages of plants, or polycultures, where multiple other animal species are also able to thrive and play particular functions. Although human-nurtured ecological lifeworlds continue to need human attention, it is possible to reorient this attention towards promoting abundance and diversity. Of course, fostering such landscapes of abundance cannot in itself turn the tides of mass extinctions and defaunation, but they can be tied to interspecies alliances that confront and disrupt capitalist agriculture. Spaces of multispecies flourishing and commoning can also help people to imagine radical alternatives and begin to build them in the ruins of capitalism (Collard et al. 2015). As Holloway (2007) argues, one of the most important actions people can take at this time in human history is the collective scream of no, a refusal to participate in the dominant ways of organizing social and economic life. According to Holloway (2010) the only way to think about revolution, or transformation, is in terms of "the creation, expansion, and multiplication of cracks in capitalist domination," and stresses that this should not be "an empty abstraction because these moments or spaces of revolt-and-other-doing already exist all over the place" (p. 56).

Caffentzis and Federici (2014) make a similar argument, insisting that spaces of commoning where neither the state nor corporations have control are the only spaces capable of fomenting the types of radical change desperately needed. Federici (2019) urges us to struggle towards a 'planet of commons', in which multispecies commons in rural and urban areas can play an important part, showing people what is possible in terms of both land uses and the practice of radical democracy. Federici (2019) argues that movements to rebuild the commons can make the world sacred to the many people for whom it has become mundane. This re-enchantment of the world must incorporate non-human animals as active participants as far as is possible. Through struggles to rebuild the commons and create landscapes of abundance, it is possible to begin to forge a better world out of the ruins of capitalism. There are multiple possibilities for how this other-worlding may look, especially when contemplating the challenges of decolonizing and re-Indigenizing landscapes. As multispecies commons take root and establish new ways of relating to each other and to non-human natures they can provide both glimpses and real-world experiments into building post-colonial, post-capitalist futures, and with this help to spark radical imaginaries for other, better worlds.

References

Altieri, M. A. (2009). Agroecology, small farms, and food sovereignty. *Monthly Review*, 61 (3), 102–113.

Altieri, M. A., Nicholls, C. I., & Montalba, R. (2017). Technological approaches to sustainable agriculture at a crossroads: An agroecological perspective. *Sustainability*, 9 (3), 349. https://doi.org/10.3390/su9030349.

Altieri, M. A., & Toledo, V. M. (2011). The agroecological revolution in Latin America: Rescuing nature, ensuring food sovereignty and empowering peasants. *Journal of Peasant Studies*, 38 (3), 587–612. https://doi.org/10.1080/03066150.2011.582947.

Caffentzis, G. and Federici, S. (2014). Commons against and beyond capitalism. *Community Development Journal*, 49, i92–i105.

Catacora-Vargas, G., Piepenstock, A., Sotomayor, C., Cuentas, D., Cruz, A., & Delgado, F. (2017). Brief historical review of agroecology in Bolivia. *Agroecology and Sustainable Food Systems*, 41(3–4),429–447. https://doi.org/10.1080/21683565.2017.1290732.

Collard, R., Dempsey, J., & Sundberg, J. (2015). A manifesto for abundant futures. *Annals of The Association of American Geographers*, 105 (2), 322–330.

Colling, S. (2020). *Animal Resistance in the Global Capitalist Era*. East Lansing: Michigan State University Press.

David, A., Botias, C., Abdul-Sada, A., Nicholls, E., Rotheray, E. L., Hill, E. M., & Goulson, D. (2016). Widespread contamination of wildflower and bee-collected pollen with complex mixtures of neonicotinoids and fungicides commonly applied to crops. *Environment International*, 88 (3), 169–178.

Ellis, R., Weis, T., Suryanarayanan, S., & Beilin, K. (2020). From a free gift of nature to a precarious commodity: Bees, pollination services, and industrial agriculture. *Journal of Agrarian Change*, 20 (3), 437–459, https://doi.org/10.1111/joac.12360.

ETC. Group (2022). Small-scale farmers and peasants still feed the world. https://www.etcgroup.org/sites/www.etcgroup.org/files/files/31-01-2022_small-scale_farmers_and_peasants_still_feed_the_world.pdf.

FAO. (2021). Small family farmers produce a third of the world's food. *Food and Agriculture Organization of the United Nations*, 23 April. https://www.fao.org/news/story/en/item/1395127/icode/.

Federici, S. (2019). *Re-enchanting the World: Feminism and the Politics of the Commons*. Oakland: PM Press.

Ferguson, S. (2021). Life-making or death-making? *Midnight Sun*, 17 October. https://www.midnightsunmag.ca/life-making-or-death-making/.

Gliessman, S. R., Engles, E., & Krieger, R. (1998). *Agroecology: Ecological Processes in Sustainable Agriculture*. Boca Raton: CRC Press.

Goulson, D. (2020). Pesticides, corporate irresponsibility, and the fate of our planet. *One Earth*, 2 (4), 302–305.

GRAIN. (2022). Peasants still feed the world, even if FAO claims otherwise (open letter). https://grain.org/en/article/6790-peasants-still-feed-the-world-even-if-fao-claims-otherwise.

Henríquez-Piskulich, P. A., Schapheer, C., Vereecken, N. J., & Villagra, C. (2021). Agroecological strategies to safeguard insect pollinators in biodiversity hotspots: Chile as a case study. *Sustainability*, 13 (12), 6728. https://doi.org/10.3390/su13126728.

Holloway, J. (2007). *Change the World Without Taking Power: The Meaning of Revolution Today*. London: Pluto Press.

Holloway, J. (2010). *Crack Capitalism*. London: Pluto Press.

Kennedy, C. M., Lonsdorf, E., Neel, M. C., Williams, N. M., Ricketts, T. H., Winfree, R. ... & Kremen, C. (2013). A global quantitative synthesis of local and landscape effects on wild bee pollinators in agroecosystems. *Ecology Letters*, 16 (5), 584–599. https://doi.org/10.1111/ele.12082.

Kimmerer, R.W (2013). *Braiding Sweetgrass: Indigenous Wisdom, Scientific Knowledge and the Teaching of Plants*. Minneapolis: Milkweed Editions.

Klein, N. (2014). *This Changes Everything: Capitalism vs. The Climate*. New York: Penguin Random House.

La Via Campesina. (n.d.). What we are fighting against: Capitalism and free trade. https://viacampesina.org/en/what-are-we-fighting-against/capitalism-and-free-trade/.

La Via Campesina. (2018). Member organizations of La Via Campesina. https://viacampesina.org/en/member-organisations-of-la-via-campesina-updated-2018/.

Landaverde-González, P., Quezada-Euán, J. J. G., Theodorou, P., Murray, T. E., Husemann, M., Ayala, R. ... & Paxton, R. J. (2017). Sweat bees on hot chillies: Provision of pollination services by native bees in traditional slash-and-burn agriculture in the Yucatán Peninsula of tropical Mexico. *Journal of Applied Ecology*, 54 (6), 1814–1824. https://doi.org/10.1111/1365-2664.12860.

Mallinger, R. E., Gaines-Day, H. R., & Gratton, C. (2017). Do managed bees have negative effects on wild bees? A systematic review of the literature. *PLoS ONE*, 12 (12). https://doi.org/10.1371/journal.pone.0189268.

Martinez-Torres, M. E., & Rosset, P. M. (2010). La Via Campesina: The birth and evolution of a transnational social movement. *The Journal of Peasant Studies*, 37 (1), 149–175.

Marx, K. (2018). *Capital Vol. 1: A Critique of Political Economy*. (Reprint, first published, 1867.) Champaign: Modern Barbarian Press.

Montenegro de Wit, M. (2021). What grows from a pandemic? Toward an abolitionist agroecology. *The Journal of Peasant Studies*, 48 (1), 99–136. https://doi.org/10.1080/03066150.2020.1854741.

National Farmers Union. (n.d.). Indigenous Solidarity Working Group. https://www.nfu.ca/about/international/indigenous-solidarity-working-group/.

Nimmo, R. (2015). Apiculture in the Anthropocene. In Human Animal Research Network Editorial Collective (eds.), *Animals in the Anthropocene: Critical Perspectives on Non-human Futures*. Sydney: Sydney University Press.

Ostrom, E. (1990). *Governing the Commons: The Evolution of Institutions for Collective Action*. Cambridge: Cambridge University Press.

Pardee, G. L. & Philpott, S. M. (2014). Native plants are the bee's knees: Local and landscape predictors of bee richness and abundance in backyard gardens. *Urban Ecosystems*, 17, 641–659. https://doi.org/10.1007/s11252-014-0349-0.

Reuters. (2022). 10,000 bees join protest in Chile, 7 police officers stung. CNN, 4 January. https://www.cnn.com/2022/01/04/americas/beekeepers-chile-police-scli-intl/index.html.

Rundlöf, M., Andersson, G., Bommarco, R., Fries, I., Hederstrom, V., Herbertson, L. ... & Smith, H. G. (2015). Seed coating with a neonicotinoid insecticide negatively affects wild bees. *Nature*, 521, 77–80. https://doi.org/10.1038/nature14420.

Seeley, T. D. (2011). *Honeybee Democracy*. Princeton: Princeton University Press.

Selwyn, B. (2021). A green new deal for agriculture: For, within, or against capitalism? *The Journal of Peasant Studies*, 48 (4), 778–806. https://doi.org/10.1080/03066150.2020.1854740.

Simpson, L. B. (2017). *As We Have Always Done: Indigenous Freedom Through Radical Resistance*. Minneapolis: University of Minnesota Press.

Von Redecker, S. & Herzig, C. (2020). The peasant way of a more than radical democracy: The case of La Via Campesina. *Journal of Business Ethics*, 164 (4), 657–670. https://doi.org/10.1007/s10551-019-04402-6.

Wanger, T. C., DeClerck, F., Garibaldi, L. A., Ghazoul, J., Kleijn, D., Klein, A. M. ... & Weisser, W. (2020). Integrating agroecological production in a robust post-2020 Global Biodiversity Framework. *Nature Ecology & Evolution*, 4 (9), 1150–1152. https://doi.org/10.1038/s41559-020-1262-y.

Weis, T. (2013). *The Ecological Hoofprint: The Global Burden of Industrial Livestock*. London: Zed.

Weis, T. (2018). Ghosts and things: Agriculture and animal life. *Global Environmental Politics*, 18 (2), 134–142.

Weis, T. & Ellis, R. (2020). Animal functionality and interspecies relations in regenerative agriculture: Considering necessity and the possibilities of non-violence. In Duncan, J., Carolan, M., & Wiskerkerke, J. S. C. (eds.), *Routledge Handbook of Sustainable and Regenerative Food Systems*. Abingdon: Routledge, pp. 141–153.

Index

Abbate, C. 10
abundance *see* landscapes of abundance
activism and advocacy *see* agrochemical industry (struggles against neonicotinoids); landscapes of abundance; movement-building
agency and autonomy of bees 7–8; pollinator gardeners 147; small-scale urban beekeeping 140–1; vs commodification 155–6
Agent Orange 65
agrarian societies and domestication of honey bees 3–10
agriculture and bee flourishing 8–9
agrochemical industry: increasing power of 85–8; influence on government regulation 78–9; responses to resistance 73, 77
agrochemical industry (struggles against neonicotinoids) 85; bee-washing 95–8; beyond neonicotinoids 100–2; EU: precautionary principle at work 89–91; EU and Ontario government approaches compared 88–9, 98–100; Ontario government 92–5
agroecology: and agrochemical approach 86–7; and landscapes of abundance 157–61
Alaux, C. et al. 117
Alex, B. 20
alien species: definitional problem 113–14
alliances: interspecies 102; in struggles against agricultural capitalism 153–6
almond industry, California 48–9, 50
Altieri, M. A. 99, 157, 158, 159; and Toledo, V. M. 158
American Foulbrood (AFB) 53
Ancient Greek myth and philosophy 10
Anthropocene, concept of 19–21

antibiotics, prophylactic 53
"*Apis*–industrial complex" 47
Arabic and Muslim texts 10
Aristotle 10, 66

Bayer Crop Science/Monsanto 74, 78–9, 86, 95; EU court case and "emergency authorization" 90–1; US court case 75–6
bee stress, migratory commercial beekeeping and 48–9
bee-centred beekeeping 121–3, 134–47
bee-washing 95–8
Bees Matter campaign 95–7
bees (overview) 1–2
Berezow, A. 75
biodiversity crisis 11, 102
blueberry farms, British Columbia 50
Bonny, S. 86, 87
#BringBacktheBees campaign 97–8
bumble bees 12–13, 31–2, 71, 78; causes of decline 119; managed colonies for greenhouse industry 111–12
Butz, E. 27

Canada Honey Council (CHC) 95–6, 97
canola/oilseed rape 48; neonicotinoids 69, 90, 91, 96
Capitalocene 19; concepts of Anthropocene and 19–23; ecosystem services 44–5; landscapes of scarcity 31–4; simplified and standardized landscapes of North America 26–31; summary and conclusion 34–5; *see also* settler-colonialism and capitalism, North America
Carson, R. 65–6
cash crops 27; *see also* canola/oilseed rape; corn and soy monocultures, North America

Index

Chile: beekeepers demonstration 154
Cilia, L. 44, 48
climate change/global warming 14, 20, 119–20
clothianidin 89, 91
Colla, S. R. and MacIvor, s. 97, 114
Collard, R. et al. 124, 156, 163
Colony Collapse Disorder (CCD) 48, 88, 117
Columbian Exchange 22, 23
commercial bee keeping *see* large-scale commercial beekeeping; migratory commercial beekeeping; small-scale commercial beekeeping
commodification: of non-human nature 44–5; vs agency of bees 155–6
common milkweed 76–7
commoning: multispecies 161–4; practices 145–6
community farming and gardening 138–9, 143, 146
concentrated animal feeding operations (CAFOs) 29, 30, 31, 33
corn and soy monocultures, North America 28–31
Crop Life Canada 92–3, 94
crop yields, pesticide ban impact on 94, 99
Crosby, A. W. 22, 23, 24
cultural and spiritual importance of bees 9–10

DDT 64–5
defaunation: mass extinctions and 10–11; *see also under* wild bees
Dolezal, A. G. et al. 50–1
domestication of honey bees and rise of agrarian societies 3–10
Douglas-Belshaw, J. 25
Dowler, S. and Clarke, J. S. 89, 91

ecological lifeworlds 115, 117; and multispecies flourishing 124–5
ecosystem services 44–5
Ellis, R. 54, 85, 88, 92, 96, 100, 110, 111–12, 115, 117, 121, 122–3, 129, 133–4, 142; et al. 2, 5, 39, 40, 42, 43, 48, 110, 153, 154; Weis, T. and 118, 159
emotion: and pain in insects 45; *see also* sensory and emotional aspects
enclosure of land/commons 25, 123, 131, 161–2
entomology and science of killing 66–8

environmental pollution 74; neonicotinoids 72–3, 91
Environmental Protection Agency, US 75
European colonization *see* settler-colonialism and capitalism, North America
European Food Safety Authority (EFSA) 89–90
European Union: neonicotinoids moratorium/ban 89–91, 99–100
expertise, conflicting conceptions of 77–9

Fairbrother, A. et al. 70, 78–9
FAO 1, 13, 31, 39–40, 159–60
Federici, S. 131, 147, 162, 164; Caffentzis, G. and 163–4
feral honey bees 7, 24, 52, 114–15
Ferguson, S. 138, 157
fipronil 90, 91, 101
floral resources competition, honey bees and wild bees 108–9, 110, 114, 121
foraging behaviour 155
foraging and worker bees 110–11
forest food stewardship 3–4
formic and oxalic acids 54
fungicides: use in combination 50, 70; *see also* pesticides (herbicides/insecticides/fungicides)

gardeners/pollinator gardeners 141–7
General Mills 97–8
genetic diversity and migratory commercial beekeeping 49
genetically engineered (GE) crops/seeds 27, 29–30, 74–5, 77, 86
global pollinator crisis 10–14
global warming *see* climate change/global warming
glyphosate 74–7, 98
Gonzalez, V. H. et al. 119
Goulson, D. 28, 64, 68, 70, 71, 76, 78, 85, 90, 101–2, 156
Government of Canada, definition of alien species 113
government regulation: influence of agrochemical industry on 78–9; *see also* agrochemical industry (struggles against neonicotinoids)
Grain Farmers of Ontario (GFO) 92, 93–5; Bees Matter campaign 95–6
greenhouse industry, managed bumble bee colonies for 111–12
Greenpeace: *Unearthed* project 91

Index 169

Hamel, M.-A. and Dorf, E. 30, 69
hedgerows and trees, loss of 32–3
herbicides: glyphosate 74–7, 98; military use of 64–5; *see also* pesticides
high-tech solutions 120
Hill, A. B. 79
hive checks 138, 139–40, 141
hives 6, 9, 10; agency of bees 155; foraging and worker bees 110–11; highways and manipulation of honey bee colonies 41–4; Langstroth 42–3; neonicotinoids in 70, 71; treatments for AFB and mites 53–4
hobbyists/small-scale bee keepers: pests and scapegoating of 55–7; urban 121–3, 134–40
Holloway, J. 163
honey-producing bees 5–6; collection from wild bees 34; global industry 39–40
honey bee harm to wild native bees 107–8; bee-centred beekeeping and healthy honey bees 121–3; climate change and role of honey bees 119–20; and commercial beekeeping 110–14; creating landscapes of abundance 123–5; evidence of competition 108–9; North America 114–18
human consumption of neonicotinoids 73
human health risk of glyphosate exposure 75–6
human–non-human relationship 154–5; large-scale agribusiness 122; pollinator gardeners 141–7; small-scale beekeeping 135–40; swarming behaviour 140–1; transformation of labour 160–1
hybrid seeds 27, 86

Ibn Magih 10
imidacloprid 69, 73, 89, 91
Indigenous societies 21–2, 113–14, 156
"insectageddon" 11–12, 88
insecticides *see* DDT; miticides; neonicotinoids; pesticides
integrated pest management (IPM) 56, 93
intellectual property rights 87
interspecies alliance 102
"intra-species mindfulness" 139–40
invasive species, honey bees as 112–14
IPCC 119, 120

Johnson, D. 75–6
Johnson, L. 145

Kentucky bluegrass 130

La Vie Campesina 101, 157–8
labour, transformation of 160–1
landscapes: honey bee and wild bee competition 108–9; of scarcity 31–4; simplified and standardized landscapes 26–31
landscapes of abundance: agroecology and 157–61; creating 123–5, 156–7; multispecies commons as 161–4
Langstroth, L. L. 42
Langstroth hives 42–3
large-scale agribusiness 27, 33–4; 'get big or get out' 27, 30, 47, 99–100, 161; human–non-human relationship 122; vs post-capitalist agroecological system 161
large-scale commercial beekeeping 39–40, 57–8; pollinator services *see* migratory commercial beekeeping; and small-scale urban beekeeping 134–5
Latin America 119, 154, 157–9
lawns, North America 129–33
livestock: concentrated animal feeding operations (CAFOs) 29, 30, 31, 33; meat 160
London Urban Beekeepers Collective (LUBC) 133–4

Malm, A. 21
Marx, K. 135, 159
mass extinctions 19; and mass defaunation 10–11
Mehta, L. et al. 123
migratory commercial beekeeping 40–7; and honey bee vulnerability 47–57; honey bee and wild bee competition 110–14; recommended strategy 120; and small-scale urban beekeepers 135
military use of herbicides 64–5
military–industrial complex 66, 67, 85–6, 132
mindfulness 136–7, 141; "intra-species mindfulness" 139–40
mites *see* varroa mites
miticides 53–5
Monbiot, G. 11, 88
monocultures: lawns 129–33; nutritional deficiencies of bees 50–1; and pollination services 47, 110; as sacrifice zones 114, 115, 117; soy and corn, North America 28–31
Monsanto *see* Bayer Crop Science/Monsanto
Montenegro de Wit, M. 153, 159, 161

Index

Moore, J. W. 21–2
Moore, L. J. and Kosut, M. 139
movement-building 152; abundance in ruins of capitalism 156–7; alliances 153–6; *see also* landscapes of abundance
multispecies flourishing 124–5
multispecies flourishing in cities 129; North American lawn 129–33; rise of urban pollinator people 133–47
Muslim and Arabic texts 10

Nagamatsu, S. 20
National Farmers' Union, Canada 101, 158
native bees *see* wild bees
native plants: pollinator gardeners 143, 145–6
neoliberal governance and agrochemical corporations, Ontario 92–5
neoliberalization of knowledge 67
neonicotinoids 29–30, 67–8; arguments for and against ban 78–9; evidence of harm 70; impact on other animals 72–3; and nutritional deficiencies of bees 51; resistance 73–4; structure, mechanism of action and uses 68–9; and wild bees 70–2; *see also* agrochemical industry (struggles against neonicotinoids)
Nimmo, R. 14, 47, 155
non-domestic bees *see* wild bees
non-human nature: commodification of 44–5; *see also* human–non-human relationship
Noxious Weeds List, OMAFRA 76–7
numerous vs thriving populations 118
nutritional deficiencies and artificial feeding 50–1

OECD 74, 86, 87
Ontario: common milkweed 76–7; corn and soy monocultures 29–31; imported queen bees 43; OMAFRA 51–2, 53, 55, 76–7; *see also under* agrochemical industry (struggles against neonicotinoids)
Ontario Bee Working Group 92–3
Ontario Beekeepers Association 53, 92
orchard industry and commercially managed bee species 112
organic beekeeping practices 135
organic farming 99, 161
oxalic and formic acids 54

pain and emotion in insects 45
pastureland, loss of 33

pesticides (herbicides/insecticides/fungicides): lawns 132–3; and migratory commercial beekeeping 49–50; uncertain science and conflicting conceptions of expertise 77–9; war, agriculture and entomology 64–8; *see also* glyphosate; miticides; neonicotinoids
pests and pathogen transfer 6–7; bee-centred beekeeping and healthy honey bees 121–3; honey and wild bee competition 108–9, 110, 114–15, 116; Langstroth hives 42; managed bumble bee colonies 111–12; migratory commercial beekeeping 51–7; small- and large-scale beekeeping 39; small- and large-scale farming 34
plantation economy 25–6
planty agency 142
playful work 138–9, 143–4
pollination services *see* migratory commercial beekeeping
pollinator people, urban 133–47
precautionary principle: EU struggles against neonicotinoids 89–91
propolis 122

queens: bumble 71–2; reduced life span 54; and swarming behaviour 140; transported mated 43, 54

Ransome, H. M. 10, 66
rape *see* canola/oilseed rape
Reade, C. et al. 111
resistance: antibiotic 53; glyphosate 77; miticide 54, 56; neonicotinoid 73–4
Robbins, P. 129, 130–1, 132, 142
robobees 120
Roundup 74, 75, 86

sacrifice zones, agro-industrial monocultures as 114, 115, 117
scarcity, landscapes of 31–4
scientific research: agrochemical R&D 87; insect control and harms 66–8; lab vs field 78–9; public vs private funded 76; and uncertainty 11, 77–9, 89–90, 94, 153
seed coatings, neonicotinoid 69, 72, 73
seed corporations 86–7
Seeley, T. D. 2, 7, 8, 52, 54–5, 122, 140, 141, 155
semi-domesticated nature of honey bees 4–8

sensory and emotional aspects: of pollinator gardeners 142–7; of small-scale beekeeping 135–40
settler bees 24
settler-colonialism and capitalism, North America 21–2; honey bees 23–6, 41–2; and Indigenous societies 21–2, 113–14, 156; lawns 131; non-native species 113–14
simplified and standardized landscapes 26–31
skeps 43
small-scale commercial beekeeping 43–4, 117–18
small-scale farming: alliances 99, 100, 101, 153–4; potential of 159–61; settler-colonial 26
Snopes website 98
solitary bees 32, 71
soy *see* corn and soy monocultures, North America
spiritual and cultural importance of bees 9–10
Spivak, M. 97
standardized and simplified landscapes 26–31
Steffen, W. et al. 19, 20
STEM disciplines 67, 76, 120
stingless bees, Columbia 119
stress, migratory commercial beekeeping and 48–9
Subramanian, M. 20
superweeds 77
Suryanarayanan, S. 45, 78, 79, 90, 102; and Kleinman, 78, 85
Swan, H. 45
swarming behaviour 6, 7, 24, 155; commercial beekeeping strategies to inhibit 122; migratory commercial beekeeping 114–15; small-scale urban beekeeping 140–1
sweat bees 145
Syngenta 86, 89, 91

thiamethoxam 89, 91
thymol 54

tomato production: managed bumble bee colonies for greenhouse industry 111–12
Toronto Beekeepers Collective (TBC) 133–4
Toronto Pollinator Advisory Group (TPAG): Pollinator Protection Strategy (PPS) 107
trees and hedgerows, loss of 32–3
Tsvetkov, N. et al. 30, 69

uncertainty 11, 77–9, 89–90, 94, 153
urban beekeeping: pollinator people 133–47; *see also* honey bee harm to wild native bees
Urban Toronto Beekeepers Association (UTBA) 107

van der Sluijs, J. 11; et al. 72, 100
varroa mites 51–3; miticides 53–5; scapegoating of hobbyist beekeepers 55–7

Wall Kimmerer, R. 31
water pollution 72–3, 91
Watson, K. and Stallins, J. A. 40, 100, 115
Weis, T. 11, 22, 26, 27, 29, 33, 40, 73–4, 90, 115, 118, 153–4; and Ellis, R. 118, 159
wild bees 12–13, 14, 28, 29; and agriculture 9; defaunation 40, 44, 46; defaunation and proper response 120; and glyphosate 76–7; honey collection from 34; landscapes of scarcity 31–2, 33; and neonicotinoids 70–2; as pollinators 46, 47; and small-scale settler-colonial farms 26; *see also* bumble bees; honey bee harm to wild native bees; stingless bees; sweat bees
wildflowers 74
winter mortality of honey bees 48, 55
Wojcik, V. A. et al. 108–9
worker and foraging bees 110–11
World Health Organization: International Agency for Research on Cancer 75

Printed in the United States
by Baker & Taylor Publisher Services